Value Creation and the Internet of Things

This book is dedicated to Herman Manu, my extraordinary father.

Value Creation and the Internet of Things

How the Behavior Economy will Shape the 4th Industrial Revolution

ALEXANDER MANU

Routledge
Taylor & Francis Group
LONDON AND NEW YORK

First published 2015 by Gower Publishing

2 Park Square, Milton Park, Abingdon, Oxon, OX14 4RN
605 Third Avenue, New York, NY 10017

Routledge is an imprint of the Taylor & Francis Group, an informa business

First issued in paperback 2020

Gower Applied Business Research
Our programme provides leaders, practitioners, scholars and researchers with thought provoking, cutting edge books that combine conceptual insights, interdisciplinary rigour and practical relevance in key areas of business and management.

British Library Cataloguing in Publication Data
A catalogue record for this book is available from the British Library

ISBN 978-1-4724-5181-1 (hbk)
ISBN 978-0-367-73790-0 (pbk)

Library of Congress Cataloging-in-Publication Data
Manu, Alexander, 1954-
Value creation and the Internet of things : how the behavior economy will shape the 4th industrial revolution / by Alexander Manu.
pages cm
Includes bibliographical references and index.
ISBN 978-1-4724-5181-1 (hbk) 1. Technological innovations--Economic aspects. 2. New products. 3. Value. 4. Consumption (Economics)--Psychological aspects. I. Title.
HC79.T4M3487 2015
338'.064--dc23

2015003792

Contents

List of Figures

About the Author

Alexander Manu is a strategic innovation practitioner, international lecturer and author. He works with executive teams in Fortune 500 companies in industries as diverse as consumer packaged goods, media, advertising, mobile communications and manufacturing. Alexander lectures around the world on innovation, imagination, change agents and strategic foresight. He is a Senior Partner and Chief Imaginator at InnoSpa International Partners, teaches Innovation, Foresight and Business Design at the Rotman School of Management, and is a Professor at OCAD University in Toronto. In his client and research work, Alexander is involved in transforming organizations by exploring and defining new competitive spaces, the development of new strategic business competencies and creation of imaginative innovation methods. Alexander has an exceptional and sustained activity as an international lecturer, being invited to give over 500 keynote lectures in 24 countries.

Acknowledgements

This book grew out of the daily nourishment I receive from my students, who challenge me constantly to provoke them with new knowledge, and the nourishment of collaborators who generously offered their brilliant knowledge and insights. My deep appreciation and gratitude to Sergey Kovalyukh and Carl Hastrich for their important contributions to this book, and for being part of this journey from the beginning. My thanks to Matthew Jones, whose research perspectives defined many of the ideas covered in Chapter 4, 'Reframing Value: Duality in the Internet of Things', and for the elegant articulation of ideas contained in 'Perspectives in Conversation' which enriches Chapter 8.

To Kristina Abbotts and the team at Gower Publishing – Donna Shanks, Sara Hutton, Adam Guppy and Bryan Campbell – my thanks for their enthusiasm and passion, and for their generous professionalism. Special thanks to Adam Kereliuk, whose inspired design for the book cover dynamically frames both the challenges and opportunities described within.

Finally, to my wonderful family, Sophie, Sasha, Bella and my father – their moral support and guidance allow my spirit to stay young and curious, as it should.

Reviews for

Value Creation and the Internet of Things

How the Behavior Economy will Shape the 4th Industrial Revolution

To date, few have really delved as deeply into what the 'Internet of Things' is and will mean to us beyond the technical and product wizardry of what's possible. Value Creation and the Internet of Things *is refreshing in its ability to frame up the opportunity and the challenges by focusing us on the most impactful questions and changes it will require of us as a society, a culture and our businesses. Alexander Manu succeeds in building the so-needed thread between business, technology, culture and humanity.*

Cybelle Srour, Managing Director-Strategy, Resource/Ammirati, USA

Alexander Manu has been able to put into words the transformation that is ongoing in the global economy. The economic downturn that has been challenging many countries in recent years seems to be more than just a normal fluctuation of the recession cycle. It is not products that people are buying anymore, but rather experience platforms. The Internet of Things is extending this transformation to involve not only the consumer businesses, but businesses altogether independent of the nature of the actual customer. Manu explains the framework needed to operate in this new economy, what the behaviour economy is all about, how value creation differs from conventional industrial economy and what kind of leadership is needed in this new context.

Solveig Roschier, Director, Social Sciences,
Helsinki Innovation Services Ltd, Finland

Introduction

Value in the Behavior Economy

When my son was turning five years old, I bought him a desk globe. It had raised reliefs, was illuminated, and had touch controls that allowed one to set it to spin from five to 60 minutes.

It had the physical and the political cartography of the Earth, and was 12 inches in diameter, with an aluminum die-cast meridian, and a rich cherrywood base. I wanted my son to have a sense of the Earth; I wanted him to learn the relationships between continents and between countries. The globe had physicality in his room, as well as a practical application. He could show this globe to his friends, and show off his knowledge of the various countries and capitals, by pointing to them with precision on his globe. In the course of time, in less than two years, this thing was no longer a favorite, and found its way slowly to the basement.

A few years later, on his eighth birthday, my father bought him the Leapfrog Quantum Leap interactive 'smart globe,' a rotating plastic globe of about 14 inches diameter, that with the simple touch of a 'magic pen' would open up with facts, phrases, music, games and challenges. You can hear the national anthems of various countries, you can hear about the demographics of the place and population numbers, anything you wanted to know about the geography of the place or the economic system. This globe would teach you about the oceans, the continents, the animals, the languages spoken in the various countries you might be looking at, or be curious about. And just when you thought you were bored, you could start playing a variety of games based on your knowledge of each country's characteristics. This is about as smart a globe can be for its times. It was 2002.

By 2009 we had four personal computers in our house, one for each member of the family, and each one with the full screen version of Google Earth installed. Indeed, the first image on the screen looked just like a spinning globe, but as soon as we started navigating towards a country, everything magically changed. And the magic continued every year since then, with the introduction of more and more features and more and more details which makes Google Earth such a fascinating platform.

People get to create and place their own data on Google Earth, can add three-dimensional buildings, can change content on the platform in ways that were not possible with the Quantum Leap or the classic spinning globe. Add to that the Street View feature, and you can spend hours in any city on the planet, seeing details that were impossible to see before, without going there in person. A new universe of possibility, on everyone's desktop. No longer imagined, but made visible and real, at the touch of the computer's mouse.

Google Earth typifies the behavior economy, by being a platform for intellectual engagement, continually upgrading its value for the user, and involving the user at all times in its growth. By contrast, the products of the industrial economy represented by the first spinning globe, and by the Quantum Leap version, diminish in value, engagement and interest with the passing of time.

Google Earth is just the beginning. It is the new breed of an engagement platform, one that increases its value and its usefulness in somebody's life, with the rate of technological developments that makes its features possible. One could view maps of the Moon or Mars, or could see the depth of the oceans. One could get directions for street names, or fly from one place to another using the flight simulator feature, and obviously, and naturally, one can navigate through the streets of any major city, at street level, in Street View.

Google Earth functions as a knowledge platform with multiple layers of information that can be turned on or off. This is *Value Delivery* in its most intrinsic form. In one's control, at any time.

There are big differences between these three ways of experiencing the world. In a classic rotating globe, the afforded interactions are between a very small group and the product, and they are restricted to the limited functions of the product, and the limited space for allowing information on the surface of a 12-inch globe. The Quantum Leap version is a *tactical value* creation example, where a product is enhanced by the new technology available, and the experience is expanded by the multiple features connected to geography, and the knowledge the user seeks about it which technology now affords. The Quantum Leap is, at best, enhancing and expanding an experience. This is representative of the traditional model of technology development, and as far as strategy, it is an easy prediction to make, using forecasting. Given the number of technology developments of the time, and a reduction in the cost of components, certain features will be present on certain products. If we have a candle that sings 'happy birthday' once lit, how long before we have a spinning globe that speaks, and sings the national anthems of the countries on the globe?

Both the traditional globe and the Quantum Leap version are examples of the industrial economy, where products are used by dedicated users, one at a time, and company growth is proportional to the number of products the producer can sell. Scaling up in this model means really 'scaling up.' Producing and selling more. Consuming more energy, more material and more labor, at every step in the value chain.

By contrast, Google Earth is a strategic value creation example. This is value creation that redefines the experience a user will have with knowledge, and with geography. Google Earth is not an expansion of the Quantum Leap product, because none of the experiences possible with Google Earth were possible before. *Strategic value always redefines the experience.*

The Quantum Globe was a bridge between the industrial economy and the behavior economy. It was the necessary schooling that our behavior required in order to comprehend and seek the value of Google Earth. Just like the movie *Toy Story*, which was the bridge to a new form of entertainment, one created exclusively on a digital platform.

A platform where we can tell new stories, in a completely new way. A place where we can imagine worlds that don't exist, but make them real for viewers. *Avatar*. *Gladiator*. A new territory for the human narrative, and for the human experience.

Google Earth exemplifies the behavior economy by being a platform for behavior on which the value increases with a number of behaviors possible. In the behavior economy, platforms *are value variable.* The growth of companies that develop platforms is not connected to how many platforms they make, but to how many users are connected to this platform. Growth in this case is also connected to the depth of engagement and to the relationship a user has to the platform, and the multiple layers of experience that one can participate in while on the platform.

A World Where Everything is Connected

The grounding question that will allow organizations to emerge with purpose from these transformative times is simply this: *how many times a day do you use the Internet?*

Answering this question grounds you in the sense of allowing you to understand the importance of the Internet in your life, and in the life of your organization, and thus of the importance of the Internet of Things about to emerge. We are living in monumental times, times in which transformation requires the resetting of our frameworks and mindsets, towards possibilities we can't even describe.

We are looking conveniently at what is about to happen as an extension of what we already have, and what we have is life with the Internet. While saying this, we need to pause and ask a very simple question: *what is the Internet?*

The simple answer is that the Internet is a series of *connected computers*. Another answer would be an attempt at describing the multiple benefits that connected computers might bring into one's life, or into an organization's life. And without thinking too much, we can all make very long lists of how the Internet, the fact that computers are connected between themselves, has affected and shaped our life in the past 25 years. In the Internet's connectivity, what is important is not that computers are connected, but the fact that *people are connected* through computers. The real definition of the Internet, and the real answer to the question 'what is the Internet?' might be something like this: *people connected through computers*.

Now let us look at the meaning of the Internet of Things. A technical definition of the Internet of Things defines it as an ecosystem in which people, places, and objects are connected to one another. In other words, the Internet as we defined it before, but now extended to objects and places.

It is wrong to think of the Internet of Things as connecting people, because people need social objects to connect with other people. People need reasons to connect, they need to understand what is the 'benefit,' the value of connecting, what we are connecting for? The real definition of the Internet of Things might be: *people connected to people they care about through everything being connected.*

When things are connected they must be connected for a purpose, and that is the purpose of communication, for the purpose of a value exchange between them. At this point we need analogies in order to unpack the potential of the ecosystem of everything being connected, in order to understand its potential, its rules and its benefits.

There are a few models—analogies—we might look at, trying to understand the potential of the ecology of everything connected. Let's look at nature. Take a tree for example: the leaves are connected to the branches, the branches connected to the trunk, the trunk is connected to the roots, and the roots connect to the ground. The human passing by is connected through the sense of smell and touch; the flower nearby is connected through the ground and the air, and the bee that just touched its petals.

These are all organic connections, where contact is made through matter. In an organic connection, everything provides value to everything else. The bee provides value to the flower, the flower provides value to the tree, and the tree provides value to the human. I see the '*everything connected*' ecology in much the same way.

The generative question in the '*everything connected*' ecology is:

> *If every person, object and place could communicate to one another, what would be the subject of their conversations?*

To answer this question we have to further ask:

- How can we add value to each other?
- What do people want to know in places?
- How can a place add value to an object?
- What do places want to know?
- How can two objects add value to each other?
- What do objects want to know in places?
- What do objects want to know about people in places?
- What do objects want to know about objects?

The reality is that we're not yet ready to answer these questions in a comprehensive way that includes a new frame for thinking about what the Internet of Things is. If we assume that life will continue to be what it is, but this time with *'everything connected'* by the Internet of Things, we will be looking at change, and the future, as being nothing more than the status quo plus the new thing. But this is not how change works. We are not looking at *life as it is + the Internet,* post the acceptance of the World Wide Web, we are looking at life *transformed by the Internet.*

Change involves transformation. Remember the grounding question at the beginning of this section and your answer to it. Now multiply that answer about 3.1 billion times.[1]

Transformation requires rethinking of possibility. Rethink what is possible and what new benefits we can bring into our lives when everything is connected. When applied to sectors of the economy, the future of entertainment, as an example, is not *entertainment + 'everything connected,'* but entertainment redefined by *'everything being connected.'* And the same can be said about the future of gaming, or the future of education. It will not be education as usual but now in a new ecology, it will be education *transformed by everything being connected.*

We need a great deal of foresight, and a lot less forecasting when thinking about the potential of the Internet of Things. Forecasting allows us to make a prediction about when a technology becomes affordable and mainstream, and how it is to be used to add value to an existing product.

The forecasting question is simple and precise: *'**How** will this technology allow me to expand and enhance the experience users have with my product?'* The Quantum Leap desk globe is one such example of expanding and enhancing an existing experience. By contrast, the foresight question is ambiguous: *'**What** could be possible?'* While answering this question with foresight, we are creating strategic value, reframing life and redefining our capabilities.

'Everything being connected' is forcing us to reconsider our limits, and most of all the limits of our imagination. In the Internet of Things, the rate and speed of possibility is far surpassing the rate and speed with which we can imagine it. We need to move beyond imagination, into a state of inspiration, triggered by the sheer possibility we can sense.

1 Available at: http://www.internetlivestats.com/internet-users/ (accessed: July 16, 2014).

Strategic foresight is a methodology that creates strategic value. By contrast, forecasting results in a prediction—by such a date, at this rate of, these features will be available at this cost—which creates tactical value, exemplified as a new and enhanced interaction between users and a product. The Internet of Things will result in a massive release of possibility, transforming organizations into a behavior economy enterprise, because most things will be connected, and they would have to behave as if they are.

Our imagination is no longer enough because we can only imagine what we've experienced. The imagination is the place in the brain where we create images of objects and concepts not present to the senses. The prerequisite for this ability is for us to have an understanding and previous experience of the

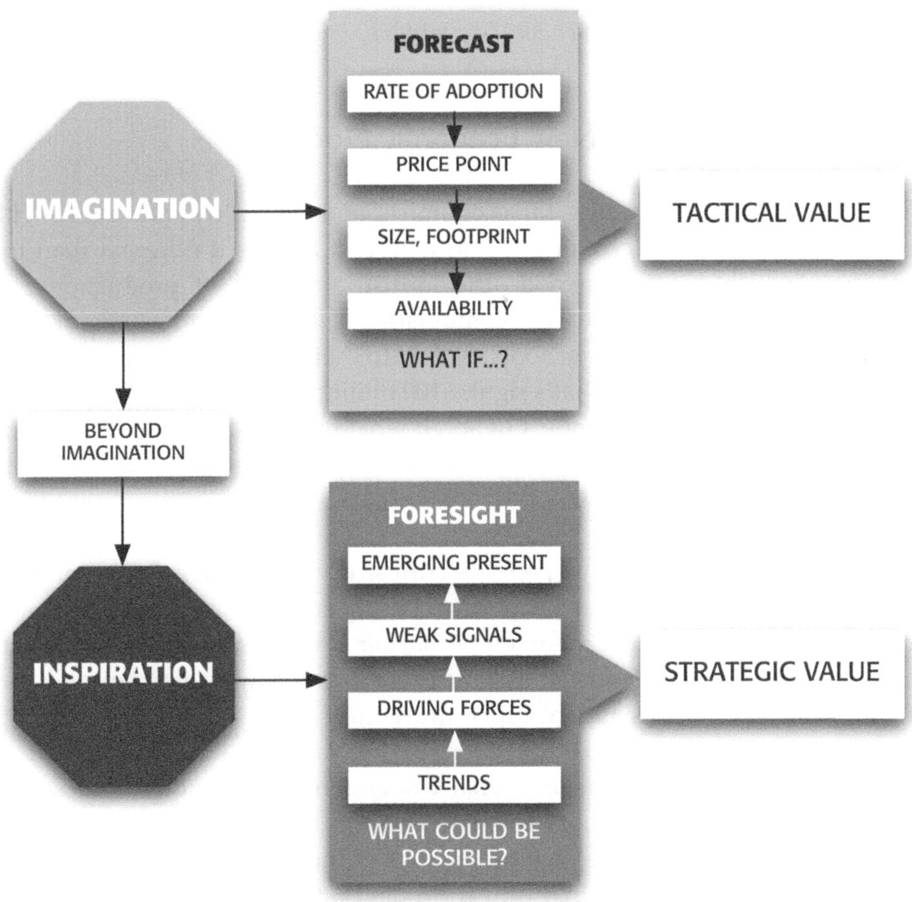

Figure I.1 Beyond imagination

thing we are imagining, or what is called apperception. A past experience or the memory of an experience of what the thing looks like, or feels like. If you think of the Statue of Liberty, you can see it even if it's not present to your senses; you see it in the imagination. Which means we cannot imagine things we have not experienced, seen, or we remember. This also means that everything you are thinking right now about a possible future, the most outrageous scenario you can imagine about is actually doable right now. Tomorrow. And why? Because you can only think of what you know, of what you have perceptually experienced. The task here is to surpass the limits of our imagination, to turn off our disbelief in things, and to start designing benefits for people's lives not based on what we know, but based on what we know to be right and necessary.

Imagination is about answers to the question *'what if?'* Inspiration is about answers to the question *'what could be possible?'*

Intrinsic Behavior as a New Economic Model

There is a perplexing reality for economists and media commentators with regards to the Internet economy, what is it, and how is it different than the economy which we understood—the industrial model of production and consumption, in which value was a combination of labor + materials + marketing + profit = price. Do business schools explain to their MBA cohorts how Google makes $100,000,000 a day (that's right, $100 million per day)? This observation is not about millions in revenue, but about what that means. Google is making $100 million a day because we, the users of Google, engage in behavior worth $100 million to someone.

These revenues are tied to people's curiosity and thirst for discovering the right thing at any given time; people are chasing something that leads them to a Google search. And what people are chasing is value; value in the products and services they purchase, value in their relationships with enterprises, value for their travel or entertainment expenditures and so on.

We are all chasing value and what Google does is provide it, one search at a time. And so do Facebook, YouTube and Netflix. These are all enterprises taking full advantage of the new ecosystems of interconnected data; these are all platforms for behaviors that transform data into individual value for each user. They are also platforms for revenue 'extraction,' which is a different metric than revenue 'generation.' Generating revenue is the result of an exchange of extrinsic value: *I want to have* something you have, and I will exchange for it. On the other hand revenue extraction is the result of intrinsic behavior. *I want to be* on Facebook.

We now live more and more in a behavior economy, an intertwined eco-system in which people no longer engage with brands by just purchasing things, but they look for engagement with services that allow them to behave, to leave a mark, to participate with others. In this economic space, people seek the best value for their engagement, in unprecedented numbers and with unprecedented empowerment. And by 'value' they do not mean 'value for the money'—most of these activities are delivered for free—but the satisfaction of multiple dimensions of value, from physical to emotional, from social to intellectual, and from spiritual to occupational.

One could argue that we always lived in a behavior economy, as it is human behavior that generates economic transactions: our desires, wants and needs motivating our actions. But what we are witnessing today is passive behaviors originating in *intrinsic motivation*— passive in the sense that no material value is exchanged between the parties—triggering vast economic transactions between multiple parties. One's presence on Facebook triggers a series of transactions that benefit both Facebook and third parties. Without us being there, these transactions will not exist. *Our time is our new currency.* And this currency has more and more value, as we are moving through a new space in which the physical and the digital are linked not through dedicated and stationary nodes, but through every person, place and object. Yes, the Internet of Things and the imperative of connecting at multiple layers of engagement.

On the user side, mobility, location proximity and full accessibility on any number of possible displays, makes content delivery a unique new opportunity as well as a unique new user experience.

Add to this the convergence of a few technologies—Google Glass, Near Field Communication, Augmented Reality—and I see in the very near future an explosion of location specific experiences—*destination broadcast streams*—with content that will invite the participation of all senses, or what I call later in this book, a Full Spectrum Experience, engaging the user in multiple layers of experience.

On the enterprise side, there is visible value shift from traditional enterprises—which performed in the economic model of production and consumption (Figure I.1), in which people exchanged money for the purchase

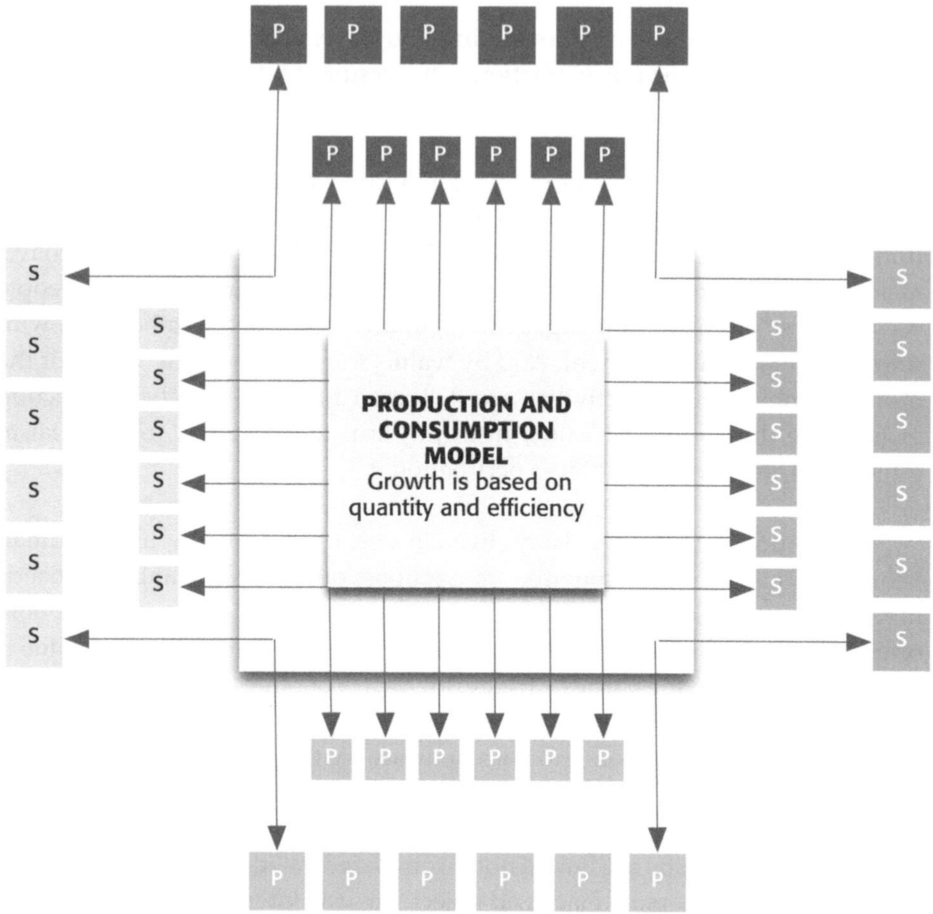

Figure I.2 Production and consumption model

of products (P) and services (S)—to enterprises that do not offer goods, but rather they offer 'platforms.' These enterprises are models of the Data Enabler Organization and a new type of business now made possible by digital technologies: the networked data business. A new form of company is being born (Figure I.2), a company that does not grow along traditional metrics—more products, more sales, more efficiencies—but grows in relationship with the user engagement in the platform it controls, along new metrics being redefined by the network size and the quality of each node.

Once the up-front costs have been incurred and the platform is established, the more people there are who are sharing the benefits, the greater the net

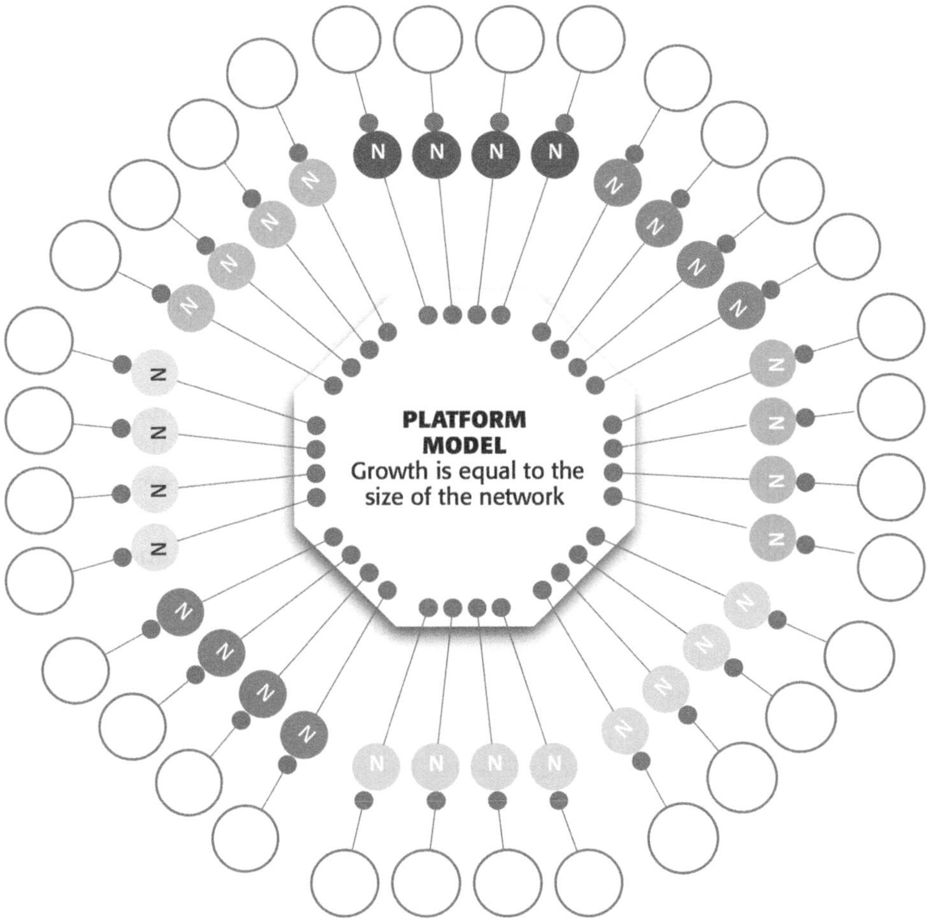

Figure I.3 Platform model

present value of the whole value system becomes. A platform company is as open, as accessible and as supportive as possible, to as many users as possible. Optimum value creation means attracting as many users as possible to a behavior platform that gives them multiple opportunities, in both the breadth and the depth of engagement (Figure I.3).

In such a context, a company does not have to physically grow; what needs to grow are the depth of engagement with users, the duration and the equality of the experience.

Extrinsic and Intrinsic Models

I mentioned earlier the industrial model of production and consumption, one in which value was produced by manufacturing goods or creating services that might be beneficial to identified users. In this model, value is often extrinsic to the user, it is a feature of the product or service, it concerns the physical attributes of the system, its mechanical performance, or the performance of the personnel engaged in the service. All these are components of a system, and because they are parts they can be improved in terms of material quality or fabrication process, in visible ways, giving a user the sentiment of 'value for the money.'

All of these aspects of a product are extrinsic to an individual user. They need to be explained, advertised, promoted, and learned. Once a user learns the operational principles of the product, he or she engages in a short-term behavior. However, behavior is not the goal here, the goal is the accomplishment of a specific task, for example making coffee, mixing dough, cutting the grass, and so on.

In the behavior model—Facebook or Twitter as examples—behavior *is the only goal*. There is little value in the physicality, the material, or the technical features of the system. The user is only interested in these as a bridge between himself and the behavior platform. How do we create value here? The value we can create is the *value of the experience.* The more dimensions of experience we can fulfill the more compelling the value we create. The two models have two different value metrics: Intrinsic Value is what the thing is worth to you, and its meaning. Extrinsic Value is what the thing is made of, what it does, and how it does it.

The two models illustrated here are models of two economic systems where *motivation is key*. The consumption economy operates in a discourse of monetary value, which is a media of exchange of physical goods or services that must be measured in order to achieve fair trade: how many ships do you need to trade for a pile of wood to heat you up during the winter.

The platform economy operates where direct exchange is possible—we are talking about the direct exchange of stimuli between individuals that takes the form of:

- Spiritual exchange (beliefs about the universe and meaning of humanity).
- Mental exchange (attention, inspiration, ideation).

- Emotional exchange (love, aspirations, admiration).
- Power exchange (feeling of empowerment, teamwork).
- Passion exchange (desires and wants—it feels good when you resonate with someone who's passionate about the same thing as you).
- Safety and well being.

Platforms allow for this exchange at the interpersonal level. You feel the need and you get it resolved—not via a purchase of goods or a service from someone, but via engagement with other individual who either can give you the stimuli you need, or can consume the stimuli that you have in abundance.

Why This Book Now?

Because the Internet of Things is not an elective for enterprises operating in the behavior economy. Just like the Internet was not an option, just like social media participation is not an option anymore. The platforms for new behavior that the Internet of Things will make possible, will increase considerably the footprint of the behavior economy at the expense of the old industrial model, with casualties in the rank of any incumbent not willing or able to adapt to the behavior economy. It is Polaroid who should have invented Instagram, not Kevin Systrom and Mike Krieger. It is Blockbuster who should have developed Netflix. And so on. The fact they did not shows that these companies did not fundamentally understand that they were in the business of behavior, and they did not understand the motivation at the root of that behavior. Why users choose their products or services. It is by looking at the behavior of users that a company will truly understand what business it is *really* in. What is it that you have that the user wants? And why?

Apple is *not in the computer business*. Apple is in the *empowerment business*. Nike *is not in* the sneakers business. It is in the *personal goals business*. Heineken *is not in* the beer business. It is in the *party business*.

Forgetting where the economic system comes from—I want something you have and I am willing to exchange value for it—distances corporations and individuals from the perceptive reality, keeping them in the world of abstracts and theories. If an oil producer cannot connect oil extraction with Facebook or YouTube, then we cannot expect the economists to do it either. Why is it hard to connect a decline in economic activity—retail sales in a month—with five billion videos being watched on YouTube the same month in the same territory? Exactly who do you think is watching these videos? If their consumption time is taken over by an exchange that does not register on the GDP, why is the downturn a surprise?

This book describes the mechanisms by which new value is captured and created in enterprises dedicated to play a role in the behavior economy. It all starts with learning a new language—the language of ideas—and with establishing frameworks of possibility in the ideology of the enterprise. Value creation is the expansion of relationships enabled by a disruptor media and the creation of new behaviors as a result. This opens two needed capabilities for a business. *The first is upstream,* creating the platform services people want to engage with. *The second is downstream,* marketing, distributing and selling these platforms as services.

By the nature of the activities involved, the upstream and downstream capabilities are quite different in scope, inputs and outputs. The downstream calls for *methodology*—what do we have to do and how?—while the upstream calls for *ideology*—why and for whom are we doing this? In the context of enterprise, ideology is a way of being, behaving and influencing the world. An attitude. A mindset.

This is also a book about *enterprise* in the true sense of the word. 'Enterprise' means a bold and courageous undertaking. What is the difference between a business and an enterprise? Business takes care of the day-to-day mitigation of the affairs of the company. Enterprise is an undertaking that aims towards permanently outdoing its latest accomplishments. Businesses are run by pragmatism, enterprises are run by poetic visions. The incomparable Steve Jobs had it right in 1983, when he made his memorable pitch to entice John Scully—at that time the youngest president in the history of PepsiCo—to leave his position and join Apple Computer as President:

> *Do you want to sell sugared water for the rest of your life? Or do you want to come with me and change the World.*

This book is the culmination of ten years of practice and research in the potential of the Internet of Things; it is also the culmination of my early belief that the Internet of Things will reframe the existence of the ones enriched by it.

PART I

THE EMERGING PRESENT

Chapter 1

Chasing Value in Everyday Experiences

It is in the ambiguous domain of 'value' that most products succeed or fail; some fail because their value is temporary and accidental, as they were designed from the 'outside–in,' from the form of the object to its interactive features; others succeed because their value was the very starting point of the design process. They were designed from the 'inside–out,' from the value proposition outward, from the desired outcome to what makes the outcome.

But what is *value* in this context? Value gives things their worth in the eyes of a user. It also gives the thing its appeal to users. Value is the worth of something to someone. And in this sense, it has a diminishing scale or worthiness.

In marketing, value is sometimes referred to as perceived value, which is how a user might look at the product in comparison with another product. Value is subjective and relational, it is how we relate one thing to another, and this is why value depends so much on perception and cognition, and memory.

Another way to look at value is to look at what we are willing to exchange in return. And in this sense, not where we need to exchange in terms of material goods and services, but what we are willing to exchange that is immaterial. Our time. Our behavior. The more behavior we invest in a product or service, the more value it holds for us. Which means that technology is never what is monetized; it is behavior that is monetized. And this behavior diminishes in importance or value as we move through the behavior cycle of a product or service. The more we use something, the more we demand new value from it. Is the new value of something that maintains the satisfaction of our relationship with that something.

As we invest ourselves in using a platform, the nature of our desires, goals and motivation changes, and we end up seeking more, looking for more from the same product or service. This is the perpetual dynamic of a behavior cycle

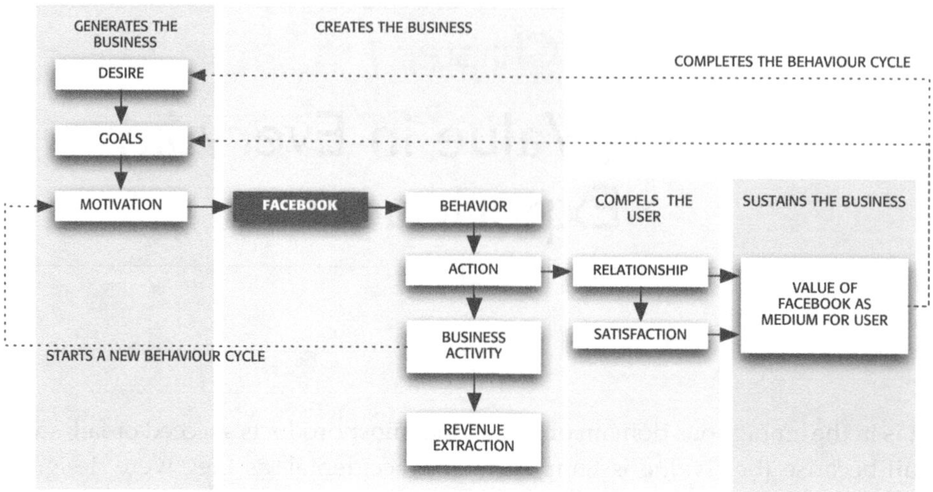

Figure 1.1 The behavior cycle

(Figure 1.1), rooted in our perpetually-seeking mediums for bettering ourselves in the near future, and the means to achieve our best selves in the present. The value of a product or service is proportional with its capability of becoming the perfect medium by which our motivating goals are satisfied.

Value has a personal dimension, in that it is purely subjective. Value evolves over time with the accumulation of life experiences and the exposure of the individual to a variety of 'value moments.'

Value and personal identity are interconnected—we are the sum of our value moments and value assessments—which is why people place so much value on their online social presence and activity. This stems from the human condition of 'plurality'—discussed later in this book—and from the desire to leave a mark and participate. More than anything, we value the image people have of ourselves, an image we are trying to construct and reconstruct by any means technologically available.

What we do all day in our online activities is chasing value moments, expressed as emotional connections with ideas or with others. Facebook, Pinterest and Twitter—to name just a few well-known platforms—are means by which individuals express their worth in the community of others. These behavior platforms are 'stages' on which individuals perform from their intrinsic motivation, because they want to be seen, they want to be heard, and they want to be measured on these performances by others.

The Value of Behavior Platforms: The New Presentation of Self in Everyday Life

The Merriam-Webster Dictionary[1] defines value as:

1. *The amount of money that something is worth: the price or cost of something.*

2. *Something that can be bought for a low or fair price.*

3. *Usefulness or importance.*

We learn in schools about meanings 1 and 2, but very little about meaning number 3, about 'usefulness and importance' or about why Facebook, Twitter and Pinterest are important and thus useful to people. These are three manifestations of the passage from the extrinsic economy of *having and consuming* to the *intrinsic economy of being and becoming.*

The *self* was always the center of the economic system, but now even more so, as the self needs, according to Erving Goffman,[2] 'fronts' and 'vehicles' for presenting itself in everyday life, and Facebook, Twitter and Pinterest present themselves as these fronts and vehicles.

With Facebook, the individual has the opportunity to be in the presence of others, and present to others most of the time. This is different than in the past, when we could only be present with others while in their direct proximity, in physical locations.

Facebook and other social media I just listed are vehicles that allow individuals to express themselves, and give to others impressions of themselves, more often than ever before. Social media vehicles also allow individuals to give signals about themselves, signals which are manufactured and very carefully choreographed. This control over one's image to the plurality of his or her own community is of intrinsic value to individuals.

To understand how the presentation of self in everyday life is so different today than it was forty or 50 years ago, give some thought to the examination of what were the vehicles then that allowed people to present themselves

1 Available at: http://www.merriam-webster.com/dictionary/value (accessed: June 26, 2014).
2 Goffman, E. (1959). *The Presentation of Self in Everyday Life*. New York, NY: Anchor.

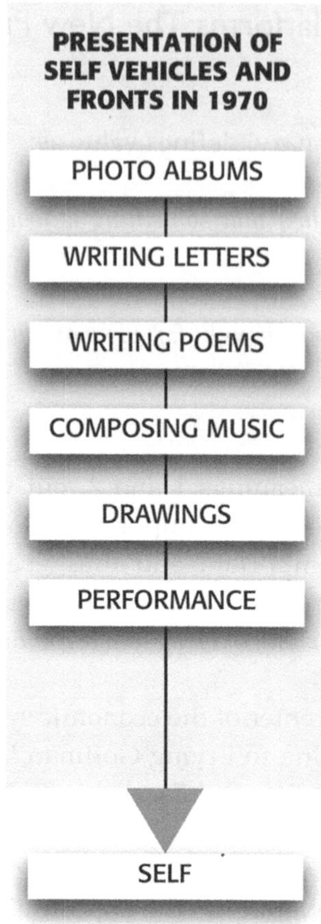

Figure 1.2 Presentation of self in 1970

to others. The list can be counted on one hand: writings (or other forms of creation such as music, painting) photographs and physical presence (Figure 1.2).

Individuals have always found it important to design their image in the eyes of others, and broadcast it on all available vehicles, and found value in every one of the vehicles allowing us to broadcast our image. Today, we are encountering even more value: we have many more vehicles and an ever-expanding array of opportunities to shape and broadcast our image (Figure 1.3). Shaping our image constantly is our performance in front of others, and Facebook offers us the tools to control our social image, and design ourselves, as we want to be perceived by others.

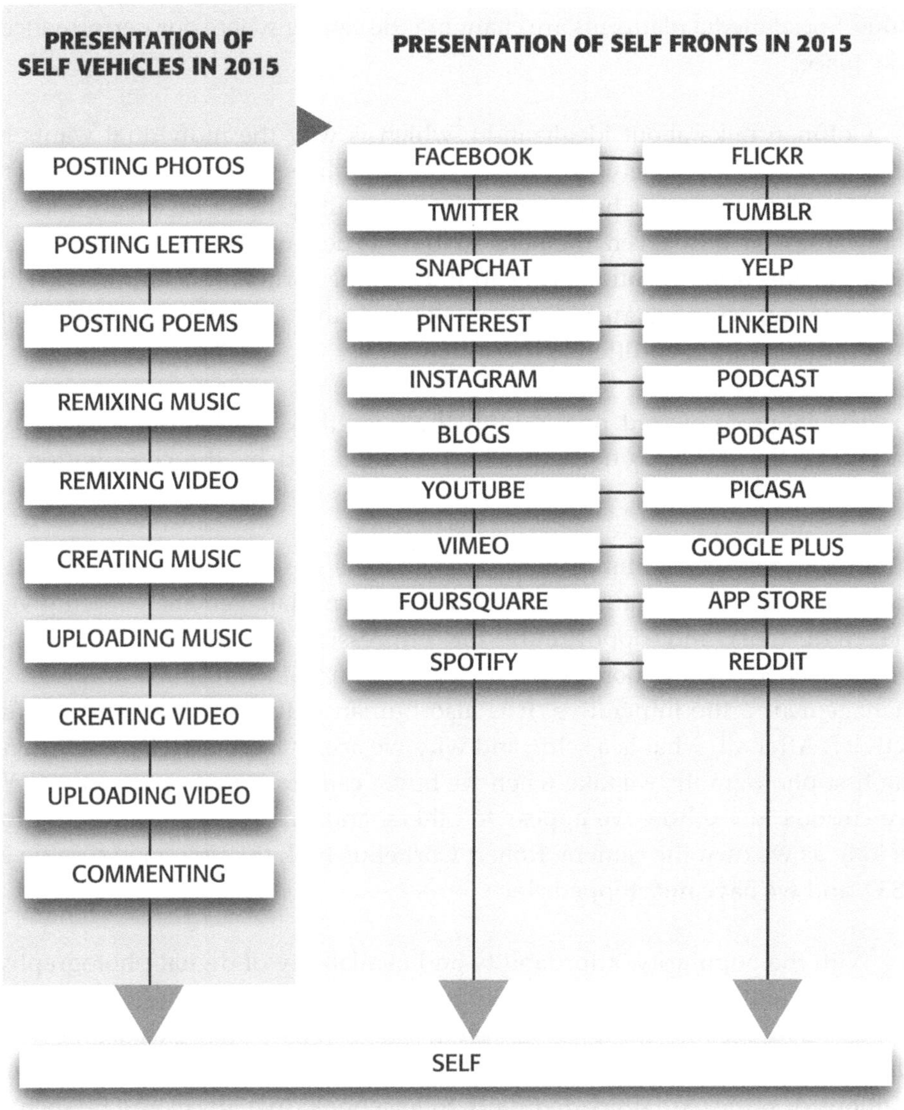

Figure 1.3 Presentation of self in 2015

These social media vehicles allow us to play different roles for different groups, in front of which we are going to perform. We would perform one role on Facebook, and quite a different one on Pinterest, and then another one on LinkedIn. We do find value in the multiple performance opportunities that the social media platforms are offering us, and we also find value in their reach and the provision of self-expression tools available to us. More tools more value. Social media platforms are changing the setting where our performances take place.

Goffman talks about idealization, which is way the individual wants to present himself in society, based on what he thinks society expects them to be. This ideal version is based on the individual's pursuit of society's ideals and values, at any given moment in time. The performance on Facebook takes its cues from the audience, and thus the performance is approved. This performance includes a great deal from others, either as a commentary on their own activities, or in addition to these activities.

The more connected one is with the cues they receive from others on Facebook, the more his/her expression is enhanced by the contribution of others, and by the value others give to this expression.

In the post www. Internet era, individuals are deeply concerned with the ways and means that affect their 'impression management.' When given the right tools and opportunity for impression management—which is what Facebook is all about—it is in our human nature to make impression management a life imperative. It is also human nature to find value in this activity. After all, what is a selfie and why we are so fascinated by them? One the first photographs we take when we buy a camera is that of ourselves. We are curious to see how we appear to others, and this curiosity continues for as long as we own the camera. Robert Cornelius took the first known selfie in 1839, and we have not stopped since.

With the popularity, affordability and availability of digital photography, as well as with the immediacy of the image generation in the digital medium, selfies have become the photograph we take most often. According to a Digital Trends study in 2013,[3] selfies are the most popular genre of photo. Millions of selfies are uploaded daily to Facebook, Instagram and Snapchat. A selfie is an immediate connection to the Self as perceived by others, and this connection allows us to modify the impression we give to others. The millennial generation is focused on the self and more connected to it than ever before. For them, 'being connected' does not mean with others, it means first being connected to the Self. From there you construct the fronts that you want others to see as yourself, and that becomes a new form of communication.

---

3 Available at: http://www.digitaltrends.com/social-media/selfies-are-now-the-most-popular-genre-of-picture-and-in-related-news-everyones-the-worst/ (accessed: November 22, 2014).

For Goffman, the role of expression is in conveying impressions of Self. This is the key to social interaction and its raison' d'être: to convey the self onto others. Social media platforms and tools are means by which we can manage the impression of Self and thus create a perpetually relevant Self for others. What is interesting here is the measure by which this Self is in effect a co-creation, as our audience has unprecedented access to the same tools, and more often than not, participates intensely in this creation. One 'like' on Facebook triggers multiple 'likes' in a cascading effect.

The intrinsic value of an Internet-based behavior platform, is the propagation of fronts and vehicles for the shaping and broadcasting of an individual's Self in Everyday Life. No industrial model, product or service, has ever achieved this power, this penetration and this relevance in people's lives. The 1.24 billion monthly users of Facebook make this very statement.

The *Perceived Significance of Self* as Value

It is due to Carl Rogers[4] that we have the benefit of one of the simplest, and most elegant, theories about the self. For Rogers, individuals exist in the changing world of experience, as the center of that world. Our perceptual field is whatever we feel and see every day, and that becomes reality for the individual. The more perception, the more reality. And the Internet gives us more perception. Add Facebook to your life, and now Facebook becomes part of your perception field, expanding it to proportions never encountered before, and establishing new targets for the self.

When we interact with our immediate environment, and more so as a result of evaluating our interaction with others, the structure of the self is formed and reformed again. It is organized in a dynamic and synchronic fashion, with what we perceive as changing values in our perceptual field. In all this time, the individual has only one basic tendency and striving, and that is to *actualize, maintain* and *enhance* the experiences perceived at any given moment.

The best vantage point for understanding behavior is from the internal frame of reference of the individual. For Rogers, behavior is a goal-directed attempt of an organism to satisfy its needs, as it experiences them in the field of perception

4 Rogers, C. (1951). *Client-centered Therapy: Its Current Practice, Implications and Theory*. London: Constable.

in which the organism—the individual—is placed. Emotion accompanies and facilitates goal-directed behavior, the emotion being related to the perceived significance of the behavior for the maintenance and enhancement of the organism. The key here is the notion of *perceived significance*. From this perspective, how can a 21-year-old student not be using Snapchat? What significance will she/he have for others if not present as often as possible on their social media platforms?

If I am exposed for a long time to Facebook, and if I participate in the life of others interjecting my experiences and allowing them to interject theirs, I start valuing experiences which are not directly mine, but become mine as they become part of my self structure, part of my perceptive field. Once part of a perceptive field, experiences become *symbolized*, in order to correspond and be consistent to the structure of the self. *The value of Facebook therefore, is the number of experiences which one can retrieve and symbolize, in order to enhance the structure of the self.*

Meaning as Value

The value we place in objects is directly proportional with the meaning we assign to that object in our apperception. We value less the perceptive—the stuff that we can see and touch—as we value the apperceptive, which is the relationship between what we perceive now and memories of experiences of the past. Apperception is the comprehension of what we see based on our past experience. This is why, in the *context of behavior*, value is an individual variable that has little to do with money.

Apperception makes a piece of fiberglass made by hand, one of 20 ever made, be worth $20,000, if that piece of fiberglass happens to be one of the Cylon helmets used in the original series *Battle Star Galactica*. This is no longer material + labor + energy = price. This is material + labor + energy + *meaning* = price. Interestingly, meaning has value especially in artifacts that have no other 'function'—in other words they do not really work—and the only function is their meaning.

Is this not the case in art? What exactly are we valuing in the Mona Lisa? It is estimated[5] that Cezanne's 'Card Players' has a value of $273 million. How many experts do you know that could explain, in a reasonable and logical way, why this piece of canvas is worth more than a Boeing 777–200, and why the

5 See http://en.wikipedia.org/wiki/List_of_most_expensive_paintings (accessed: July 9, 2014).

value of the painting will keep rising, while that of the jet will progressively move downward?

Meaning is the fuel we use to create our perception of reality—we are meaning-making machines.[6] We constantly try to make sense of our life by forming schemas about our experiences, actively constructing a context for identity that varies from person to person. These individual perceptions are what we base our values, goals, and aspirations on, and in turn, those drive our behavior and preferences. The reality is that value as meaning is a deeply rooted and deeply personal percept. Certain things are meaningful beyond reason and for no reason, except our attachment to symbolic artifacts that attest we have spent time on Earth, and left our mark behind. These artifacts—paintings, sculptures, literature, and music—are the constructs of the human mind, and they propagate our organization, our forms of being.

How we assign meaning and value defines who we are, and the choices we make; those patterns set the precedent for future behaviors. What we've designated as significant in the past will affect and influence what we designate as meaningful in the future. If a bouquet of flowers was sentimental in the past, a token of love or affection, we are inclined to see any bouquet we come across in the future in much the same way. More than anything, for something to become meaningful the connection we make with it has to be relevant, so we permanently ask of everything we encounter 'What does this mean to ME, to MY life?'

The Present as Value

The economy is a space for being, a place where we seek satisfaction in the present. Period. This is what makes us consume any medium that holds the promise of delivering satisfaction. And nothing—with the possible exception of chocolate—delivers such immediate satisfaction as posting a picture just taken on one's Facebook page, for all his/her friends to see. This immediacy of sharing is satisfaction in the present moment.

For millions of people Twitter has supplanted blogging, and other types of online broadcasting of one's condition; Twitter is the easiest and fastest way to broadcast yourself online. It is a broadcast with a precise address, precise audience, reaching its target every single time. The real value of Twitter as a company is the value of the social infrastructure it has created. It is also the

6 Manu, A. (2006). *The Imagination Challenge*. Berkeley, CA: New Riders, 8.

value of the indispensable service that Twitter provides for millions of people. With all these ingredients in play, Twitter may turn out to be one of the most valuable companies on the planet. For some people, Twitter is just an extended 'party line,' a bunch of people that know each other talking to each other. No value in sight. Except if you're looking at what they're talking about, how frequently they are talking about it, and where from they initiate conversations. With all this data combined, you now have a multilayered behavioral map of places, people, interests and opinions; you know what people think, moment by moment, and from where. The wisdom that one can access by aggregating this knowledge has absolutely no metric. Twitter is becoming central to how people communicate with each other, constructing a new social framework in which a limited number of characters serve to focus thinking, and communication, between people that believe that sharing their present state is a prerequisite. Twitter is just another vehicle for people that want to present themselves to others, in ways that are controllable and manageable at their own end.

The industrial model business analysts will tell you that they are skeptical of Twitter, because they find it tedious and don't use it, that they are not on Facebook and never use social media platforms, so they don't really understand what is the value of these platforms for people in general. Or their value as a business. I have heard this time and time again, followed by the qualifier:

> *None of my friends are on Twitter and none of my relatives are on Facebook. As far as I can tell, nobody that I know can be bothered to belong and contribute to these online platforms.*

So what is the meaning of this? Value is rarely a visible attribute. Everyone is used to valuate a company based on financial multiples. But this is not the case of Twitter, Facebook or YouTube. The financial multiple is replaced by depth of engagement multiples, as every one of these platforms have become masters at monetizing engagement by extracting revenue from third parties. The value may reside in all of the work that cannot be immediately quantified and qualified. Behind the scenes, Twitter is engaged in defining and qualifying the nature of conversation between the people that find it necessary to continue using the service, as a measure of their belonging. Twitter deals in the *now*. Right here, right now, this is what I'm thinking. This is how I feel. This is how I belong to my time. Twitter doesn't make products. Twitter doesn't make anything. Twitter waits for you to create your own value moments, and the value resides in your engagement with the platform. The more you are engaged, the richer that platform becomes. And the more you need that platform as a means of expression, as a means of existence, the more Twitter is worth.

How can you place value, and more so a value metric, on the ability of an individual to announce his location to his friends anytime he wants? Go to the gym; let your friends know where you are, and feel really good about it. This is *intensity value,* for a user that wants to gain a new performance stage he/she never had before. Someone wants to broadcast to their world:

> *yes, I am taking care of myself, I just spent two hours here taking care of my body. And I want you all to know. So I would post my exercises, my calorie counts, the pounds I can push or lift and everything else I can share with you, so you know that I'm really serious about taking care of myself.*

A Platform for Now: Snapchat

Snapchat is 'the fastest way to share a moment with friends.' You control how long your friends can view your message—simply set the timer up to ten seconds and send your photograph. Your friends will have ten seconds to view your image and then your message disappears forever. Snapchat is not a new behavior—it is what we were doing already, sharing our photographs with our friends on any number of social platforms. The difference now is that the author of the picture has to let go of the image at the same time as his audience does. So this is not about photography or about memorialization, as the 'memory' is erased in seconds, but about building a community of experiences with synchronic collective moments, on a scale as small or as large as one's network of friends. This again, is *intensity value.* There is no past and no future in the Snapchat collective. There is only the *now,* this moment in which we all share the same image. Snapchat maintains the ephemeral quality of each moment while adding unprecedented scale.

In celebrating the moment with friends, something larger happens to us: our sense of plurality deepens, and our connection to the other deepens as well. This has nothing to do with an image that disappears in ten seconds, but with allowing us a new dependency to participate with others in our own life.

What can we learn from this? Snapchat is a temporary front allowing people to share themselves one moment at a time, the way they want to be seen, as a measure of how they see the world in this very moment.

Social Capital Value and Valuations

Let's look at the financial value of Facebook from the perspective of its users. That is, let's put a value on each user page, a value that includes building the page as well as maintaining it. A 'proper' web site will cost you around $30,000 to develop, and, providing you are in charge of its maintenance, you will be saving some $35,000 per year. I believe that for an active Facebook user, their presence on the site is much more important than that of having a personal webpage. So it is good math to look at the value of a user's Facebook presence in the same way we look at the value of a website. Even at a discounted average of $20,000 per user page, when we multiply this by the number of Facebook users (1.2 billion), we end up with, yes, $24 trillion. This is the sum of what the collective aggregate of memories hosted on the platform is worth; this is the valuation of Facebook's social capital.

Facebook functions like a recording of one moment in time. What is the value of a recording? How about Nat King Cole in a duo with his daughter 40 years after his death? So ask yourself, what is the value of retrieved memory, the memory of you, to your daughter, 20 years from now? How much would you pay for that? The trouble in valuating Facebook[7] as a business is that we lack the tools to do so. We are adept at measuring the book value of any business based on inventory, accounts receivable, the value of real estate and so on, all measures that refer to the past but not to the future. We lack the tools to valuate behavior in economic terms. Behavior is not a raw material, and yet it is *behavior that gives value to raw material.* We need imaginative new metrics to evaluate the economic value of manifest behaviors, the behavior that we can see and document, as well as *retrieved behaviors*, behaviors that are now possible due to new spaces being created. To valuate the potential of behavior platforms we need a good measure of foresight.

Foresight as Value

Consider Google's purchase of YouTube in 2006 as an example of the company's foresight. Activated in February 2005, the domain YouTube went live in October 2005, and by mid-2006 was averaging 20 million visitors a month, who were watching about 100 million video clips daily.[8] According to its 2006 SEC

7 Manu, A. (2010). *Behavior Space*. Farnham: Gower Publishing, 37.

8 See http://googlepress.blogspot.ca/2006/10/google-to-acquire-youtube-for-165_09.html (accessed: April 7, 2014).

filing,[9] the site generated almost $15 million per year from advertising revenues. For this, Google's acquisition price was $1.6 billion, or an astonishing $80 per user. For the many cynics that were questioning at the time YouTube's staying power, this deal made no sense, on any of the known metrics. For Eric Smith, Google's CEO at the time, YouTube was the 'next step in the evolution of the internet.'[10]

This was a declaration of understanding the concept of *behavior space retrieval* and its specific dynamic: the speed of behavior retrieval compresses the time frame between a 'precise' signal[11] and a 'sensed' signal. The degree to which a technology retrieves latent behavior is the rate by which a sensed signal becomes precise. The faster, deeper and wider the adoption of YouTube as a behavior platform, the faster this activity becomes mainstream. So how many users does YouTube have today? Daily? The ultimate strategy for Google was to focus on the sensed signal and ask the question: *at its intended penetration, what value will YouTube represent and what are the constituent components of this value?* In other words 'where will the full value come from?'

The answer is simple, and it is connected to the massive behavior data gathered by the actions (retrieved behaviors) that YouTube enables: *the value of YouTube is the value of the behaviors it has successfully retrieved. YouTube is a Retrieved Behavior Space.*

A retrieved behavior is a latent behavior, a behavior that did not have a media to make it manifest (you did not know you wanted to send texts of 47 characters in length, until the medium allowing you to do so became manifest, which made your latent behavior manifest. Latent behavior is an action you might be engaged in if given the right tools.[12]

Latent behaviors derive from *latent goals*. We want, and permanently seek the conditions that will allow us to satisfy these latent goals. It is here, in the satisfaction of these goals, that humans find 'value.' The success or failure of any technology, service or concept is directly related to its capability to be a medium for the satisfaction of our motivating goals.

9 See http://techcrunch.com/2007/03/06/youtube-revenues-15-million-per-year-or-per-month/ (accessed: March 19, 2014).

10 See http://www.nbcnews.com/id/15196982/ns/business-us_business/t/google-buys-youtube-billion/#.VFzRe75cT8s (accessed: April 7, 2014).

11 Sometimes called 'weak signals,' these are information bits about behaviors that are emerging and trending upward toward the mainstream.

12 Manu, A. (2010). *Disruptive Business: Desire, Innovation and the Re-Design of Business*. Farnham: Gower Publishing, 30.

Chapter 2

To Have and To Be and the Language of Ideas

Present day capitalism assumes that the moving force of the economic system is the access to energy resources and the possession of the same resources. Everything else is discounted to favor energy. For a long time, market sentiment agreed, and Exxon was the company with the largest market cap. This is not today's reality any more. Apple Corporation has the largest market cap, and everyone seems, at times, confused as to why. Breakthrough capitalism has already happened! Apple, Google (with YouTube combined) and Facebook, just the three of them, have redefined what capitalism is all about. Some are focusing on the wrong things when looking for the constant of a business enterprise, and not the variable. The variable is behavior. And in this new context, to 'be-have' means to have in order to be, and in order to become. The economic system is all about what we want to be now, and what we want to become in the near future.

The definition of value discussed in the previous section, contains the best differentiation between the having and being mode of humans. In the having mode, we feel comfortable with understanding value as the *amount of money* that something is worth, or something that can be bought for a low or fair price.

In the being mode, we are interested in the *usefulness or importance of something to our being*, to our life, in this or the next moment. Usefulness or importance has nothing to do with numerical value or with money. It is something 'felt,' something experienced, not something 'reasoned.' The *importance of something* connects to our 'being mode' and less to our 'having mode.'

The entertainment industry is the typical sector where value is understood as the condition of being—relative worth to an individual, importance and usefulness, and where the only functionality is derived from meaning. On a fee basis, this industry is worth $2.1 trillion annually. This is about four times the budget expenditure of the United Kingdom … Which makes it imperative that we look at how the economic system is connected to the being mode of humans.

We desire pleasure in any form, and we also want specific forms of pleasure in the manifestation of artifacts. As George Santayana commented, 'beauty is pleasure objectified.'[1] We learned from Abraham Maslow[2] that human behavior is goal directed and our goals stem from:

> *Basic desires for the nourishment of the body*: The search and desire for Smooth, Soft, Shiny, Sweet, Fragrant, Intoxicating, Beauty and Pleasure.
>
> *Motivating desires*: To participate, to leave a mark, to maintain, to enhance, to propagate, and to actualize the Self.
>
> *Ultimate desires*: Knowledge, Understanding and Hope.

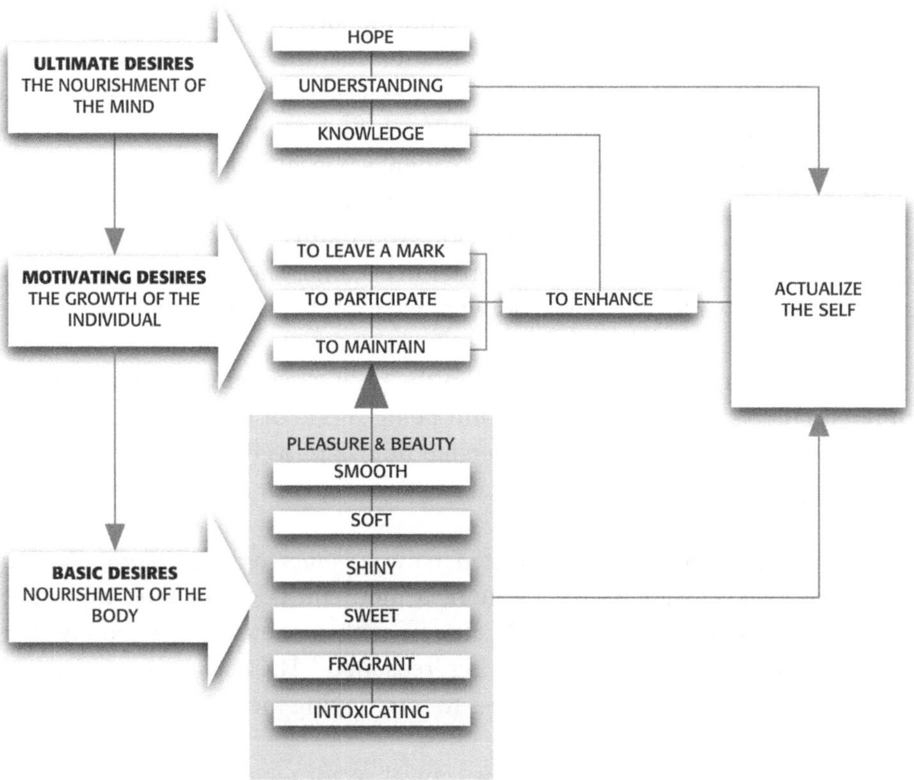

Figure 2.1 The map of motivation

1 Santayana, G. (2008). *Sense of Beauty: Being the Outlines of Aesthetic Theory*. Available at http://www.gutenberg.org/ebooks/26842 (accessed: April 12, 2009).

2 Maslow, A. (1943). 'A theory of human motivation.' *Psychological Review*, 50(4), 370–96.

We frame our life around strategies designed to experience some or all of these desires. We permanently seek higher and higher mediums for the satisfaction of these goals, as our goals change with our accomplishments, and new behavior patterns emerge, which in turn give rise to new motivations, and new goals. It is in the meeting of beneficial goals that humans find value; the benefit of the *felt* experience of satisfaction, the experience of pleasure, the experience of being (Figure 2.1).

Seeking satisfaction through experience rather than performance through interaction with objects and spaces is the higher calling of experience design. To achieve this, it all comes back to understanding humans. Not consumers, not users, not demographic targets, but simply the human being, as all human action is instigated by the desire for, and in the pursuit of, something.[3]

Intrinsic Motivation and the Behavior Economy

The search for a new state of being is one of the primary motivators of the economic system, and the reason we originate ideas, which become products or services. According to Erich Fromm,[4] the human brain has two distinct modes, and so does the human personality; the Having mode on one side is concerned with the survival instinct, having plenty for the nourishment of the body, having a roof over your head and so on. The Being Mode on the other side, is concerned with transcending our animal condition, and with creating long-lasting memories of our accomplishments during our time on Earth. In other words, the being mode is concerned with Becoming.

To have, means to have *things*. And things must have a purpose, and purpose leads to a function or a number of functions, and function leads to our search for better performance in the things we own and use. This performance can be measured, and our Having Mode seeks objective measures for the quantity of things in our life. These objective measures of performance create the motivation for possessing the thing. But this motivation is extrinsic, because we often want things because we desire to be like other people.

Things that belong in the having side of the human brain are perfectly suited for metrics and because of that, they are perfect for management because they could be managed. Management loves the having mode, because one could design

3 Manu, A. (2012). *Behavior Space*. Farnham: Gower Publishing, 32.
4 Fromm, E. (1976). *To Have or To Be*. New York, NY: Harper Row.

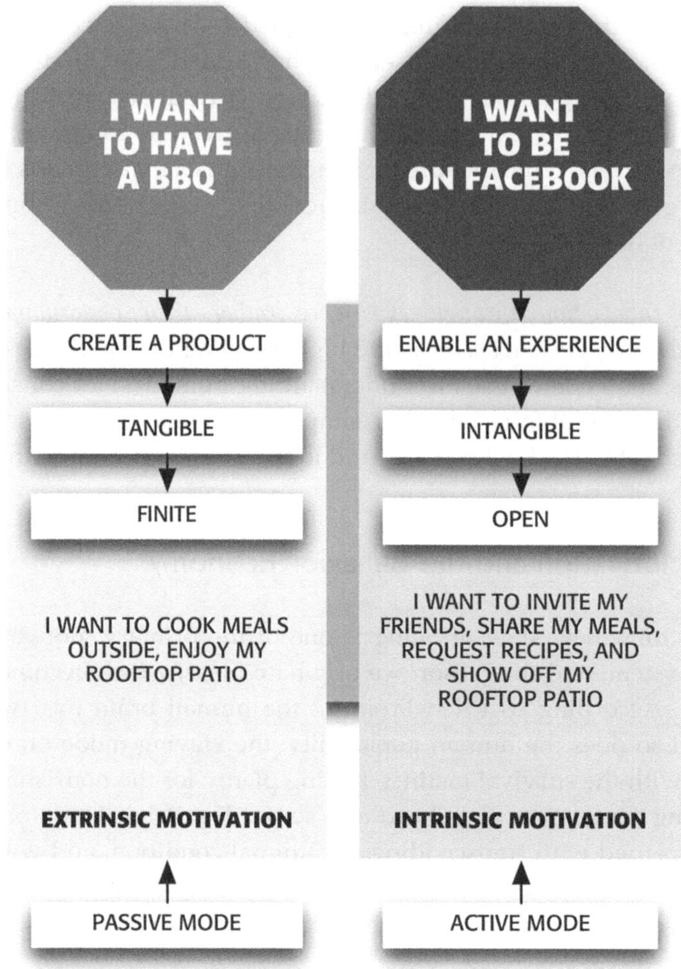

Figure 2.2 Having and being modes

processes that are understandable, because they produce things and things have a purpose. Every time somebody proposes a new thing, the only question that is asked is *what is its purpose?* As soon as a reply is given in a manner that satisfies the questioner, we are happy to accept this new thing in our life (Figure 2.2).

The Goal of Being

To be means *to experience*. It means to feel in a certain way when you look at a flower. Or to paint pictures in your imagination when you listen to a song. It means to experience all those things that create the relationship between us as physical beings, and our feelings. This relationship leads to the Manner in which we address the world around us, how we react to it, and how we participate in it with others. Manner is critical in our interaction with the world; especially in the way we experience our own actions.

Having and Being are modes that lead to two development models for products and services; one which is eminently measurable, because it contains both the quantity and quality of a thing, the other ambiguous, as it defies metrics, while at the same time having a very clear perceptive response to the experiential quality of a moment, be that the taste of chocolate, or the aftertaste of Bailey's Irish Cream. Or Mona-Lisa's smile.

In our ideal experiences, both the having and the being mode are satisfied, and we consider ourselves to be in a relationship with the *thing*.

The being mode requires however much more before it declares itself satisfied; being an active mode, it seeks for ways to be creative, rather than to be just productive, and also looking for ways in which we can have more fun, for experiences that challenge us deeper and deeper, moving us forward in our life. While the having mode seeks connectivity and productivity, our being mode is looking for something that is fun, challenging, rewarding, and absorbing. This is more or less someone's activity and experience while searching on Google. Looking for something means coming up with a search string, and that is a creative process. The more creative you are, the better the search results. Productivity without the creativity of a clever search string does not mean much. It is the being mode that ensures that our results are fast, and more accurate, and thus we are productive.

Let us look at the metrics of Having and Being. We understand how to measure the performance of a locomotive or of an automobile, and how to calculate efficiency given any number of variables. And because of that, if performance is our goal it is rather easy to build a really good automobile. If I say the word 'performance,' you have a picture in mind and an expectation as far as metrics go. Performance is a physical attribute; we need performance in a thing because we want to accomplish a task in the most efficient way, and in the shortest amount of time.

On the other hand, if I say the word 'comfort,' you have another picture in mind. So if 'comfortable luxury' is our goal, things change somewhat. We start adding to the performance of the automobile attributes that we associate with luxury and comfort. But these attributes are not a guaranteed measure of success for every individual's taste preference, because both luxury and comfort are concepts and thus not measurable in the same way in which the performance of a chain link can be measured. For describing the attributes of luxury, we need to move from the having mode to the being mode, a mode in which we need the language of ideas. Your hear 'luxury' and you think of …? How many people will give the same answer? For some people luxury might mean something shiny. Other people will think immediately of the softness of a well-worn leather couch. Or maybe a combination of shiny and soft might do.

In the being mode we are dealing with totally different ways of measuring the attributes of a thing, and if we try any metrics they might be inaccurate because of the variety of personal experiences people have had in their life, which in turn has given the objectification of the concepts of comfort and luxury many personal interpretations.

The Benefit of Value and the Benefit of Meaning

What is then the connection between having and being and the creation of value? Having creates the means that allow humans to pursue meaning. The having mode seeks the transformation of matter through labor into *means*, while the being mode seeks the transformation of matter into *meaning*, through creativity and imagination. For thousands of years, while the material was physical in nature—stone, marble, steel, glass, and ceramics—the union of means and meaning was somewhat in balance. Objects were made of materials present to the senses, and thus an individual or group was able to assess the value of the object, based on its material qualities, the labor involved and the meaning assigned the object. We are now in the presence of a new material, and that is data, a material that has no physical presence or volume, and a material whose value is the content itself: the value of data resides in the meaning it represents.

In the absence of the having mode, and all its attributes leading to an assessment of value—function, performance—we have a hard time with placing value on data.

We take steel and we make a bridge. We take metal and reshape it as a hammer. We transform these things by labor. We take plastic and make celluloid, and that becomes a substrate on which we can print moving pictures.

But movies have meaning, so making a movie and using that celluloid means matter transformed by imagination.

We find coffee in a coffee bush, dry it, roast it, grind it, and we pump water through these grounds at high pressure, transforming it in a wonderfully foamy and flavored espresso. That is not the matter transformed by labor, this is matter transformed by the imagination that can conceive a moment of pleasure, in the experience of a cup of espresso. A moment we value. This is value as Benefit. Value is a benefit not a solution. Value is a mental process. People don't want the coffee bean; people want the flavor of coffee as a benefit, transforming a moment of life into a pleasurable experience, in our perpetual quest for becoming and for pleasure by any means.

Some executives have a hard time addressing the being part of humans—with the exception of executives in the cultural industries, fashion and cosmetics—because that part is hard to measure, hard to quantify and it is hard to manage. When Steve Jobs was calling for business education to be closer to the liberal arts, rather than technology and science, he was pointing out the reality that business is not a science, but an art, with its own aesthetic, that of the relationship between the having and being mode of an individual. Jobs continues 'the reason that Apple is able to create products like the iPad is because we always try to be at the intersection of technology and liberal arts, to be able to get the best of both.'[5]

For understanding of what the being mode is after, we need to understand the language of concepts, and then understand the ideas that we associate with each concept.

The Language of Concepts and Ideas

Language is a human ability that allows us to communicate with one another, complex concepts or simple ideas. In the absence of language, we are blind as to the value of things in our surroundings, as we lack the ability to express their value to others. So it is fundamental in the creation of value for others, to have the ability to express the attributes of an experience, to use analogies and symbolic images that trigger associations. The lack of an appropriate language is usually the main reason executives are unable to understand the relevance

5 See http://fortune.com/2010/01/27/live-blog-steve-jobs-presents-the-apple-tablet/ (accessed July 13, 2014).

of a competitor's product; if you cannot express what is great about a product, you are bound to ignore its relevance.

This is precisely what happened when the iPhone was introduced into the market place, by a company that was not an incumbent in the communications sector, as both Nokia and Research in Motion (today's Blackberry) were. These incumbents where blind to the potential of the iPhone to disrupt their market not because they did not see the iPhone, but because they *lacked the language to define what it was*. That language is not technical, that language is not English or German, and that is the language of ideas and value creation.

Mathematics has its own language. So do physics, biology, finance, marketing, etc. They all have terms with definitions that mean something. $E=mc^2$ has a specific meaning that transcends time and space. It doesn't matter what century it is, what business you operate, or who you are. $E=mc^2$ is a universal truth that applies across all cases across all time. That's equally true for ROI in finance, or DNA structures in biology. These are examples of universal truths expressed in a *technical* language.[6]

But what about value creation? What are the universal truths about that? How many universal truths can you name (with terms and definitions) that explain value creation across all times and in all environments? So this is not only about seeing, it is about understanding what you're seeing, and being able to describe what you are seeing. In education at all levels, but especially at the undergraduate and graduate level, where are the courses in 'value creation'? We teach our MBA's to manage value assets, how to increase value in products and services, but who learns in a business school anything about how to create value? If one lacks the elements of language when one is faced with describing something new, there are no frames of reference left. When we don't have frames of reference, all we have left is our own experience, so we are faced with describing the new experience based on a previous experience, defining value creation from our perspective, the perspective of the business we are currently engaged in.

My collaborator, John Sutherland, has proposed a new definition of value that takes into account a framing of the experience new value creates. In his definition, the *creation of value is the expansion of relationships from new behaviors enabled by a disruptive media.* Any time our relationships are being expanded

6 Sutherland, J. (2012). 'Afterword: Getting started.' In A. Manu, *Behavior Space.* Farnham: Gower Publishing, 211–22.

into a new behavior, or a retrieved behavior due to a disruptive media, we can call that moment value creation or new value.

This definition works in describing why we find value in Facebook, why we find value in Twitter, YouTube and other social platforms.

If we look at life as being composed of relationships between our environment and ourselves, life becomes a system of relationships between ourselves and time, our location in time, in space, or where we are at any given moment. We also have a relationship with our own self, which is the quest of understanding it and promoting it to others, which brings us to our relationship with others, either by themselves or in groups, and the relationship with our objects and with our ideas. Every one of these relationships is being enriched by the disruptive medium we call Facebook. In the context of these multiple relationships and in proportion to their depth and complexity, what creates value in our interaction with a new medium is the measure by which this medium improves both the size and quality of our relationships. Improving the size means allowing us an easy reach to a greater number, while improving quality means introducing new layers of experience, be that by means of images, sounds or motion pictures/video.

The language of value creation uses *concepts*, and concepts use *ideas*. A concept is a platform for an idea, the place where ideas come from. Value is in itself a concept. Breakthrough leaders of the new economy are talking about concepts, and plan strategy in conceptual terms. *Connectivity* is a concept. *Access and empowerment* are concepts. *Beauty* is a concept, and many ideas can express it. Concepts have attributes which compel us to describe them, thus entering into a conversation about the concept. For each individual the attributes of concepts are personal, as we assess concepts based on individual frameworks for value.

What are the attributes of 'elegant'? Elegance is beauty. Once I say or write the word elegant, I have to describe in which way something is elegant. Once I say something is 'nice' I have to be more specific. So these idea words invite elaboration. They invite development. They invite descriptive examples of their properties. If something is beautiful in my opinion, I am bound to explain to my peer group which attributes of this product or experience are beautiful and why. I would use analogies, I would use metaphors, and I would probe my audience for any experiences of the past that might contain characteristics of the experience I'm describing as beautiful.

The language of ideas is not a science. In the context of value creation, the language of ideas is something felt, something that has to be experienced. It is something that uses somebody's imagination because one cannot access the concept of beauty without imagination.

Ideas about things are attributes. One of the toughest concepts to describe is probably the concept of 'cool.' What makes an experience cool? The description that follows uses idea words which in turn might be concepts, but understood nevertheless by the audience from their own experiential perception. An experience that is categorized as being cool is something that has a sense of *novelty*, something that is *technologically advanced*, something that has a *sense of uniqueness*, something that has a sense of *special*, in the sense that it is a special kind of experience, not part of ordinary life, and it is something that you encountered only a few times up to the moment in which you are describing something is a cool experience.

A cool experience is a transformative experience. Spending the week at the Burning Man festival is probably very cool. Because of the attributes I just described, the coolness factor of something disappears as the frequency of use increases.

The Internet of Things is another good example of a concept. To make someone understand what is the promise of the Internet of Things, you will have to give a few examples of some of the tangible benefits of this new technological capability in people's lives. And the language used in these examples would undoubtedly use more concepts and ideas, things such as *the connected fleet*, or *predictive maintenance*, or *smart cities*, or *smart shopping malls*, and so on.

Each one of these ideas fall under the big umbrella framework of the Internet of Things, which is a concept holding other concepts, each one requiring further explanation detailing the benefits of predictive maintenance, or manifestations of what a smart city is in daily life. What is a smart city all about? Well for one thing, it is a city that is aware of its inhabitants, it is aware of its consumption needs in terms of utilities, it is aware of the location of the inhabitants at any given moment, it is aware of the transactions that take place and the interactions between the city's inhabitants, their objects and their spaces. A smart street understands when to turn its lights on or off, based on the number of participants in traffic at any given time. A smart street corner can talk to a smart car, in order to understand where that car wants to go, and where is it coming from, so it can adjust accordingly all the traffic lights towards the destination.

Concepts are forcing us to imagine ideas about creating new benefits in people's lives, benefits that balance the having and being mode to a new degree of satisfaction.

Concept is to idea what vision is to mission. Vision is where to go and the mission is how to get there. An idea allows individuals to perceive the reality that doesn't physically exist. How does this translate to enterprise?

Concurrent sets of ideas are key in organizing the missions that implement the vision of an enterprise.

Chapter 3
Dimensions of Value

Our expectation of value is only based on our most recent perceptual experience. Imagine your life 15 years ago. It is the year 2000, and you have a partner and two children. You live in a nice house and you have everything you need. Everything you think you need for a comfortable life in the year 2000. Everything you need for a 'connected life' which makes you equal with your peers.

Everything you need means that you have one TV set in the living room and maybe one in the basement, all the appliances you might require in the kitchen, you probably have a microwave and nothing more. And you might have one personal computer. This is the year 2000. The Internet is only nine years old. You have no use for a computer in the house, there is barely Google, and there is no Facebook. There is no Internet streaming. Napster is illegal and Netflix is maybe a glimmer in someone's eyes. It simply does not exist. The big boy is Blockbuster, and for them you have a VHS handily connected to your TV set.

Your value judgments are essentially based on what you think you need, and the measure by which what you have supplies your needs. And you have enough. You have enough because you never thought of more. Because you never sat down one day and asked this question yourself: *what would I really want in my life?* What will really make me happy? What will really give my kids the opportunity to explore, discover, learn and become better people?

It is now 2015. Every member of your family, your wife, your children, and yourself own a personal computer. But it doesn't stop here. Each one of your family members has a phone, which is also connected to your Wi-Fi router. And, you have a legacy of other devices that you purchased along the way. A few MP3 players, CD players, your old film camera and your VCR video recording machine. What is value in this context? What do you have in the year 2015 that you did not have in the year 2000?

I am proposing the value depends on the behavior cycle you are in, as you cycle through life gaining insights and expectations, from experiences that transform you and improve you. Value assessments change, as we complete more behavior cycles and desire more and more (see Figure 1.1), and what was value to you in 2000, has no value now.

Background to Dimensions of Value

What is the value of 'time' in the economy of 'being'? Asked another way, why do we value the manipulation of time so much? Because we know human life is limited? Because we have a sense of our own mortality? This is worth considering:

We value time shifting. Fast forwarding. Netflix binging is the result of our need for time compression. The first value here is *time compression*. We see this value manifest in many forms: spending considerable amounts of money on a bottle of aged wine. Why? Because we are shifting time in our favor. We can taste the wine *today* without waiting 12 years. Same with single malt scotch, where we shift time by 15 years every time we buy a bottle of 15-year-old malt.

We also value compressing *physical distance* and we value *expanding physical presence,* by all available means: Facebook, Instagram, Pinterest, YouTube. We want our images, our ideas and impressions expanded on as large a territory as possible. In our Spiritual, Intellectual and Professional dimensions we like to fast forward the understanding of things. That is why we like to watch TED Talks, read books and magazines, and subscribe to podcasts.

Value and the Condition of Being Human

Of all animals, we are the animal that knows about our limited time on Earth; we learn very early in life that we will die. As a result, our life becomes a series of plans for achieving, in any way possible, continuity on Earth. Continuity in the form of the objects we create, which in turn create our ways of life, manifestations of our transcendence from our animal nature. It is in the plans we make to insure our life has meaning, that we can find the seeds of change and transformation. As humans, we think and act from the gut, through the heart, and into the brain. This is where we *live from*. This is where we have created masterpieces from, the monuments that we leave behind for our children, as proof that we have existed. We exist only in the measure of how we exist for others. This is why Facebook has value for us. It allows for the coexistence of an ideal self with others, with hundreds and thousands of others. It allows us to belong to a community in which our contribution—our Facebook postings—adds value to the community itself, as well as to our life.

Every time we consider concepts like the concept of value, we need to place in the center of this conversation the main actor for which value has meaning, and that is the human being. There is no value in 'things' if the human element is removed; because it is this human that gives meaning to the 'thing' and thus value. Value is not a fact, it is not a number and it is not a particular tool. Value is a feeling, a way of becoming something that we like about ourselves, at the moment of encountering something that has the power to transform us. We permanently seek the best circumstances for the way we experience life, and this is where value resides for us.

It is these circumstances that form the Human Behavior Space, and the richness and variety of the human experience of life. In the next few pages I will explore the drive humans have towards becoming more than they are, which is the drive *to be human*, the drive to leave a mark, and the drive to participate. These are the value creation activities that humans engage in; these are the metrics on which we judge value.

The Human Context: Meaning and Human Life

Humans are not just a species any more. Human life is not about efficiency any more, and not about the lowest energy state. We need culture to survive[1] and grow, and so, human life is about storytelling, literature, and music, about meaning.

The Condition of Being Human

Hannah Arendt[2] outlined the human condition as being the artifacts that define our life as humans on this Earth at any given moment. At any given moment,

1 Manu, A. (2013). 'Sustainability and the condition of being human.' In S. Walker and J. Giard (eds), *The Handbook of Design for Sustainability*. London: A&C Black.

2 Arendt, H. (1964). *The Human Condition*. Chicago, IL: University of Chicago Press.

things—the objects, services or ideas we use—condition us. We are equally conditioned by the Internet, as we are conditioned by cooking protein on the kitchen stove, ironing our shirts, brushing our teeth, reading and writing ideas on paper. Our purpose—what conditions us—is the desire to leave a mark and to participate. Leaving a mark and participating is what we do right now on YouTube, on Facebook, on Flickr and on Wikipedia. We participate. Keep this idea in mind while you consider the Zulu concept of 'Ubuntu,' which means 'Me through Your eyes.' In other words, *'I exist because you see me.'* Therefore, I will do whatever it takes to exist in a way in which you will see me as the best possible 'me' at this time. I will wash, wipe, smell good, look good, know more, and want more. Be more, become better in your eyes. Better. I will do whatever it takes to exist at a new level every time you see me.

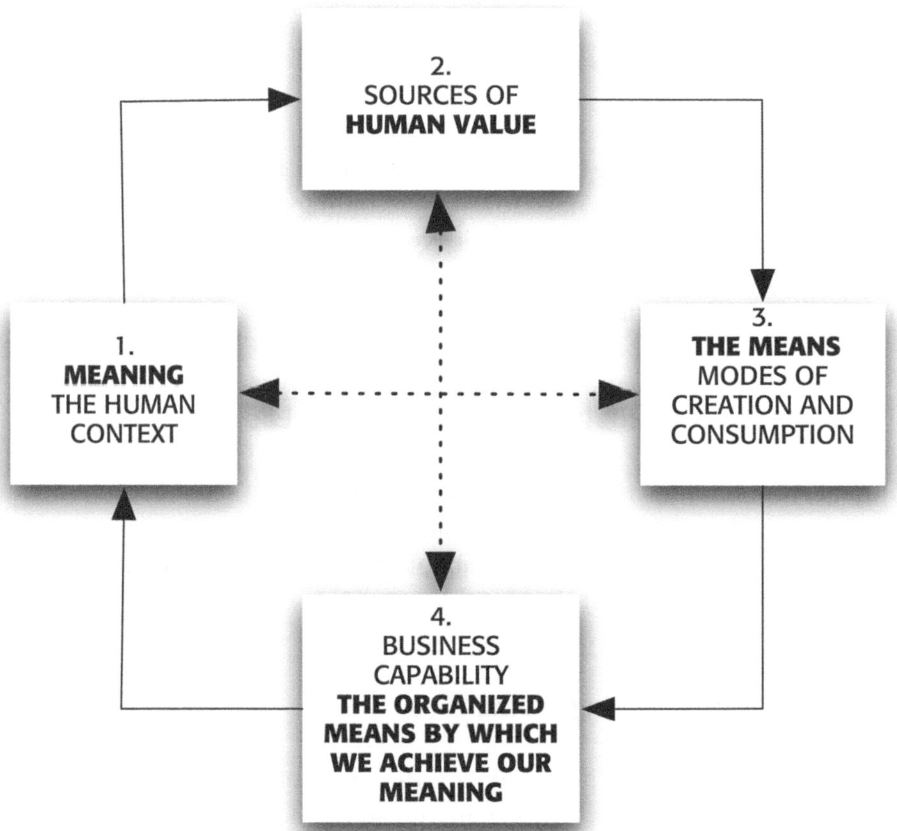

Figure 3.1 **The human behavior space**

Sources of Human Value

For Arendt 'Humans are conditioned beings because everything they come in contact with turns immediately into a condition of their existence.' Arendt introduced the concept of 'vita activa,' which helps in understanding the nature of the questions we pose, when coming in contact with any event that has influence on our life activities. Vita activa is the Human Behavior Space (Figure 3.1). It is the *why* and *what* of human activity.

> *With the term vita activa, I propose to designate three fundamental human activities: labor, work, and action. They are fundamental because each corresponds to one of the basic conditions under which life on earth has been given to human beings.*

Labor, work and action, are the activities for which we design, the activities for which we have built and created the world of tools, the world of education, and the world of laws, as well as all the constructed spaces we now call civilization. This is the world we refer to with the generic term 'technology.' Arendt defines labor as:

> *the activity which corresponds to the biological process of the human body, whose spontaneous growth, metabolism, and eventual decay are bound to the vital necessities produced and fed into the life process by labor. The human condition of labor is life itself.*

In this condition, the question asked is in the realm of the tactical: the question is 'How?' *How do I survive? How do I find food? How do I build shelter?* This is a condition related to the 'having' side of the human being, a side interested in the *quantity of things,* their performance, durability, appropriateness for the task, numbers and the sequence of action. A condition concerned with the tactics of life.

Perfecting the performance of tools is also a 'how' question, suitable to the 'having mode,' a mode dominated by our interest in acquiring things which are fixed and describable. According to Fromm:[3]

> *Most of us know more about the mode of having than we do about the mode of being, because having is by far the more frequently experienced mode in our culture. ... Being refers to experience, and human experience is in principle not describable.*

3 Fromm, E. (1976). *To Have or To Be*. New York, NY: Harper & Row.

Fromm points to a quality unique to humans: the quality of being, of becoming through experiences and learning. This is the quality that completes us, and gives meaning and reason to why we need to move always forward, searching for more ways to experience life, for why we need to learn, to explore in order to have more worth and merit. *The quality that allows us to become.* To leave a mark through our work and deeds. To have mattered, for others. To be seen through their eyes.

For Arendt, work is the activity that corresponds to the unnaturalness of human existence. Work provides an 'artificial' world of things, distinctly different from all natural surroundings. In other words, the creation of worth, using our tools, and the answers to the question *Why?*

Desire and What We Find of Value in Human Life

Earlier, I discussed briefly the role desire plays in creating the ethos for developing products, services and the ways of life these create in return. Anytime we develop something new, we are in effect the development: we redesign ourselves every time we create new tools for our survival and betterment. We are re-designed by these tools and we re-design with them our human behavior space.

'Desire is the ultimate source of action.'[4] The desire to survive, the desire to achieve a different level of existence: these are the ultimate sources of action. The question for you right now is: What do you desire? How open are you to understanding what you desire and to believing that this desire can transform the way you look at everything else? Understanding the nature of your desire can create a path for a new journey of life.

What is it that we desire? *The media that both define where we are, and where we want to go in life.* We exist not because we are here, now, but because we want to become and we strive for more, and because we made the choice of defining ourselves as different than other animals. Striving for more and wanting to become, are foundations for the architecture of existence and the primary value metrics in human life. Looking at everything around us you will see statements about who we have become through our desire and striving. The buildings, bridges, paintings, technologies, music, roads, all you can see and hear are manifestations of our desires to leave a mark, to participate, to know,

4 Aristotle (1986). *De Anima.* London: Penguin Books Ltd.

to understand, to maintain, to enhance, to actualize and to propagate. The Taj Mahal would have never been built, if we didn't desire to leave a mark. Most of the monuments that you know are about us, making sure that we are being seen through other people's eyes.

Somebody needed to be seen, and that's how the Eiffel Tower was built. Every human artifact that is of value to us must answer this singular question: *How is this a medium for me? How can this allow me to satisfy, to actualize, to propagate, to participate? How does this allow me to leave a mark? How does this allow me to reach my next destination?* Facebook is an exemplary model of a medium that answers precisely these fundamentals.

Value in Change

Humans are always in multiple states of being: who we were yesterday, who we are today, and who we will be tomorrow. We are on a perpetual journey towards a dynamic destination. This is what 'becoming' requires. We are in constant need of mediums, because we need a constant tool for our new direction in life. Every tool that we create is an expression of our current understanding of the destination, and these tools always modify our destination. We are in constant need for tools as new platforms for possibility, and through them, new destinations for becoming. Wanting to become means both recognizing and desiring new conditions. Beneath this desire is a value judgment—an implicit personal assigning of value to change—an embracing and ranking of different states of existence. Wanting is the pursuit of possibility, and implicitly assigns value to change.

Me Through Your Eyes: Wellness and Purposeful Transformation

I want to be the best I can be so you can see me as the best representation of myself. So far, so good. But how do I measure this condition and how do I label it? We use the term Wellness to generally describe the absence of disease and a generally positive and productive state of mind. According to the National Wellness organization and Ray Meyer Fitness & Recreation Center, of DePaul University, there are six dimensions[5] of wellness that are necessary to feel healthy and be happy in this life. Health and wellness is a state of being that is more

5 Six Dimensions of Wellness. Available at: http://www.nationalwellness.org/?page=Six_Dimensions&hhSearchTerms=%22six+and+dimensions%22 (accessed: April 10, 2015). Also, see http://c.ymcdn.com/sites/www.nationalwellness.org/resource/resmgr/docs/sixdimensions factsheet.pdf (accessed: April 10, 2015).

than an 'absence of disease.' When you attain a balance in the six dimensions of wellness, you feel more energized and excited about living. You will be more proactive, self-determined, joyful, and healthier. All six dimensions are needed to feel totally fulfilled, and depending on your personality, you may find more satisfaction and joy in one area than another, but you should not neglect any one of the areas. All six dimensions of wellness are integrated and influence each other; the first dimension needs the most attention as your ability to do all the other areas is curtailed if you fail in the first.

Because of the importance we give in life to each of these six dimensions, they become dimensions of what we value.

Intrinsic Dimensions of Value

Social

Occupational

Spiritual

Physical

Intellectual

Emotional

These are dominants of our daily life, as we seek media for the satisfaction of each one to a degree of maximum potential. In this context, maximum potential means either faster time compression or a larger and more expansive physical presence. Facebook is a medium for our Social, Emotional, Physical and Intellectual dimensions, and it has intrinsic value precisely because of this.

In the *social* dimension, we value contributing to the common good and the wellbeing of our communities. Being social means to live in coexistence with others in a harmonious way. We value our impact on society and the environment in which we work and actively seek ways to enhance our relationship with others, through better communications, and for increasing our impact and relevance to them.

In the *occupational* dimension, we value gaining personal satisfaction from our work, and more so we value when we work from passion rather than constraint. We value and find satisfaction when our intrinsic likes are aligned with our chosen profession. We value the pursuit of fundamental questions as much as we value the answers we might get, and this is our *spiritual* wellness. As we grow spiritually, we seek awareness and an understanding of the origin of things, and value when our emotions are in harmony, and our actions are guided by our sense of right and wrong.

Physically, we value living well. This means understanding the limits of our bodies, knowing we have the strength and endurance to partake in the activities that we enjoy, and proactively being engaged in pursuing ways to get better at everything we do.

In the *intellectual* dimension, we value stimulating our mind and all mediums that do it, all ideas that increase our awareness, expand our knowledge and skills. We also value being in the 'know' when we need to, and we get satisfaction from sources of knowledge that expand our depth of understanding of the world around us (Google anyone?).

The *emotional* dimension seeks and values the acceptance of our emotions and feelings by others, and the ability to realistically evaluate our limits when faced with stressful situations. We do not like to lose control; we like to cope with everything life throws at us. We value the emotional balance that brings about and maintains a healthy and satisfying relationship with others.

The Means: Modes of Creation and Consumption

Of all the examples I could give here, I will just give the one most connected to the first chapter of this book, Chasing Value. The need for remembrance is intrinsic to the human condition of worldliness, of transcending just being and wanting to become more for others, to leave a mark. We expend incalculable resources in order to be remembered and to remember others. Remembering is part of our human narrative and part of sustaining civilization; the pursuit of memory might be one of the most intrinsic—in the sense that we spend no time thinking about it in a logical fashion, or debating its merits, instead we simply do it—actions humans engage in. One of its manifestations is the *Retrieval and Preservation of Memory as Human Condition.*

Consider the photographic camera. Or Instagram. Or the camera on your smart phone. Why do people take pictures? Images of Memory. What is a camera all about? It is about the retrieval of a life's experience. We seek the full recovery of ourselves in one specific moment in time. This is not about the high definition of the image; it is about the moment being captured in any way, shape or form. The moment is about what you perceived in a particular place, at a particular time. About what you felt, what you sensed, what you experienced. Most of all, about what you want others to share of this moment. You will want to keep that moment and share it with the group that defines your plurality as a human. Memory is about retaining, recalling, and sharing information that defines who you are for you, and for others.

Our purpose as human beings is to create something that attests to our presence on Earth. We need to survive for sure, but after that, we are involved in a quest for meaning, a quest for worth as measured by others. We need to create and let others know we have created. This fulfills our human condition of plurality. To make sure others know we exist. We did not build the Eiffel Tower because we wanted shelter or we were trying to survive. We built the Eiffel Tower because we were trying to tell something about ourselves, to ourselves, in the present and in the future. We need to leave a mark; it is the condition of our humanity.

The desire to memorialize is not restricted to historic times; it is a modern preoccupation that substantiates our humanity, as different and more complex than the life of other animals on our planet.

Business Capability: The Organized Means by which we Achieve Value

Memorializing is not a trivial pursuit; it is not about the self, but about the perceived significance of the self to others. This is the real value of our digital legacy on Facebook; through Facebook we are leaving a trace that, from our perspective of today, looks like immortality. *Facebook is the organized means by which the human condition of plurality receives its current manifestation, and its most compelling value platform.*

What is the business model that will deliver the values we hold as primal to our being? It is all a question of how one defines 'business.' I define the role of any business as *the organized capability of creating and delivering any medium for the manifestation of human behavior.* The tools we use, the staples we consume

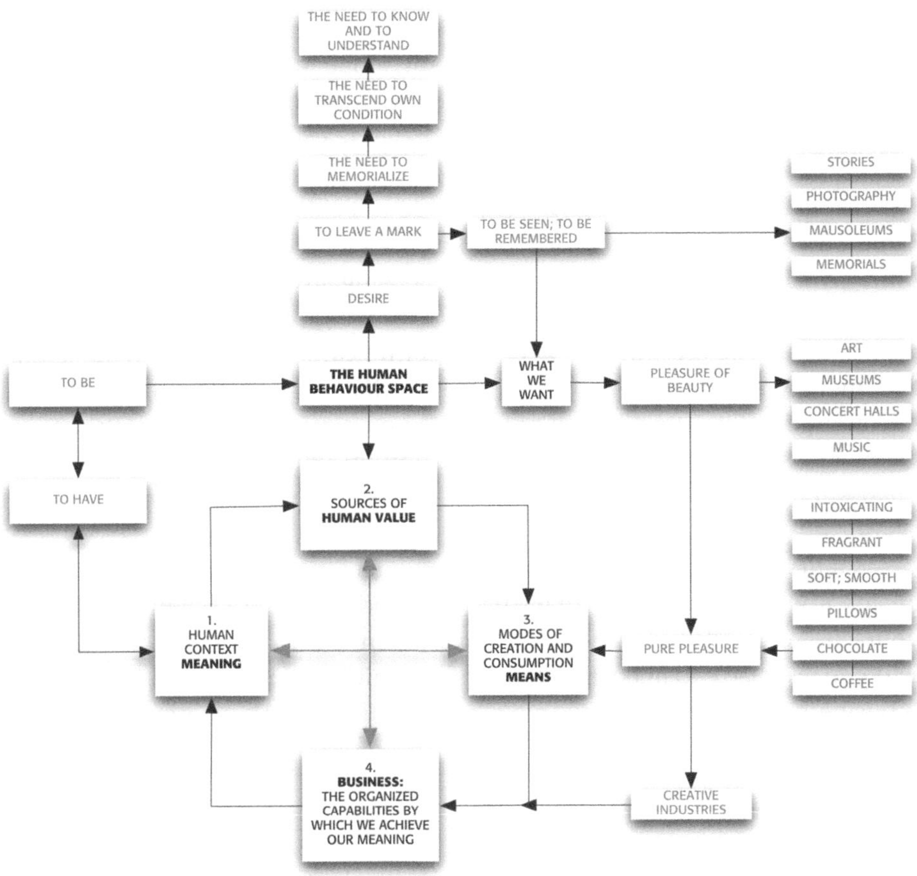

Figure 3.2 The simplified map of the human conditions and its means

every day to maintain who we are, and to become more than what we are. The means (Figure 3.2) that deliver on our primary dimensions of value, by allowing us to *become* and to *belong.*

The Primary Dimensions of Value

The goal of becoming—rather than just simply being—may be unique to the human animal, and it is at the root of our behavior of engaging in new experiences of learning, of exploration, of permanent search for more. More understanding, more value. Our goals are closely tied to our purpose; that of creating objects, methods, images and ideas that will transcend our mortality, and will attest to our presence on Earth.

Plurality. The condition of being human; you cannot be human without being plural. Being human means not being alone; it also means sharing what and who you are. From the moment we are born to the moment we die, we strive not to be alone, and we will do whatever necessary not to be alone.

Ubuntu. It is the condition in which I do not exist without you. Our worth is measured in what we are worth for others, in their eyes. It is our condition of plurality. Human survival is more than just being alive; it is the quality of being alive that matters to most of us. This is why we go to school, this is why we participate in society, and this is why we build careers. We are leaving a mark for others. We are telling them what our destination was. We are asking them to continue our journey. For all of us, in the community. These are the choices we make as humans, choices that define not only the journey, but also likely, the destination.

In a first reaction to these ideas, you may feel they have nothing to do with business, with markets, or with the financial and economic system. Think inside yourself. You will discover that you want something, and you will discover that you are ready to make the choice of engaging in an exchange to get it. This is business. And the choices we make on the journey to transform ourselves are the economic system.

Chapter 4

Reframing Value: Duality and the Internet of Things

Becoming Through Plurality

When thinking about new value, we must first accept a period of questioning everything and reframing our understanding of what is now of value to people first, and to organizations second. In this context, 'now' means an emerging reality in which individuals are both connected and existent in each other's life, being at the same time physically linked and virtually present. Every time I post pictures of my food or my bread on Facebook, I am reminded of this, as I sense at all times the virtual presence of all my Facebook contacts. I have a duality of being, as I am present in people's lives and they are in mine, without a physical proximity in flesh, but with proximity of intent and purpose. What I do seems to matter to 'them' and what 'they' do matters to me. It matters at least enough that I keep an eye on their posts on my Facebook feed. The 'me' on Facebook is constantly broadcasting to others, even when I am asleep. This is a duality of being, a state in which both my physical presence and my virtual avatar presence on various forms of social media merge, forming a new entity in which Duality is the whole. *This duality is a continuum of becoming through the plurality of others.*

The dilemma of Duality is inherent in the condition of being human. This is the simultaneous truth of life in both a physical body and an intangible mind. This condition carries with it a challenge to meet the needs of the body, while satisfying the needs of the mind. This is what our actions on Facebook prove, that we are concerned with both. However, the Internet of Things introduces a duality to non-sentient physical entities, by giving physical objects a persistent virtual presence.

In the Internet of Things, every Enabled Person, Place and Object has more than a physical presence; they have a communication presence. This communication presence is the ability of a Person, Object or Space to inform each other through data transfer.

The result of everything connected to everything else that *makes sense*, is a Link-Enabled ecology, a complex ecosystem of interdependent and networked organic elements. The ecosystem is the very relationship between organisms and their environment, a community of ecological parts functioning as a unit, determined by and dependent upon its members.

Navigation in a Link-Enabled ecology will be the meaningful navigation of physical and virtual data transfers, forming and informing interactions of everyday life, where people live and work in virtual settings such as Facebook, YouTube, blogs, eBay and video games. The borders between virtual and physical space blur further, as smart phones have extended online environments into more and more physical settings.

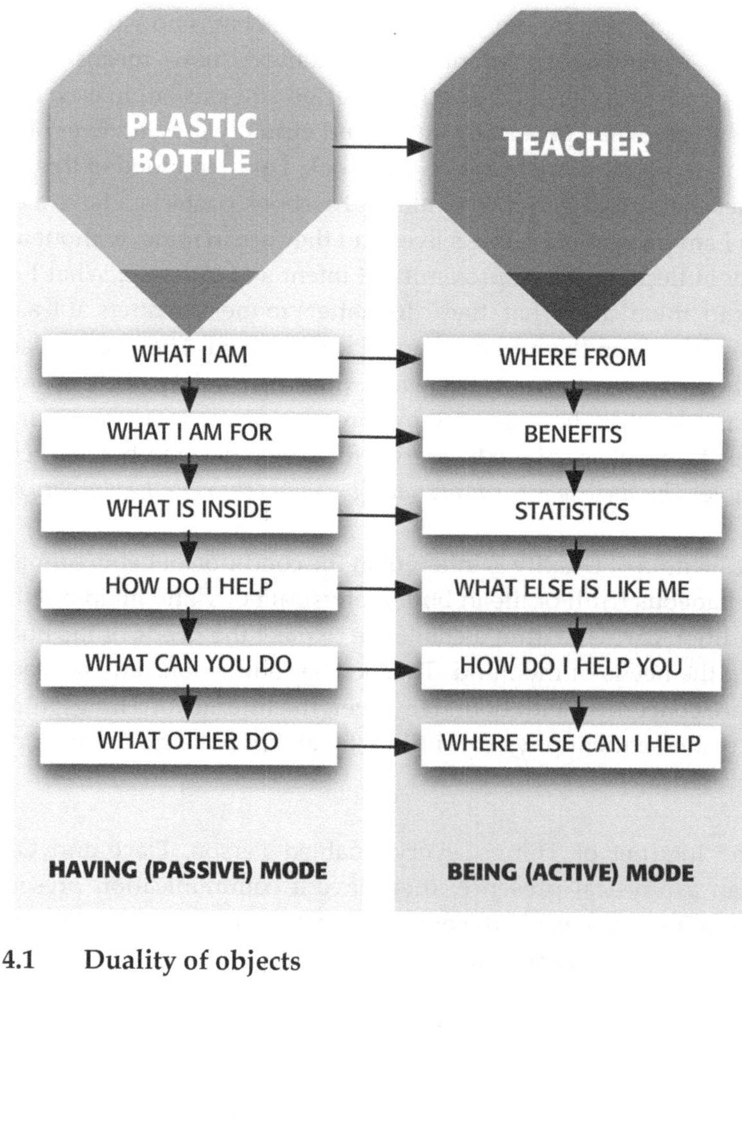

Figure 4.1 Duality of objects

When objects and spaces gain the capability to communicate digitally with our devices through Near Field Communication (NFC), Bluetooth, iBeacon, etc., elements of the physical world will require a sensory representation in virtual space. Thus, each element of the Internet of Things will have a dual social role.

They will *be something*—a street car, a lamp post, a mail box, a park bench—while at the same time they will *mean something*—a connection to granularly filtered knowledge about the context of the object itself, tailored for individual interests and needs. The rules that guide the representation of any object or space (physical or virtual) should aim to express this social role.

By examining the relationships of objects, people and spaces under the concept of Duality, we expand our understanding of the emerging potential of Link-Enabled ecologies as behavior platforms, and we gain a better understanding of the possible value that can be created for the monetization of these platforms (Figure 4.1).

Dimensions of Duality: Duality of Self

As the fabric of the physical world becomes interlaced with elements of the virtual world, reality is split in two. I do not refer to a split between reality and virtual reality—I am suggesting a split of the real and virtual self. Life in the emerging present is the challenge of living in both worlds at once. This dual life must become a union rather than a fracture, since each world lends itself to its own natural interactions and exchanges. The physical world is the arena of an intuitive pursuit of discovery, while the virtual world lends itself to thought exploration. This new paradigm will change the way we perceive the places we live in, the demands we place on our tools, and even the way that we see ourselves.

As we move forward in the Internet of Things, objects and spaces will gain the capability to communicate digitally with our receiving devices. The integration of the real and virtual world frees *place* from *location*—in the sense that now a place can do more than just 'be there,' and can mean more than just its latitude and longitude coordinates—and fill them with the capabilities of the people who bring in these places their goals and desires, and in return have a meaningful experience. To the physical attributes of places that hold meaning to people, we can now add their attributes of meaning, all in a digital form, making them searchable, filtered and organized, in ontologies of significance to people's lives. What places mean to people is not physical, but a world that exists in our collective imagination. Think of the Taj-Mahal, the Louvre, the Uffizi Palace, the Smithsonian and Disney World, to mention just a few.

Maximizing Value in Duality

How do we maximize our current capability to create value and provide benefits? How we can maximize interactions in physical space to provide benefit in the digital landscape? In truth, these are not distinct questions but two sides of the same question. Tools, for example, are conditioned by purpose—shaped to suit the way that they will be used. So the design of a tool is the study of the capabilities that they enable. In the paradigm of duality, we cannot presume that the tool will be strictly tangible or strictly virtual—we must begin with an understanding that life occurs in both realms at once. Is Facebook strictly virtual when people begin their day checking the latest updates from their friends? Once one 'likes' a post is that not a tangible action that takes place in 'real life'?

Two Worlds

The virtual world is not the world of the digital; it is the world of the imagination, the world not present to the senses. Leonardo da Vinci's portrait of Mona Lisa exists in both the physical and virtual world. In the physical world, it is a 77 x 53 cm piece of wood coated with dried pigment. In the imagination of the viewer she becomes a woman with an intriguing smile—this smile does not tangibly exist since the woman exists only in the mind of the viewer. In art, literature and science, people have long explored ideas through virtual incarnations of real or imagined worlds. Artists create sensual stimuli to evoke response and change perception. Writers create immersive worlds in which avatars grow and share human experiences. Scientists use metaphor and symbolic diagrams, to model relationships that are beyond direct observation.

I refer to these representations as *virtual* insofar as their meaning is virtual and not explicit—found not in the traits of the physical, but in the interpretation of the receiver. These worlds are able to convey ideas that transcend explicit physical demonstration.

From Location to Place

A geographical map traditionally shows the location of places in space. 'Spaces occur between places' or we could say 'a place is a space with meaning.' The notion of place and space are often attached to the labeling of a location, but this association is not necessarily truthful. A location is a fixed and indexed position that can be described by referencing the origin of a chosen coordinate system. A place however is the personal or collective understanding of the reason for a location—'place' is *best described by illustrating the experiences that occur there.*

To demonstrate, I am now at *a location* on Martinique Beach, E. Petpeswick Rd, Musquodoboit Harbour, Nova Scotia, Canada, with coordinates 44°41' 19.74" N and 63°08'43.35" W. But it is also *the place* where I am writing this document. It has certain attributes that enable the task of writing. These attributes are physical—a task chair, a table, electricity, a lamp, etc.—as well as social (a generally relaxed and quiet environment, etc.). This human understanding of place defies any top-down indexing system because the notion of purpose is a continuously evolving spectrum.

New Purpose means new meaning, and new meaning increases the social capital we attach to a place. The more social capital we attach to a place, the more monetization potential this place holds. In the context of mobile digital environments, the distinction between *place* and *location* is more than a semantic argument. Since virtual capability is increasingly mobile, the notion of place ceases to be necessarily attached to a specific point in space. In other words, *places no longer have necessary well-defined locations.* Because of that, behavior platforms such as Google and Facebook are trying to define with as much granularity as possible where the user is at any given time, and more importantly, *for what reason.*

The New Meaning of Travel

Virtual travel is distinct in nature from physical travel, because travel in virtual space is a process of pulling a destination toward the traveler, rather than pushing a traveler toward a destination. In virtual travel it *is the places that move*, not the person, so the traveler does not need to leave one place in order to arrive at another. One can move from the destination platform Facebook to the destination platform YouTube, without much more effort than lifting a finger. Behavior Platform Places are not fixed in space, but are defined and refined by the purpose and experiences their participants engage in. Crowds of people could arrive simultaneously at one place in physical space, and crowds of places could arrive at one person in virtual space. This is not a trivial point because each place is linked to purpose, so the integration of multiple places is the integration of multiple purposes, and the integration of multiple dimensions of the person creating the experience. Understanding these dimensions and cataloguing them for each user, provides the opportunity to tailor *value experiences at the individual preference level.*

Latent Value

Most of today's objects and spaces are blind, deaf and mute; however, sensor technologies are increasingly being embedded into their very fabric. This will result in more than just a perceptual extension of ourselves; sensors placed in objects and spaces will potentially become an extension of ourselves, a distributed sensory organ that will read, reflect and respond to us in a way that is beneficial and valuable. The perception capabilities of things will be directly proportional to their ability to read the invisible relationships present in our environment. The Internet of Things is not about the objects, or the spaces themselves, but about their new capacity as socio-cultural barometers, just like letters are not about words, but about the meaning they convey. In this sense, objects and spaces will be active participants in the co-production of meaning.

The Internet of Things will forge new links between objects or spaces in proximity to each other, creating new forms of social capital. When every object, every place and every person will have the capacity to receive, generate, transmit and store data, a communication-ready ecosystem will be shaped as a Link-Enabled ecology. With this expansion capability, the density of participants in the ecology will increase exponentially and reveal new forms of social capital. By expanding the notion of social networks to include Link-Enabled ecologies, we find in the network participants previously not engaged, namely objects and spaces enabled now to store, transmit and receive data. As social objects and social places, these new participants bring with them new sets of relationships; the key to converting this network into net-worth will be the recognition that relationships contain reciprocity, and reciprocity creates value.

This reciprocity between people-place-object will be transformed into net-worth, once the taxonomy and ontology of the Internet of Things is undertaken as a strategic business activity. Understanding the meaning—ontology—of a categorized action—taxonomy—is a mandatory step in the creation of value, and a core capability leading to the monetization opportunities of any social network.

Value Themes[1]

1. LINK-ENABLED SPACES

When entering a Link-Enabled space, a person transforms that space through the chain of links they provide. This transformation is not unidirectional; the space will in turn leave its mark on the person, thus touching all subsequent spaces that person will enter. These spaces will shape and be shaped by human experience. Once enabled to do so, people will reveal their needs and wants through their interactions and behaviors. When places and objects are data enabled, they take meaning from people, they become what people need them to be at a given moment in time and for a given purpose. Any smart-phone is an example of this. It becomes what you need it to be: a game console one minute, a communication tool the next, and a business device minutes later.

The meaning of the object shifts with the user's intentions and purpose. In a Link-Enabled ecology every combination of people, devices and places will create a wealth with a unique social capital possibility. Every setting and every interaction will determine a one of a kind ecosystem of opportunity. The crucial question: Upon entering a Link-Enabled space, how do people transform the space itself through the links they provoke?

2. VALUE IN OBJECTS

Objects have specific value to individuals for specific reasons, and they have a potential general value to the network for different reasons. A set of keys has value only to the owner of the locks the keys open. Or to anyone that knows which key opens which lock, and is interested in the contents. While the social value of a space resides in what we do there, what transforms it in a 'place,' the same can be said about objects; their value resides in who is using it and for what purpose. The value of networked objects is exponential with the network size and composition. Objects will know the capabilities of other objects like them. How does social capital value in a network change, when we introduce Link-Enabled objects in that network?

1 Manu, A. (2012). *Behavior Space*. Farnham: Gower Publishing, 175–7.

Traditionally, objects allow individuals to make manifest their value thus contributing to increasing the social capital of the network. The object also allows for an individual to self-actualize his potential. A piano in a room full of piano players has a different meaning than the same object in a warehouse. Objects mean something somewhere, but may not have the same meaning anywhere else. The meaning of objects in the right place at the right time is their intrinsic potential value.

What is the difference between our objects and us? Our objects are *us*, as they serve to propagate us, as they serve to enhance us, as they serve to augment the Self. We look at people, place and object as distinct when in effect they are one: *People are actualized through Object and Place*. We exist and produce through objects and places. Objects do not exist without People. Nor do Places exist without what makes them meaningful—and that is People. With traditional objects, the social capital of the network depends on the physical proximity of the participants. That piano produces no value if a piano player is not present as well.

With Enabled Objects, a Link-Enabled network is created in which physical proximity is not necessary. Value resides in what the Enabled Objects know—how to feel and sound like a piano for example—and in what Enabled People can do with that knowledge, as well as in the value the Enabled Object brings as an avatar of other objects. This may be a confusing argument, but think of your smart-phone again: this is the avatar of any object you might need, as long as you have the right application installed. The value of your smartphone is equal to the number of avatar objects it contains and can become at any given time. Imagine then releasing this capability in all other objects you are surrounded by, and further imagine that every object can perform as *every other object at any given moment of need.*

Everything will be Everything Else that makes sense. This is the value in Link-Enabled objects.

3. CONTEXT IS THE VALUE VARIABLE

On June 24, 2014, England played Costa Rica in the World Cup in Brazil. The score was 0–0. The data for all concerned is 00110000 00101101 00110000. Yet, in the context of England—at that time placed 13 in the FIFA rankings—the information the data contained was seen as a defeat. In the context of Costa Rica—number 31 in the same ranking—it was seen as a victory. The faces of

British and Costa-Rican fans, as well as the media reports in both countries expressed precisely this. Without context, information is just Data.

A *space* becomes a *place*, when actor X has a *value* relationship with C. When both X and C have a mutual benefit, P (place) is created. Place is Context. A *space* becomes a *place* when actors have a *mutually beneficial* relationship to each other, expressed as information transformed in wealth, due to the place as context.

4. OBJECTS IN CONTEXT ARE CONTENT

Link-Enabled objects contain, retrieve, receive and transmit data and can be searched, filtered, and aggregated. Their intelligence and presence will create a new language of experiences and opportunities within the built environment, experiences that will be shaped by what is close by, and what links THE environment contains. These new experiences will not only create new relationship models between objects, spaces and people, but ultimately they will strengthen the relationships between people. Content is no longer king. In Link-Enabled ecologies, *context is King.*

5. WHAT ELSE DO YOU NEED ME TO BE?

The capability to recognize, articulate and transform the purpose and scope of our experience, to provide maximum benefit to all participants, is not to be found within new technological applications or interfaces, but within the latent human behaviors they retrieve, and how those behaviors are leveraged to strengthen and affect the system at hand.

In the Internet of Things, all objects would be empowered with the ability to transmit not only their location and capability, but also their composition. In this context, the existence of a material in any form will generate and answer the implicit question *where else could I be?*—or more accurately *what other place could I make for you right now?*

PART 2

VALUE CREATION AND DELIVERY

Chapter 5
Frameworks and Mindsets

Why is opportunity so hard to see when it is staring you right in the face? There are signals of opportunity everywhere around us, but until we assign meaning and value to them, we act as if they don't exist.

The poet Goethe said that 'the hardest thing to see is what's in front of your eyes,' and that is because within the world of reality we see according to the frameworks we have constructed in our mind. We design these frameworks in order to clarify the purpose of things in our life, in order to give them meaning, and in order to arrange them in a sequence that we can understand. Organizations are such frameworks, as are relationships we construct within. The framework is designed to allow us to arrange the furniture in the room without any preset lines, because we can see it all in our head, because the reality we are organizing is a reality that corresponds to a framework in our mind. In the same way we arrange guests at the dinner table, and in the same way we arrange the flatware and tableware on that table.

We like dealing with precise frameworks because we like measurable outcomes, and because this is what education is mostly about, teaching us frameworks. When looking at something for the first time, we are searching for frameworks so we can understand the meaning of the thing. We design these frameworks. And so we can redesign any framework to achieve the mindset we are after. It is therefore imperative when considering the changes that the Internet of Things will bring about in the behavior economy, to purposefully redesign our frameworks and mindset about enterprise and business in this new context.

A Few Words about Frameworks and Ways of Seeing

People in organizations become limited by what they are looking at rather than what they see. What you are looking at is usually a physical object, or an objectification of something that is an idea. A lot of people and organizations have lost the art of understanding *what is the concept* that is at the core of a physical object. What are you looking *at* when looking at a plastic bottle? You are looking at the concept of portability in hydration devices, objectified as a plastic bottle.

Looking beyond the visible to the possibilities inherent in an object is the talent required now, as we move from an industrial model to the behavior model in the economic system. We are surrounded by advanced technologies and we need to surround ourselves as well with new innovative ways of thinking, and with new practices. New practices allow us the ability to see beyond the immediate application of a technology, and to see and understand the real possibilities present. And the real possibility is connected to behavior and not to technology.

The context for our frameworks has changed from tangible surroundings to abstract ideas, but our mind, and this is in large part because of the education system, is still fixated on the physical and looking for cues that tell us how things might work. We are still focused on the machine, on performance, on comparing things from the past, and that limits how much we can see. In the emerging present, we need flexibility of mind in order to comprehend the next generation of technologies and the opportunities it represents. The Internet of Things is not just computers connected to the Internet; it is *everything connected*. And that means our mind has to expand its notions of possibility in an unprecedented way.

Since we have no archetypes against which to measure new possibilities, we need strong ideological frameworks for decision-making, and for strategy planning. Leadership in this environment requires philosophy much more than engineering. We can no longer subcontract our mindsets to other people because we have no time to think for ourselves. We can no longer be told what to think because everyone is in the same boat, asking the same question: *what could be possible when everything is connected?*

Sense Makers, Note Takers and Tricksters

Management has depended for too long on note takers and sense makers, authors of books proving either a prescription for *what you should think about*, or insight into *how you should think about it.* While socially relevant as a conversation starter at a party, sense making is dealing post facto with the reasons a behavior cycle has ended, and new markets are formed around new behaviors. Note taking and sense making leaves little room for action, and no strategic advantage can be gained from this knowledge.

The capability required to sense and deliver on possibility is that of the trickster, who is defined as *a medium into the possibilities.* Tricksters are one of the oldest archetypes of human civilization, and the trickster's longevity as an archetype is due to its capability for adaptation and transformation, and its value in interpreting the earliest signs of change as the possibility they represent. Tricksters are expert at extending the possibilities of our imagination, because they rarely respect authority or regard any values as un-mutable; this is the reason they have a flexible mind ready to uncover new knowledge and new meaning. This flexibility also gives a trickster the ability to tear down old frameworks and to build new ones. If in this description you recognize Steve Jobs you are right. He was a trickster. Each one of us has a trickster within, waiting to be uncovered and to be allowed to perform his magic. We need this capability more than ever when we encounter the need for transformation and change, when things seem uncertain, and when we need to imagine what future we can shape for ourselves.

Why Reframe Mindsets

One of the reasons that we need to reframe our mindsets about the economic system is the confusion people generally have about the Internet economy, or as we call it in this book, the behavior economy. The confusion comes from the meaning of *scale* in economics. As we discussed in the introduction to this book, a behavior platform type of business, does not have to physically grow, as was the case with an assembly line for an automotive company. What a behavior platform needs is to spread the behavior across multiple users, in which case it is the user base that grows and not the company. This is the network effect, where value is proportional with the number of people using a product or service.

The size of the firm in the industrial economy was a function of how much technology the firm was capable of owning, and not as much a function of its economic impact. Size was also connected to the supply chain, the distribution networks and so on. With the arrival of new technologies it has become much easier for a small firm to coordinate production plants overseas, and to effectively be in charge only with the marketing aspects of a product line. Once the Internet became mainstream, it enabled the shift from manufacturing intensity to marketing intensity, by allowing access to online markets and to users from every quarter of the world that has access to the Internet. In the behavior economy, the focus has shifted from the size of the company, to the size of the marketplace.

New Framework: From Adding to Creating Value

The value chain is a point of departure for developing products or services that assume that users can identify and articulate missing needs. The value chain is one of the frameworks we designed to make things measurable and understandable, and also to mitigate risks as much as possible. Take a crowd of users into a focus group, ask them a set of questions, and they will tell you what's missing in their life. You take notes, you let your development team know what the users are and then you deliver a new product or service. During this entire process, if successful, you would have *added value,* because your starting point was conditioned by the existence of user needs, in the defined framework of an existing product or service.

The new value chain has to start with mapping emerging technology as well as mapping emerging behaviors. Once these maps are done, one needs to carefully examine and understand people's motivations, which are the reasons people engage in new behaviors. It is not just the mapping of Facebook as a data point but also the understanding of Facebook as an activity with multiple meanings. Once you understand the deep motivation that compels people to engage in new behavior, you can engage in the creation of strategic value. It is *strategic* because it does not start from an existing artifact or human activity, but rather from understanding the opportunity present at the meeting of technology and behavior.

While the old value chain was good at creating tactical value, the new value chain creates strategic value, which is pre-competitive in nature, because it starts by creating a new platform for behavior. Creating tactical value protects a business while creating strategic value creates new opportunities. Tactical value uses skills applied creatively, while strategic value uses the imagination. Strategic value is the transformation of matter into something that did not exist before.

Understanding value in this context is very important, because many individuals engaged in the technology space often confuse the number of features a product has with value. Features deal with the 'how' and value deals with the 'what.' The value of engagement to the product or service is the value of the user experience, and the '*what*' is accomplished using a product. The '*how*' is how we get there, and that is frequently of no interest to users engrossed in the experience of a product. Very few home cooks know how a microwave works, and no one other than people developing microwaves really cares. We just want the results.

Some organizations do not focus necessarily on the end-user as the core recipient of the value proposition. But instead they focus on their distribution partners, which they call their customers. For Motorola or Blackberry the customer is Verizon, or AT&T, Rogers, or Telecom X. It is the carriers that these companies want to satisfy and it is this partnership that is perceived as more valuable than a relationship with the end-user. This is not happening just in the telecom industry, this happens in almost every sector. If you work in a CPG company (consumer packaged goods), your customer is the distribution partner in the supply chain, the stores that sell your product and the buyers that you meet frequently to determine their needs. This distorts the business model because now you are focusing on value for the store buyer instead of focusing on value for the end-user. The distortion comes from the fact that you are removing the experience of use, and you deal only in numbers.

New Framework: From Consumer to Audience

In the new behavior economy that the Internet of Things will make possible, key elements that organizations deal with will be changing, and that requires a rapid change of mindset. Some of these changes are mentioned in other parts of this book, so I will focus here only on the elements that we call 'the demographic' and 'the market.'

'The Market' has made it imperative for every company to become an Internet company; every company is now relying on the Web to guide production, to market, to sell, and to distribute goods. Every company with a connection to the Internet is connected to millions of users at the same time, for which they need to provide content. And this content is above and beyond the purpose of the company or the products and services it is developing and marketing. This is content that needs to compel, surprise, provide insights, and needs to expand the relationship people have with a company's brands, products and services. This means that the companies now need the capability of creating and managing content, which is distinct from the capability of physical products.

Physical products are used or consumed by a user, someone that exercises use over an object, a service or a space. *Content is experienced*, it is felt, by an audience. An Audience watches a performance or a broadcast as a collective activity. Content is entertainment, which means that every company with an audience is now in the entertainment business as well. What are the attributes of an audience member? Attention. Involvement. Participation in the telling of the story. The shift from users to audience is critical, and this is where companies need to move from technology to entertainment. When done right, technology is entertainment, something giving pleasure, an agreeable moment, and a welcomed diversion from daily life. Reframing the mindset from User to Audience involves answers to a few questions.

HOW IS AN ENTERTAINMENT COMPANY DIFFERENT FROM A TECHNOLOGY COMPANY?

An entertainment company has to master the creation of stories that compel an audience to watch them, and to participate in the evolution of each character. An entertainment company has to be good at manipulating time, understanding that engagement with an audience takes place in the course of time. It needs to grasp how to create a character, and how to transform this character into something the audience will identify as a hero or a villain. Entertainment companies deal at all times with the feelings and emotions of their audience.

HOW IS A TECHNOLOGY COMPANY IN THE BUSINESS OF ENTERTAINMENT?

The answer here is simple: technology is magic. Technology when first introduced, surprises users and delights them, and that is the definition of a compelling experience. As one gets used to the use of an object, the surprise and delight diminishes, and what was one's favorite gadget becomes, in the course of time, just another tool. Remember when you bought your first laptop computer? You couldn't wait to spend time on it; you couldn't wait to play with it. The same applies to today's tablets or iPad's. People can't get their hands off of them. So how is this not entertainment?

Entertainment needs a story in order to compel, while technology needs to perform new and surprising tasks in surprising ways. Technology entertains because it opens our mind to new possibilities and makes our own life experience the narrative. Which is why these little gadgets we call smart phones are so compelling.

New Framework: Entertainment Everywhere

What is the future of entertainment? There are two ways to answer this question: one is by using forecasting, which is thinking that takes into account the current direction of entertainment as an industry, and adds to it current developments in technology. Using forecasting assumes that little else will change, and entertainment will benefit from growth by adding elements of storytelling which correspond to what the audience expects, as well as adding elements of technology to make the visual style engrossing and compelling. And this is how we get to the common predictions that see the future of entertainment as including the audience which may participate in the development of the narrative, the destiny of certain characters and even the ending of the movie.

This linear thinking is similar to the thinking that leads the development of the Quantum Leap spinning globe described earlier, as an extension of the common and featureless rotating globe of old. We add a few technologies that are now more affordable—small speakers, small memory cards that hold sound, touch control surfaces and so on—and we now have an interactive experience.

This is forecasting leading to prediction, and this adds tactical value—you do the same things as before but better, as well as you do new things on the same platform. Tactical value expands the experience and sometimes it may enhance it.

By contrast, foresight thinking adds strategic value, redefining the experience: you now engage in new experiences on new platforms.

Google Earth is a redefined experience and a strategic value example. If we apply the same type of thinking to answering the question about the future of entertainment, we are bound to look around us at all the developments that lead to emerging technologies and emerging behavior. If we look around us we will understand that many other activities are now holding the attention and interest of the audience, which means that many other activities that are not dependent on the location of a movie theater, or TV screen, can be now considered entertainment. Posting, surfing, commenting, reading, and tweeting: this is what is considered entertainment today, in both form and meaning. The amount of time spent in other forms of entertainment that are not monetized by Hollywood or by the large TV networks might give us an indication of what the future of entertainment is. Traditional forms of entertainment such as storytelling, music, dance, drama and various forms of performance will migrate into everyday activities, as brands will respond to the imperative of becoming cultural operators, and purposeful storytellers. Add to this the Link-Enabled capability of every object and place, and the entire field of entertainment would be redefined beyond the obvious.

What are the Attributes of the Experience that Compels an Audience?

Any experience that affects the tension of the audience or its emotional state is a compelling experience. If a story can take you from boredom to anxiety, and from pleasantness to unpleasantness, that story compels your attention and draws you in. Storytellers achieve this by providing the stimuli that attain the right response on the part of an audience. The stimulus is objective while the response is subjective. In a piece of music, the composer has about 3.5 minutes to take an audience through a journey in which the only stimulus is sound, modulated in such a way as to release an emotional response. The subjectivity of this emotional response is the reason we have millions of songs.

In longer time formats, such as movies, the storyteller has more time and more objective stimuli to work with: images, sounds, and a narrative, all centered around characters which are also objectively created. The length of time and the number of available stimuli are critical in establishing a set of emotional responses that, even when subjective, are within the same range of emotion. This means that the degree to which the storyteller can control the emotional response range of the audience, is much higher when the duration in time is longer, and when the number of available stimuli is higher.

To our physical perceptive mechanisms of seeing and hearing, a long format story has the benefit of added stimuli in the areas of cognition and memory, as well as the benefit of time in which to build an emotional context, aspirational and inspirational charges that evolve in a compelling and transformative experience. Transformative experiences are the shortest and most direct route for transforming a consumer into an engaged audience.

The FLIGHT Model of Experience and Value Creation

What great technology companies realized a while ago is that the best engagement happens in experimentation, through the creation of behavior platforms that allow the users to define, side by side with the company, what the product is all about. Think YouTube: it is what users make it be.

The challenge: how does one make user engagement a mainstream activity for a new generation? Does the expertise reside in the creation of new and exciting experiences? Does it reside in marketing differently to this very defined and distinctive group—the Millennial? In my view, the expertise needs to reside in both. If one creates a new experience that is marketed in the traditional media channels—radio, TV and print—sadly none of the Millennial will be there. So where do we start?

We start with a plan and a new model. This model is FLIGHT and it consists of six intertwined elements:

- Focus;
- Language;
- Incentives;
- Gamification;
- Harmonization; and
- Transformation.

Focus

Three generative questions will help frame the strategic focus of the marketing initiative. They are:

1. What is the capability required for transforming the knowledge and experience of your brand into *social, cultural* and *economic capital* in the context of a networked, empowered and participatory new demographic?

2. What unique and *new social* and *cultural role* can your brand play in the future, in the life of individuals and organizations, and how might current developments and trends affect this role?

3. What unique *new business role* can your brand play in the lives of individuals and organizations, and how will current disruptive technology, developments and trends affect this role?

Impact, social purpose and social media are the key words that should inform any new strategy. Any experience designed for the Millennial now has to use digital media, tools and channels previously not in the domain of brand management.

The focus needs to be on enabling new interactions through technology, thus creating a *social experience,* which in turn will determine the value experience of the engagement. Improve the social experience and you will improve the *engagement experience.* I have termed this engagement a Full Spectrum Experience.

FULL SPECTRUM EXPERIENCES

I have termed this transformative typology of experience a *Full Spectrum Experience,* due to its multiple compelling attributes delivered in multiple dimensions of engagement: Intellectual, Physical (audio, video, motion, purpose, action, duration, risk), Emotional, Spiritual, Social as well as having a Temporal dimension (time and space) and a Transformative Dimension. Red Bull, a brand fully engaged in transforming their consumers into an audience, delivered one of the best examples of a full spectrum experience: the free fall from the edge of space. The October 2012 Felix Baumgartner jump had all the compelling attributes, and dimensions, of engagement of a full spectrum experience:

- Intellectual engagement.
- Physical engagement (audio, video, motion, purpose, action, duration, risk).
- Emotional engagement.
- Spiritual engagement.
- Social engagement.
- Historical.
- Temporal dimension (time and space).
- Transformative dimension.

All in the course of a timeline that started in 2005 with the first media stories about Felix Baumgartner, and the direction in which Red Bull was thinking. This was a multiyear journey, with public milestones along the way, milestones capable of attracting an audience and have them emotionally and intellectually invested, before the jump itself.

The event took place on October 14, 2012—a free-fall jump of 128,000 feet—and was watched on YouTube by eight million viewers, after a brilliantly planned teaser campaign that started in February the same year and focused on introducing the deeply human story of the little boy who wanted to break a record. The record for the highest altitude of a high jump and longest duration belonged to Joe Kittinger. The boy was Felix Baumgartner. In October 2012 he broke five records, and became the first human to break the sound barrier without engine power. Red Bull streamed the event live on its own YouTube channel, retaining all control over the broadcasting rights for the event.

Nearly 80 TV stations in 50 countries carried the broadcast. The live webcast was distributed through 280 digital partners and racked up 52 million views, making it the most-watched live stream in history.[1] What Red Bull was successful in creating is a moment in history, and a moment that has become, on the same October day, an icon of popular culture. Red Bull's YouTube channel has at the time of writing 3,697,540[2] subscribers and more than 4,000 videos.

There are many lessons that Red Bull's Stratos Jump can teach in connection with the planning and execution of an engaging full spectrum experience. It starts with a compelling story and content in the pre-promotion phase—aspirations to be the first and best at something are always compelling to an audience. This ensures temporal, intellectual and emotional engagement. A connection with the individual and his dreams and aspirations takes care of the intellectual engagement. High quality content on the YouTube platform combined with good story telling and a dramatic story to tell, supplies the social engagement and community involvement. And lastly, the records themselves provide the historical significance, strengthening the social engagement and adding a spiritual transformative dimension. Hard to beat.

1 Available at: http://www.decisionmarketing.co.uk/indepth/content-really-king-marketers (accessed: September 3, 2014).

2 Available at http://www.youtube.com/results?search_query=red+bull (accessed: September 3, 2014).

Language

The framework for creating engagement tied to a social experience—which is the precondition for achieving an emotional and intellectual connection between the Millennial and the brand—must start with the deep understanding of the frames of reference that make the Millennial different as a demographic for branded goods.

The Millennial is looking for something concrete in exchange for their engagement and participation, but before thinking about informal and formal incentives, you need to establish a connection with your participants on a more basic level—talking about topics that interest them, using a tone that they accept and feel natural with, and offering ways to join the interaction on levels, and in ways, that are possible, relevant and attractive. Thus the second phase of FLIGHT is establishing a common Language with the Millennial.

The terms of engagement with this generation are changing. They are no longer passively accepting a new technology, idea, product, or service as it was originally intended. Rather, they are increasingly encouraging and empowering each other to participate in the creation and exchange of knowledge, experience, skill and ideas—their *social capital.*

The platform of technologies currently on the threshold of emergence, require a different capability to carry through on their promises, because the nature of the promises to be made has to change. Rather than asking 'How can I transfer my existing marketing campaign on this new platform?' organizations must ask '*What else can we now say? How else can I engage now, on what new topics?*' The focus of this new capability is not on what technology can do, but on *what we can do with it.*

The new engagement must allow for the opportunity of a new narrative for brand marketing, as stories create a space where anything could be possible, a space where we all become the narrators of possibility, participating and performing as the story unravels. Organizations need to learn how to initiate a participatory dialogue with the Millennial, and empower them to directly affect the make-up of the dialogue and the substance of the brand. This is what Red Bull succeeded in doing by masterfully planning and executing the full spectrum experience of the Stratos Jump.

Incentives

There is a huge difference between the expectations of the Millennial vs the baby boomer: the Millennial is looking for the satisfaction of intrinsic motivation first and for extrinsic motivation second (if at all). In terms of incentives, or 'what's in it for the Millennial,' there are three different levels of incentives that you can employ either implicitly, by simply showing their role in action, or explicitly, by promoting them aloud:

Intrinsic incentives play on the value participants receive from simply participating in the engagement. These incentives include enjoyment from executing the activity itself, the challenge of the task, learning from doing, the possibility of mastery, etc. Intrinsic motivations are very strong, but over time they need to be rekindled. Intrinsic motivation is derived from rewards inherent in the task or activity itself—the enjoyment of a challenging crossword, or the love of engaging in physical activity, such as team sports. A person is intrinsically motivated when engaging in an activity with no apparent reward, except for the activity itself.

Extrinsic incentives refer to those incentives that the product claims as benefits. These incentives worked well for the baby boomer, which needs a reasoned approach to the consumption of goods and services, and reason is outlined by the benefits a particular product or service will bring about in daily life. A more effective way to deal with dirty laundry, a closer shave, a more spreadable margarine, a stronger tissue paper, are all physical benefits that are extrinsic in nature. These incentives do not hold any value for the Millennial; the Millennial has no concept of 'household chores,' performing appliances or underperforming fabric softener. For the Millennial, security in any life domain equals *social capital*: how big is their audience, how do they rank within their social group, what recognition markers can the game provide.

Money is an instrument for the Millennial, and not a marker of social recognition. So money—as in spend less money by buying a more efficient product—cannot be used as the primary extrinsic motivation that attracts a Millennial to a product or service.

Explicit incentives are concrete incentives that can be assigned direct monetary value. These include cash, but can also mean products, gift cards, paid memberships, etc. The Millennial is not interested in winning direct advantage as the prime motivator for engaging with a brand. They are looking for social participation and long-term social purpose. They are looking for a connection between purpose and pleasure. Any engagement tactic needs to be designed to give the Millennial the same pleasure and play value as his/her actions on Facebook, YouTube, and Twitter etc. And this can come only with their emotional and intellectual engagement. Engagement for the Millennial needs purpose, an immediate and tangible Social Object. Another score for the Stratos Jump.

Gamification

Daily life is full of transactional moments—seeing something, learning something, being in a new place, moving from place to place, doing a variety of activities—all moments that can be enhanced by a gaming experience. Gamification uses game design principles to engage audiences and solve problems, and works by making technology more engaging, and by encouraging users to engage in pleasurable behaviors. The experience includes stimuli that elicit immersive responses, allows for mastery, and sometimes it allows for strategy. The stimuli design uses the principles of play behavior and takes advantage of the human predisposition to engage in gaming. The key considerations in the design of the gaming experience are the *compelling nature of the activity* and its *play value.*

Harmonization

The harmonization needed in implementing FLIGHT is between activities that the Millennial considers to be outside the domain of a brand—shopping, travel, attending entertainment events, attending school, dining at a restaurant, all daily activities that one does not associate with the values of a specific brand at this time—and the activities which are traditionally associated with the brand. Gamification is an example of a harmonized daily activity in which a transaction has a play element built in. Be that a challenge, a quiz, a trivia contest, people look for triggers to manifest their play behaviors and the desires connected with it.

Transformation

All of us exist in time and space, and as we move through time and space we interact with the things around us. Our lives are comprised of all the many and varied relationships we have with *Time* (when we are), *Space* (where we are), *Self* (who we are), *People* (by themselves and in groups), *Objects* (inanimate and living), *Ideas* (how and why we are), all of whom contribute to the creation of our unique relationship space. Value is created when an interaction with a medium improves the size and/or quality of our relationship space. The characteristic of the interaction with the object or an idea that makes this improvement possible is the enabling of a new behavior within the existing behavioral norm for that individual. As an example of transformation, consider the opportunities that a Link-Enabled object will have to enhance, expand and redefine the relationship space of individuals, and potentially redefine how we live our life.

Changing Mindset, Changing Capability

As an answer to the challenge: how *does one make user engagement a mainstream activity for a new generation?*, the FLIGHT model of user engagement discussed earlier, is a framework for changing mindset and a blueprint for a changing capability, clearly required by marketing and communication companies, and most of all by the advertising industry. The advertising industry is one of the largest on the planet, and an industry still organized under the old mass broadcast model.

> *In a digital world, the traditional, multinational agency model is unsustainable and inefficient. By and large, legacy agencies have not caught up with technology, and their business model, though it has globalized, has not changed much in the past 150 years.*[3]

So writes Avi Dan in *Forbes*, on March 31, 2014. It is as if the Internet did not happen for lots of agencies. But more so, this is not about the Internet, but about the transformation of data as the preferred material for marketing communication and user engagement.

Agencies have not kept up with the transformation of the economic model of 'produce and consume' to a new model dominated by platform companies, where people co-create and share. As every company with an audience slowly understands, they are now in the media business, as a broadcaster of content. Agencies did not pick this up and are faced with quite a few contextual challenges:

3 Available at: http://www.forbes.com/sites/avidan/2014/03/31/the-future-of-advertising-lean-nimble-agile/ (accessed: June 20, 2014).

- More and more brands are going into the publishing business, inspired by Dove, Red Bull and Oreo.
- Digital video is exploding.
- Mobile is exploding.
- TV and online video are becoming one.

Everyone in the advertising business is complaining that project-based assignments have transformed the agency into a commodity, and that creative work should be seen as more than an hourly rate project. This is true, and it goes to the core of how we define today what '*creative*' means. A creative word-tag does not do it anymore. As recently as March 2014, the second largest retailer in the United States posed the following challenge:

> *... The retail landscape has changed and consumers—more connected than ever—have increasing expectations about how, when and where they want to shop. In response, a new breed of retailers is challenging our market share. We recognize that in order to remain a leader for the next 50 years we will need to find new, innovative ways to make money and ultimately fuel growth.*
>
> The Challenge: *If you were one of our executives how would you disrupt our own business model to compete in this new environment?*

By any measure this is not a marketing challenge, nor is it a design challenge. *This is a strategic foresight challenge.* Brands are asking for strategic value innovation—in effect placing the agency at the level of strategic partner. Yet, agencies are not equipped—capability wise—to handle foresight strategy and transform it into innovation. It is very likely that brands will soon stop sending foresight challenges to traditional agencies, opting to use—at least for the strategic elements of the mandate—foresight innovation consultancies instead.

In the new context, advertising agencies will have to understand the intersection point of technology and consumer behavior, and have the capability to deliver the right innovation (medium) to a targeted behavior group. However, *the intersection of technology with behavior is not the traditional capability of advertising agencies.* That capability belongs squarely with Strategic Foresight practitioners. Without a manifest and credible strategic foresight and innovation capability, it is doubtful that agencies will continue receiving foresight challenges they cannot respond to, and this is a danger signal for their financial sustainability.

Michael Karg, CEO International at Razorfish, was quoted as saying:

> *The agency of the future will be just a consultancy. Any creative hot-shop or a well-established network will have to understand the intersection point of technology, media and consumer behavior to deliver the right creative. So companies will look at the new consultancies for advice on how to be prepared for this change and reorganize themselves. Interestingly, when this happens media planning will have a whole new meaning. Imagine the possibilities when millions of ad dollars will be saved and pumped in creating new user experiences and content.*[4]

What is the question to which an advertising agency is the answer? The answers to this question will reveal the new capabilities needed by advertising agencies, and the needs of organizations in general to be dynamic and synchronic with the emerging present society and economic system.

4 Available at: http://www.business-standard.com/article/management/the-agency-of-the-future-will-be-just-a-consultancy-michael-karg-vincent-digonnet-114050400690_1.html (accessed: August 9, 2014).

Chapter 6
The Dynamic Enterprise

What is the question to which your enterprise is the answer?

Questions and Value

In an earlier section I talked about an organization's need to understand why people engage with its products or services, and understanding the motivation at the root of behaviors resulting in products or services being purchased and used. I suggested then that Nike's answer to the question above might be 'how do I attain my personal fitness goals'? Understanding the question to which one's products are the answer, places the organization on the center stage of someone's life, and also in their aspiration for a better life, as it is the aspiration for the quality of a thing that users value most. The ultimate benefit is what one might become as a result of engaging with a product.

Questions seek the value in things; questions seek to find the core concept that gives rise to an embodied product or service that people use. The concept *is* the value.

Take any technology or any tool that you encounter, and look at it as the answer to a question, because everything you see is a direct answer to a question. What is the question to which a plastic bottle is the answer? How do I make hydration portable? What is the question to which a chair is the answer? How do I comfortably suspend the human body above the ground?

Every technology we encounter invites also another question aside from the question that originated it. It invites the question 'what else can this be?' and 'where else can I use this, in which other context will this thing provide me with value?'

The Internet of Things is the answer to multiple questions, one of which is 'what else can I do with data?' This question is reshaping the environments in which we live and the way we live. The typology of questions that begin with *what* and *what else*, have reshaped the world many times over in the past. *What else* is a defining question for the journey ahead.

The strategic business question for any corporation[1] is: 'What is the *question* to which *your product is the answer?*' To this question, a precisely defined answer is purported to show a clear understanding of the market space. The trouble with the precise answer is that it may narrow the true monetization potential of any technology. I will use an example from the appliance industry to illustrate this point. If you are in the business of electric shavers, it is not a motor-based personal appliance that you should be trying to monetize, but the revenue generating opportunity of the behavior space a motor appliance creates.

When you look at what you produce and market with the lens of *behavior spaces*, the revenue potential of your organization expands: you are no longer seeing your business as the manufacture of electric shavers. You are seeing it as the *behavior space of male grooming*; in this space, shaving is just one of the behaviors your demographic will engage in. The product —the electric shaver—is *the platform* that enables a specific behavior. The more behaviors

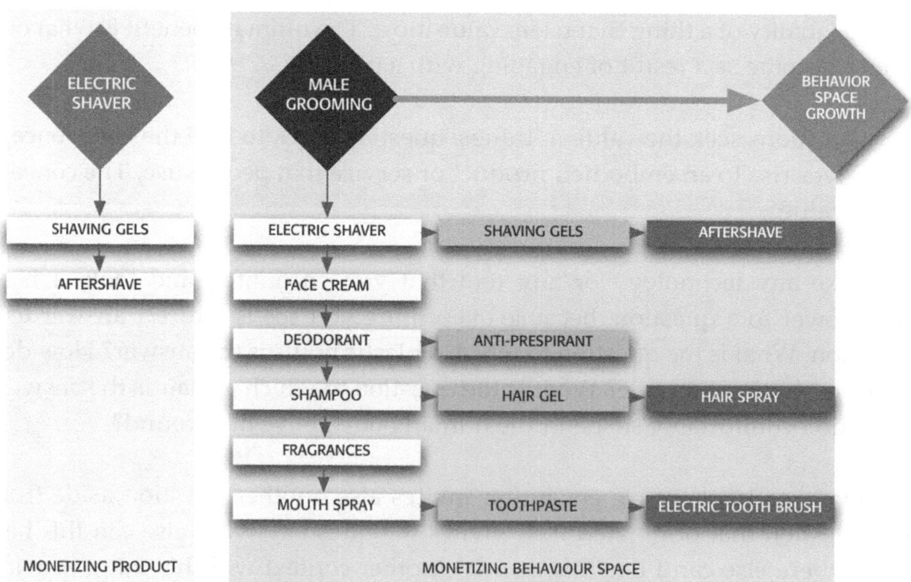

Figure 6.1 Monetization map of behavior space

1 Manu, A. (2012). *Behavior Space*. Farnham: Gower Publishing, 29.

one brand can enable within the same space equal more monetization potential (Figure 6.1). This means shaving gels, creams, deodorants, hair products, soaps, fragrances and so on. The value of a product is a measure of its platform-ability, the number of behaviors it creates and satisfies.

So, what is the question to which *your* brand/organization is the answer?

What is the Question for Which the WWW is the Answer?

Of all inventions, the World Wide Web had one of the highest rates of acceptance of any technology while solving a problem no one thought they had. This is why the question 'what is the question for which the World Wide Web is the answer' is important.

I've always believed that the World Wide Web would have never been developed if someone were trying to solve a problem. The problem-solving mindset just doesn't do it here, nor do its frameworks. When inventing things like the World Wide Web or the electric motor, we are not seeking to solve problems, we are searching for a new way of life, for a wide field of possibility that will open up multiple behavior spaces to be imagined and implemented by the ones that come after us.

It was on August 6, 1991, that Tim Berners-Lee emailed the, by now the famous, 'short summary of the World Wide Web project' at the address 'groups: alt.hypertext':

> *The WWW project merges the techniques of information retrieval and hypertext to make an easy but powerful global information system. The project started with the philosophy that much academic information should be freely available to anyone. It aims to allow information sharing within internationally dispersed teams, and the dissemination of information by support groups.*
>
> *The WWW world consists of documents, and links. Indexes are special documents that, rather than being read, may be searched. The result of such a search is another ('virtual') document containing links to the documents found. A simple protocol ('HTTP') is used to allow a browser program to request a keyword search by a remote information server.*[2]

2 Manu, A. (2006). *The Imagination Challenge*. Berkeley, CA: New Riders/PeachPit Press, 132–3.

Priceless in its precision, simplicity and purpose. But for everyone else outside the group to whom the email was addressed, within the frameworks they were operating from at the time, the question was pretty basic: *what is the problem for which the World Wide Web is a solution?* Here we have again an example of a question asked from a mindset that ignores the existence of a new framework for existence. This is the question asked from the mindset of a problem>solution framework, when in effect we are dealing with a question>answer framework. Failing to identify a problem that had a wide market need for a tactical solution objectified by the WWW, a lot of industries, and a lot of corporations and governments, lived for a few years with the illusion that nothing much will change. They lived the illusion that the World Wide Web was an *option,* that it was an elective they may or may not decide to take at one point in the future, and if conditions dictated the need to do so.

This is almost like believing that, at one point after electricity and the electric motor became mainstream, the organization you are a part of will somehow be exempted from any involvement with either electricity, or the electric motor.

After all, there is no money to be made with either electricity or the World Wide Web at the time of their introduction, as they solve no problem we know of, and no users need this outside of the few enthusiasts involved in the technology. On top of that, the value chain you are using at this time just doesn't fit this *new thing*. But what if you ask *what is the question for which the WWW is the answer?*

What answers would that reveal? What would you discover? The desire to explore and continue asking questions? The desire to play and the urgency to communicate one's ideas, artistic creations, daily experiences? The search for others of like mind or with similar interests, that may live thousands of miles away or just a few blocks around the corner? The desire for community and fellowship? The compelling empowerment of collaborating with others without geographic barriers? How about all of these!

The World Wide Web became a social phenomenon because it released our latent behaviors of curiosity, nosiness, and continuing search for becoming better by understanding more. Our instinct for becoming as much as our tools allow us to reveal, was now made possible by a new technology, with the capability to *create the experience most conducive to emerge our latent behavior*.

Human life is a quest for the higher life experience. As we learn from experience, we transform ourselves and our goals in a dynamic and synchronic fashion with the quality and quantity of the experiences we have. We seek a better experience in order to build on a previous experience. All in a quest for pleasurable moments, and for beauty, because beauty and pleasure are value-positive experiences. When looking at human action and the compelling motivation that makes us engage in actions, we notice that no metrics apply. All of these motivators are ambiguous in nature. It is this ambiguity that creates a fertile ground for interpretation and for diversity in the creation of products and services. And it is also this ambiguity that creates the need for dynamic enterprises, because the sources of value that engage the intrinsic motivation of people are in a perpetual dynamic.

Value Dynamic Enterprises

Sources of value are connected to the dynamic nature of the behavior cycle. Users are usually satisfied by the experiences products present them with, but in time this satisfaction is being eroded by the daily repetition of the experience. As surprise is one of the components of a compelling experience, products and services that do not offer surprising new features or benefits over the course of time, cease to be of value to users. Corporations need a dynamic strategy to deliver on new capabilities, because behavior completes desires in a perpetual cycle (see Figure 1.1, 'The behavior cycle'), and because humans perpetually want more. Value is a dynamic of variables, and it requires a dynamic response from the providers of value. With very few exceptions—notably the utilities sector—most sectors of the economy are affected by the dynamic nature of value, and the constancy of a user's behavior cycles. And very few enterprises respond well to this dynamic.

Traditionally, incumbent organizations are slow in their response to the changing behavior of consumers, leaving it for outsiders, organizations operating at the fringe of the market space to provide the innovation that responds to this dynamic. Incumbent ski manufacturers were not the ones that introduced snowboards, nor did incumbent bicycle makers introduce mountain bikes.

The situation changes slightly as one looks at consumer-packaged-goods companies, which prove to be much more sensitive to changing consumer

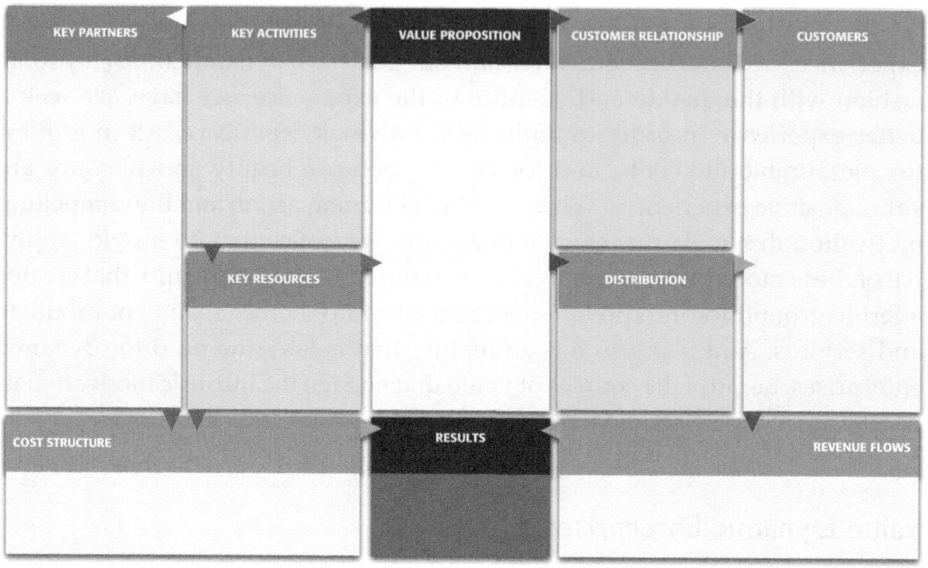

Figure 6.2 Business model canvas

attitudes—health concerns, environmental stance, changing taste palate—and respond with innovations to match.

Looking at the business model canvas (Figure 6.2) developed by Alex Osterwalder, it is easy to see that the rubrics Cost Structure and Revenue Flows, are items that by the nature of supply and demand, will always be in flow. Flow here means that they are ambiguous; uncertain with respect to attaining the revenue desired against the expenditure budgeted for. This is why everyone uses strong disclaimers when presenting these numbers, as they are simply assumptions, best guesses and ideal projections. Somehow, this ambiguity seems to be accepted as the norm while at the same time, the idea that *disruption is a constant and business is a dynamic variable* makes managers seem highly uncomfortable. If we are OK with the ambiguity of the bottom line, its dynamic nature and its flow, why are we not comfortable seeing the whole business as a variable? How can the value proposition not be in dynamic flow with the behavior disruptions it is designed to satisfy? And if the value proposition is in flow, how can the value generating activities not be in flow? The quicker leaders accept the dynamic flow of continuous transformation, the quicker they can design their way into it.

Strategic Ambition as a Value Source

Strategy means reframing reality in poetic terms, and to do that, one needs a poetic vision. The reality to reframe is not an imaginary one but an immediate one. It is what you see, and how you feel now, in the present, that you want to change. The future is the change you make to the present, and this is what poetic visionaries know.

All great leaders had and have poetic vision: Steve Jobs, Nelson Mandela, Martin Luther King, Bill Gates, Mahatma Gandhi, Winston Churchill, Che Guevara, Richard Branson, Barak Obama. This is not the ability to imagine, but the ability to understand with your heart. *See, look, feel and understand with your heart.*[3] Strategy is not about predicting the future, but about having foresight. Not about natural science, but about human science: the choices individuals make, have much more weight on the shape of the future, than any technology by itself. Foresight seeks to discover the signals that create the patterns of emergence, the seeds announcing the presence of a new behavior space. The capability to map a signal in its earliest stages, accelerates our understanding of the possibilities resident in it, and allows for the appropriate course of action to be chosen. An appropriate course of action will maximize the opportunity—or minimize the threat—for both the individual and the organization. That is strategy in its purest expression.

To maximize any opportunity, we must first recognize the *different nature* of a new variable at the strategic level, understand what must be redefined, enhanced and expanded in our business models, once a new behavior enters a behavior space. One needs to understand the change agent of the business context. The new possibilities are the result of an emerging context, the development of which is not necessarily of our choosing, but rather a convergence of multiple agents, sometimes unrelated, working toward the same goals, and in the same technology spaces. Once the context has changed—no matter how imperceptible at first—an organization's strategic intent needs to change as well.

The Ambition to be the First, the Best, the Only

Which is the winning strategy in the ideology aim? To be the First at something? To be the Best at something or to be the *Only* enterprise providing something? Which strategy can be defended and which provides

3 Bang and Olufsen's *Product Development Credo,* circa 1999.

more social and capital wealth? Apple was rarely *First* at something but they are certainly the *Best* at what they do. Try to answer these three questions about your organization:

1. In 2020 we will be the FIRST organization to …

2. In 2020 we will be the BEST organization in the space of …

3. In 2020 we will be the ONLY organization to have …

This is all about purpose. It is about having a direction and having the courage to articulate it. It is about engaging in becoming something more, and in defining what that might be. What is the common direction most likely to enlist the passions of my employees and of my executive team? Ambition!

Without an articulated ambition, the organization is about to run in circles searching for something, trying to find purpose in everyday activities. This purpose needs to be declared, this purpose needs to be articulated and made public to all and for all to see.

From Being First to Being Best

To be the first nation to put a man on the moon was an ambition that enlisted the passion and support of a nation, and then the passion and curiosity of the world. However, being the first cannot be a long-term strategic advantage, because once you are the first then what? Being the first works for as long as you are pursuing 'being the first'; when you accomplish being the first there is nothing else to maintain. For a while, you may be the first and also the only to have achieved a goal shared by many, but the market space will get crowded with other participants, and that makes your position indefensible. Being first has an advantage in that it gives you time to shape the market, essentially defining a new role and shaping a future. You are shaping a future because others see what you do, and as they try to emulate your success, they populate the market with offers similar to yours.

Apple was not the first company to produce an MP3 player, so being first there was not a strategic option. The option Apple had was to be the best, and defend being the best by introducing products that consistently obsolesce their predecessors, and provide new pleasurable experiences for users to engage with. Being the best at what you do is completely measurable: the material you select, the componentry inside your product, the fabrication plan—how things come together—all can be measured against a competitor's product.

Twitter was not the first application that allowed users to send text messages. Nor was it the first in allowing users to broadcast their current location and condition. While this was not the first SMS or messaging application, it was the first in allowing people to *broadcast themselves to a list of followers*, and to follow people broadcasting under their own handles at the same time. Their position can be defended with strong intellectual property, which is another advantage of being first in this case.

Looking at a different example, Playboy was the first to produce male entertainment in print form, which had the quality of the best and most popular magazines of the time. And this quality extended beyond the materials used, into the quality of the writing and the stories selected. While it proved easy for others to enter that market and offer the same type of imagery, it has proven difficult for the new entrant to achieve the same quality of content, or attract talent already committed to another publication. Playboy migrated from *being first* into *being the best*.

Being the best is a value judgment because being the best can only be defined in terms of value attributes. Out of the three ambitions described here, that of being first, best, or only, being the best is the most connected to value and value creation, and also gives you the ability to control the creation of value by continually creating compelling experiences for your audience. Being 'best' at something means scoring a high degree of user satisfaction over a number of identified attributes.

Once these attributes are known, the organization can start defending them strategically. Can being the best be considered an ideology or is it the natural destination of an ideology? Is Best enough of a reason to give purpose to an enterprise? I believe the answer is 'yes.'

Ambition and Business Models

A business model is all about the creation and delivery of value. It is about identifying what your value proposition is—what is the question to which I need to provide the answer and what answer do I provide?—and also identifying who is your customer base for which your answer will be relevant. But any value proposition needs value creation activities, so you need to have the people and the plans in place, and be able to extract, create and distribute value. The value proposition informs and connects all your business activities, so the key here is the organization's value creation capability.

If your strategic goal is to be the *'best at something,'* the value proposition will have to reflect that, as will your value creation activities. This ambition of being the best gives an organization the ammunition to sustain transformations, as long as the key resources employed are enlisted participants in a shared ideology. A good business model is essentially the blueprint of an ideological ambition.

The Value Proposition Objectified: Uber

The ridesharing service Uber, established in 2009, typifies building a business from the value proposition outward. Uber's business model is that of a behavior platform, and it could not have happened before it did, because of the dynamic of a market space that required the mainstream acceptance of smart phones amongst both its customer groups, the drivers and the riders. Uber exemplifies the value of asking the question, 'what is the *question* to which *your product is the answer*?', by providing a clear answer of value to a number of parties (Figure 6.3). Their answer is: *How can we enhance the experience of private transportation*

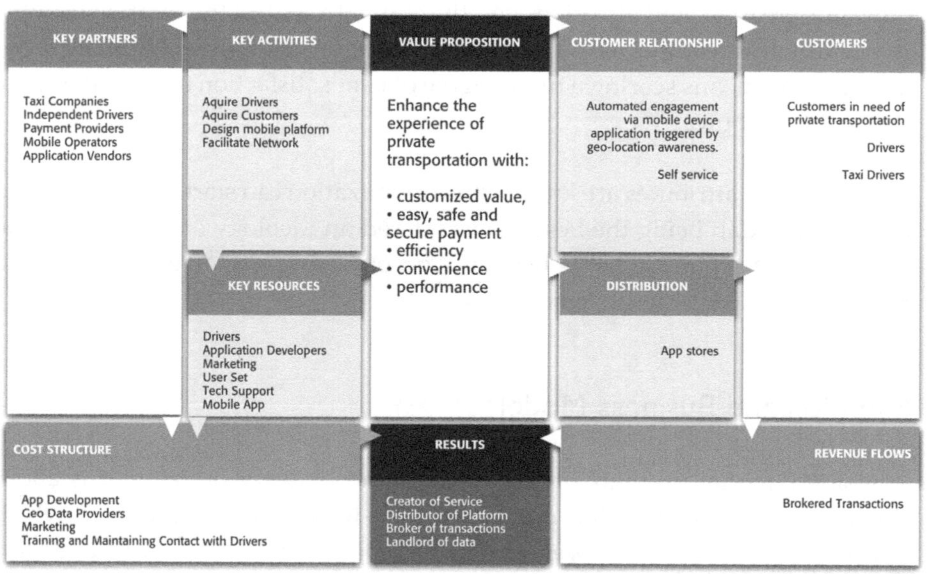

Figure 6.3 Uber business model

in an urban environment? By providing customized value in a comfortable environment, and with safe easy payments, efficiency and convenience.

Uber has disrupted the taxi industry world over, with a very simple proposition: if you need a ride anywhere in the city, there are drivers nearby willing to take you to your destination, for about the same cost as the taxi company. Uber is the middleman between a willing passenger and a willing driver, and no money changes hands, as the transaction happens wirelessly, the amount is deducted from your credit card. The concept is challenging an industry that has relied for a long time on a protectionist approach, which has resulted in long waiting periods, and unsafe cabs.

All you need is the platform on your smartphone, and you can locate within seconds the closest cars enrolled in the program. You can select one of them as your ride, and know precisely when they get to your location, what car they are driving and the name of the driver. Passengers and drivers are required to rate each other, so the system continually upgrades itself with knowledge about the satisfaction level of all of its participants. Uber is an exemplary dynamic enterprise, which at the time of this writing was active in 45 countries.

Their business model can be expanded to disrupt a large number of incumbent businesses, not necessarily in the transportation sector, but in any market space where an individual capable of performing a service is connected to an individual in need of that service. This model will undoubtedly inspire similarly dynamic business models that will create more dynamic enterprises in fields other than private transportation.

Large-scale Dynamism

The multinational corporation Bosch presents as an example of a dynamic corporation, an organization that understands its place in the structure of the economic system as a variable, in a continuing dynamic with the ecosystem in which it performs. The company produced a white paper[4] titled 'Capitalizing on the Internet of Things—how to succeed in a connected world,' published in February 2014.

It is very important that large corporations set an example of dynamism, as most often we equate size with the inability to move fast enough, or to

4 Bosch (2014). Bosch Connected Manufacturing, White Paper, September. Stuttgart: Bosch.

understand the changing circumstances with the speed needed to make a difference.

Bosch articulates the transformation necessary when leaving one industrial landscape and entering another. The company understands that in this more than disruptive Internet of Things opportunity, what are at stake are all the business models that will not adapt fast enough and deep enough. In this instance, deep means understanding that transformation is required not at the surface of things, but in the depth of the capability of the enterprise. This depth is not guaranteed unless the leadership of enterprises undertakes an unlearning of the current market conditions, and learns more about the being side of the human mind.

For Bosch, the Internet of Things is the fourth Industrial Revolution, and by labeling it this way they, the company, shows their understanding of the meaning and implications of this new opportunity. Their vision is to make the Internet of Things a reality that will bring about new values and new benefits in people's lives, as well as better ways of doing business. Because very few of the building blocks of the previous industrial revolution will be part of the way of doing business in the Internet of Things, the changes required are drastic, and will invariably result in the demise of a large number of business models made obsolete by the new demands of everything being connected. Sitting and waiting is no longer an option, which is why the Corporation is actively investigating the opportunities in the Internet of Things, and producing white papers on the subject.

This is the quintessential capability of a dynamic corporation, noticed also in the transformation of IBM in years after selling its personal computer business to Lenovo; the capability of truly understanding the landscape in which it is a participant, and what the emergent president holds in terms of realistic opportunity. The reality is that transformation is required in all domains and will affect many companies that your organization might be doing business with.

If media will be transformed, then the retail industry will be transformed, the music industry will be transformed, the entertainment sector will be transformed, and the marketing of products and services will be transformed. What will be the impact of these transformations on the business model of your organization? How will these transformations impact your ability to capture and create value, and how would it impact your key partners and your targeted customer base? The impact of these transformations is not yet visible which means again, you need quite a good measure of foresight in deciding the strategy forward.

The recent past gives us a few good examples of organizations that were not prepared for the transformations brought about by digital technology. We need to remind ourselves of a company called Blockbuster, or another company called Sony, both market leaders in their day, and both relegated to lesser if any roles at all. The choices ahead are rather simple if one decides to articulate them:

- You can either add Internet of Things technology in the products you already make, thus connecting everything to everything; or
- You can start dreaming about completely new products and services, by defining a few new benefits that can be attained *only* with the technology available in the Internet of Things.

Bosch has decided to pick their future and actively start pursuing it by looking at five key markets where the potential of the Internet of Things might be realized within the next seven years. These key markets are intelligent buildings, automotive, utilities, smart cities and manufacturing. These five areas will be transformed when the physical world will be embedded with the virtual world, and Bosch calls for management to start envisioning what opportunities will be possible.

The inspiration question again: what could be possible? It is interesting to observe that two of the five areas of focus—intelligent buildings and smart cities—are expressed as ideas, and here again we have the importance of the language of concepts. Bosch is proposing an evolutionary business model suited for innovation in the Internet of Things. They call it '*the magic triangle*' (Figure 6.4).

This is a very insightful move towards complete dynamics taking place at the same time as disruption happens. The insight understood that one couldn't look at New Opportunity from the perspective of the old business model, or the old metrics. The new success factors are tied to the ability to develop an *ecosystem* ready for the transformation at hand, and the speed with which *business model innovation* takes place. Both require the mindset and DNA of a start-up. For a large organization—the company, which employs over 300,000 people, and has subsidiaries in 60 countries—to talk about a start-up mentality as the mindset for the right conceptual approach when it comes to

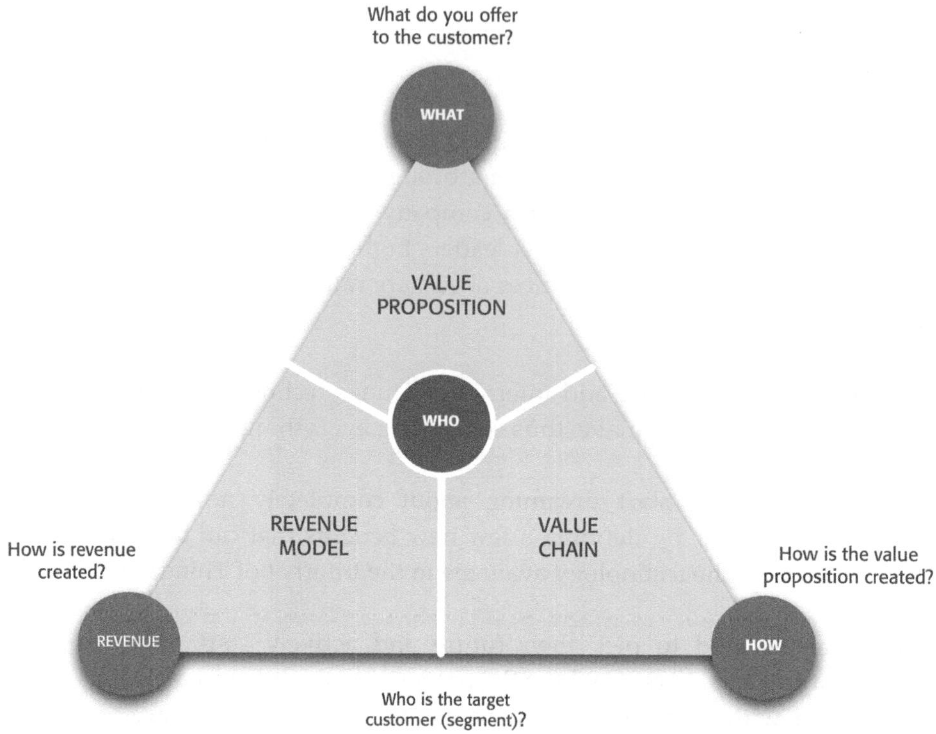

Figure 6.4 The magic triangle

Source: Adapted from University St. Gallen, Institute of Technology Management, 2013.

transformative times, shows a true understanding of the different nature of the variables that will create the disruption ahead.

In a world in which everything is connected, a business organization that is proactive in a highly volatile and dynamic environment, will actively shape its world, and make the most of its new opportunities. Embarking on such an ambitious transformation project requires not only a reframing of the organization's purpose, but the retooling of the individuals within. Their ambition to accomplish the goals of the organization will always be connected to their own ambition as individuals, to maximize and actualize their potential, and co-create value in the enterprise.

PART 3

VALUE CAPTURE AND DELIVERY

Chapter 7
The Future as a Choice

The Value Creating Enterprise

My definition of 'The Future' in the context of enterprise is this: The future is the changes you make to the present, through your *motivation, behavior* and *action.* Motivation is the internal condition that gives rise to what we want to do, based on our goals, what we can do based on our capabilities, and what we will do, based on our will. Motivation is the ethos of goal-orientated behavior.

The engagement with the future is a matter of will. Make your choice and have the Will to Engage. In this definition 'The Future' means taking a stance about what you want to be when you have become. What then when the future is not a choice? More precisely, when it is not 'your choice'? You and your organization are then just reacting; you are just mitigating an emerging condition of the market space, which was designed by others, as their future. These 'others' have imposed on you a condition of surrendering to forces you rarely understand, and even more so rare, you can fully master. Think about the demise of Blockbuster and the surge of Netflix. Think about the entire advertising industry that is surrendering every year more than $30 billion to Google. Think about the recording industry, transformed in a few years by forces they did not control or anticipate. These examples are about choices not acted upon, and futures that we imposed on incumbents, by enterprises actively engaged in designing their own future.

Designing the Future

As I write these words it is Sunday. I am on Martinique Beach, in Nova Scotia, Canada. From where I am now, the future does not mean 'next Sunday,' with every condition unchanged. While 'next Sunday' is technically seven days away, and might be thought of as 'the future,' if my behavior remains unchanged, then we will just have me, again, on Martinique Beach. That will not be 'me in the future,' but just me, next Sunday.

To qualify as 'the future,' my condition on next Sunday needs a behavior transformation. I must make a change in my condition, and a change substantially toward a better condition. That is what the future means. The pursuit of a better condition for the individual and the organization, at a defined period in time, ahead of the present time.

Another way to look at this and illustrate the difference between the future as a physical phenomenon, and the future as a psychological and physiological experience, is to place an object a few yards in front of you. A book is a good

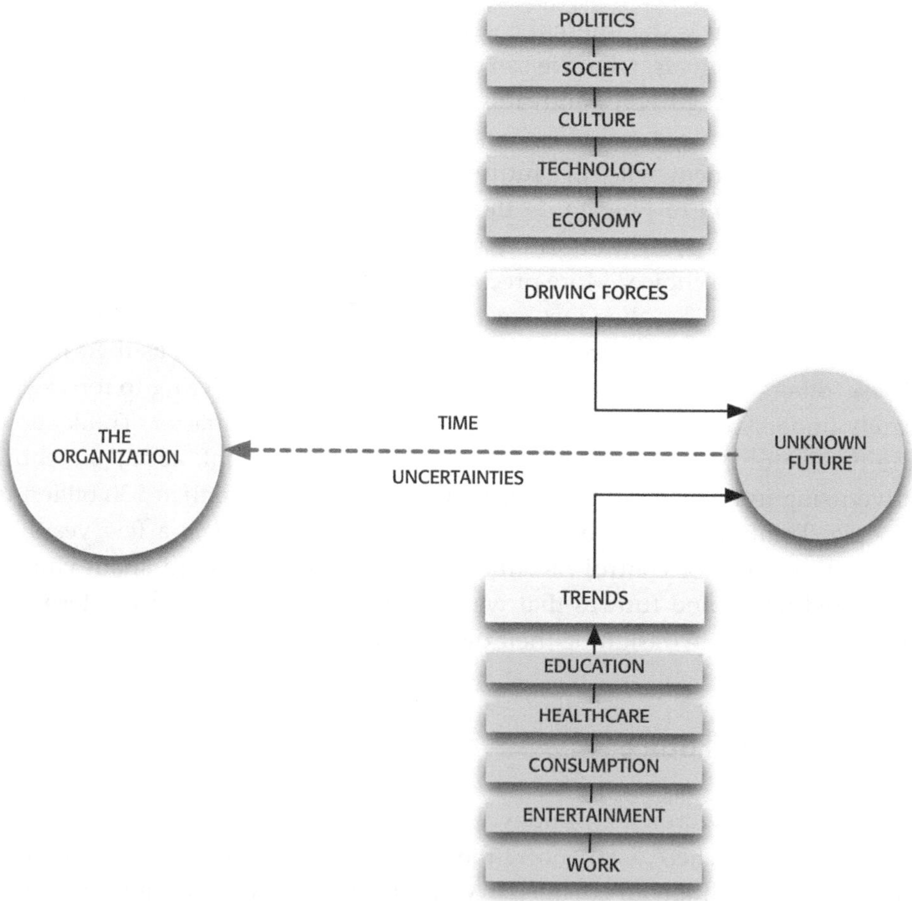

Figure 7.1 Mitigating the future

object for this exercise. There is a physical distance between you and the book now. There is also an intellectual distance between you and the book, as you are not aware of its contents. If you wait—and you can wait quite a few hours, days or months—the book will not come to you.

The placement of the book in relationship to you is physically in 'the future,' in the sense that only by an active and conscious action of moving forwards and towards the book, you can touch it, open it and become aware of its contents. And only after these actions are complete, the book's contents will enrich your life experience. So the future is an individual experience. The future is your action; it is what you do to get to it. The future includes your proactive engagement in getting there. The future does not mean 'tomorrow,' it means a move forward.

Organizations have two clear choices when it comes to their treatment of the future: Choice number one is to stay in the present and let the future flow

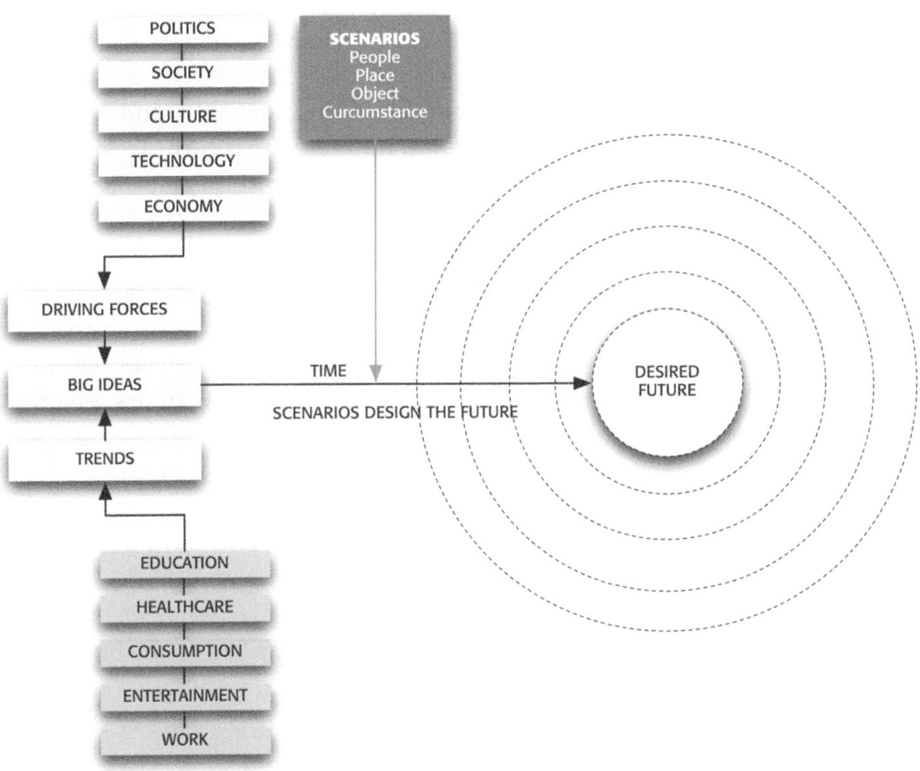

Figure 7.2 Designing the desired future

towards you (Figure 7.1). Choice number two is to design your path to where the future is and purposefully claim it as *your future* (Figure 7.2).

The Future is a Foresight, Not a Forecast

Imagine you are planning the release of a series of products or services over the course of the next five years, products that will be successful in the market and that will gradually teach users to perform more and more complex tasks. You have to start by formulating an opinion about what could be possible now, at the intersection of emerging behavior and emerging technology. And then you have to formulate an opinion about what you might sense will be possible in *the future*, five years or so from now. You need the power of foreseeing what people just like you, might be doing at a time in the future, given a number of new behaviors now made possible by emerging technology. I am mentioning a few times in this book that business is not a science, but an art, and this is worth repeating, because this is precisely the difference between forecasts and foresight. One is a *science based on mathematical predictions*, the other is an *art based on human understanding.*

What is the difference between a prediction and foresight, and which one gives the enterprise a more accurate tool to mitigate the future? In forecasting we depend on predictions that use natural sciences, and this means we study things as *phenomena.*

A phenomenon usually contains forces, and these forces are applied to objects, and when applied they will result in a change of the current state of the object. In other words, we look at the speed of the wind as applied to the clouds, and we forecast where the clouds might be in a few hours, given the same wind speed and direction (Figure 7.3).

These are forces well suited to a rational analysis, as we can quantify all of them with numbers, and numbers lead to formulas, and formulas lead to a prediction. At speed X, at this Y location, by Z time.

Can the same formulas and way of thinking be applied to the business of an enterprise? Of course, we can apply a number to anything we wish, and we can create pro-forma scenarios for the future of any product or service by making assumptions that favor our hopes for the enterprise. We can assume that the sell-through rate of our products will maintain the same momentum as in the present, for a foreseeable future of our choosing. But this is just

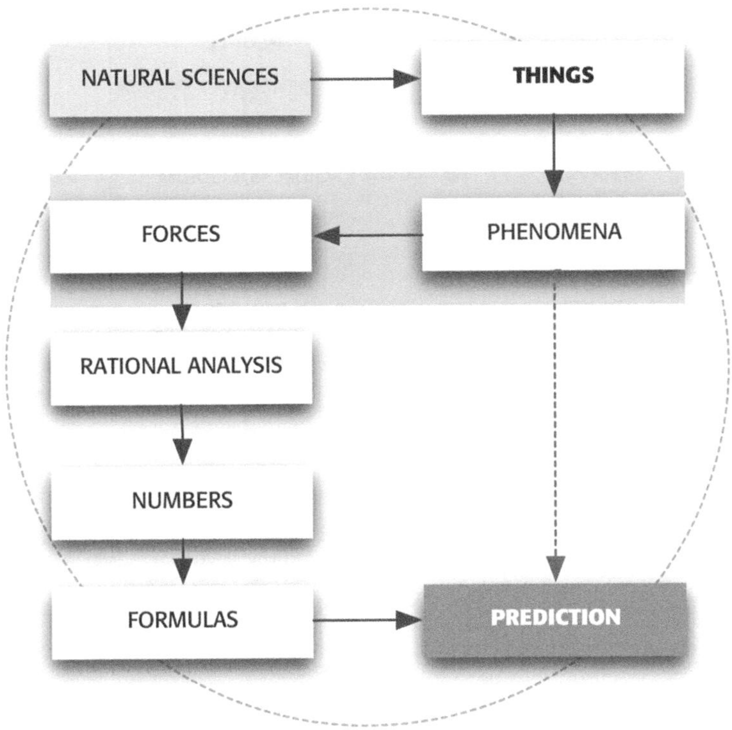

Figure 7.3 Forecasting through prediction

Source: Diagram inspired by the work of Professor Peter Collins, University of Salford, UK.

a game. We cannot predict future sales for products and services based on what we can observe today. Of course lots of companies do it, because they are looking for an entry point from where they can start thinking about the future, and the present is that convenient entry point. Harsh Muthal, Managing Partner at Biz Mantra calls this approach a *Condition Strategy* that extrapolates the present into the future, which is something *just like today* but *takes place next week*. We look at the present and the past, drive insights from this, and prepare a road map for the future based on what worked, and what we know how to execute.

There is no guarantee that the current rates will sustain themselves, and there is no guarantee that the outside risk factors will stay the same. So this means that the natural sciences formula does not apply to business forecasting. By contrast, an *ambition strategy* creates a compelling vision of the desirable future, and creates a tactical road map to get there. The ability to create this

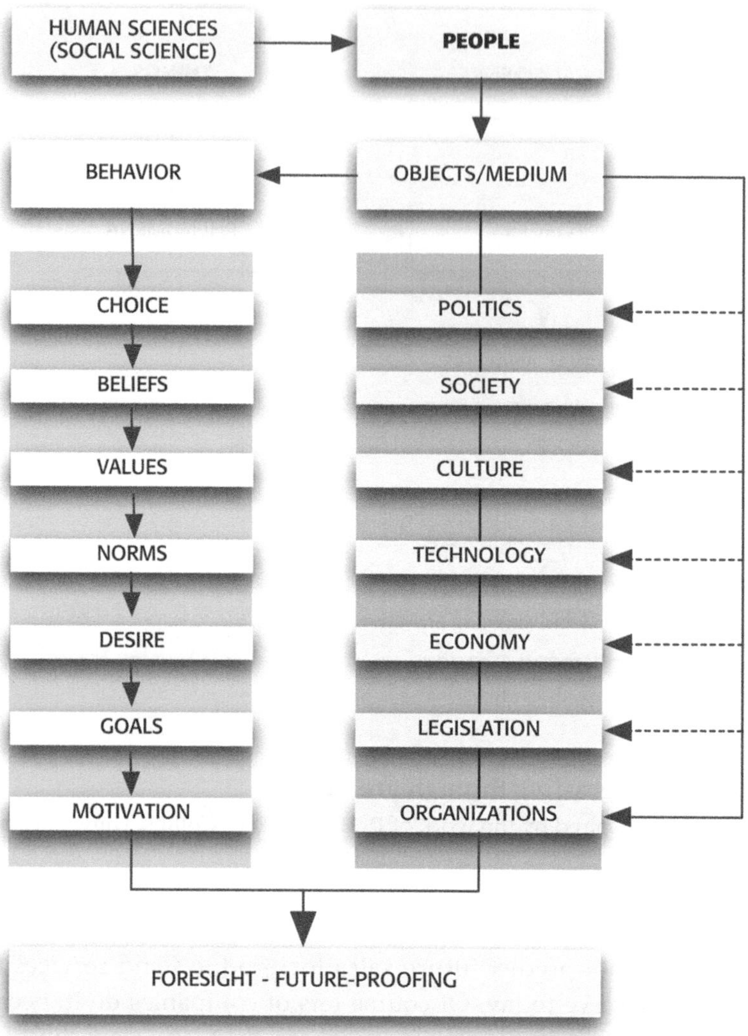

Figure 7.4 Foresight elements

Source: Diagram inspired by the work of Professor Peter Collins, University of Salford, UK.

compelling vision is based on fresh data points seen as opportunities, and is not bound by current capability.

When dealing with foresight we are looking at human beings, bringing us closer to social sciences. We are looking at people (Figure 7.4) encountering objects—and in this context object means something that affects one or more of our senses, something we can touch, feel, or taste, or something that makes us think about things in a new way. Ideas can be objects for the benefit of this explanation. Fire could be such an object, or the smart phone, or the microwave oven, and so on. When people encounter objects they engage in behavior, which is something that can be observed, and also monitored, as behavior is controlled by a number of extrinsic factors to the individual, factors such as social norms, beliefs, values, some of which are controlled at times by large peer groups, or by governments.

The engagement with the object is also the result of individual choice and individual values, which in turn are the result of individual desires, leading to individual goals, and ultimately creating motivation and completing the precondition of all human behavior: that of being goal-driven.

On the societal side, this new object has potential impact on the social realm, in politics, in the economic system, it might lead to new legislation and impact organizations, and further impact the development of connected technologies. Think about the MP3 compression technology that allowed music to be compressed in small data sectors on digital files, which made music transferable via the Internet as data. This led to DRM—digital rights management—and the reshaping of the music industry in less than a decade; from business models to distribution and sound reproduction devices, the MP3 Object impacted all the actors in the diagram depicted in Figure 7.4.

At the intersection of all these actors, we have foresight. Foresight means the act of foreseeing what could be new on the horizon, and taking active steps to get there. Any large corporation can do nothing less but foreseeing, as this is where power resides. The power comes from the sustainable nature of any enterprise that can foresee and choose its future.

Future-Proof: The Sustainable Innovation Enterprise

A sustainable innovation enterprise is an enterprise that has the ability to sustain innovation over the long term. An innovation-producing journey starts with defining an innovation challenge. The greater the challenge, the more satisfying the potential outcomes. Obviously, we are attempting to create an outcome that will create its own market space, either as a product or service, and something we can fully control in terms of the legal property—something that we can obtain Intellectual Property protection for. Also to keep in mind when setting the innovation challenge, is the size of the demographic the outcome is addressed toward. We are not concerned with identifying a user need, but we are concerned with mapping accurately the *best opportunities* at the intersection of emerging technology with emerging behavior.

Every new product introduction helps the development team in expanding its future potential, by training the marketplace into the use of new technologies. As an example, the Apple iPhone trained users how to use a multi-touch screen, and that helped many development teams around the world create new applications in which multi-touch is a prerequisite. These applications were not introduced at the same time as the original iPhone, but as time passed, users have become familiar with the multi-touch gestures, and the capability of the device. Each one of these applications serves to sustain the innovation we call the iPhone in the future, by giving users new benefits and new behaviors to engage in.

Before expanding the methodology used in sustainable innovation, let's make sure that we all understand innovation the same way, and specifically what innovation *is not*.

First of all, *innovation is not a process.* Every time we think innovation is a process, we are reducing it to the basic elements of every process, and we expect the outcome to be the result of a process within a timeline, within the deliverables that processes result in. The reality is that when you are engaged in the pursuit of innovative outcomes, you simply don't know when you will be done, and simply don't know what the outcome will be. And this is where the art comes in, knowing when you have found something worth developing, and knowing when to stop searching. If innovation is not a process then what is it? *Innovation is an outcome.* Innovation is the thing you are creating as a result of a process that might involve design, might involve engineering, and might involve creativity, imagination, inspiration and multiple iterations of concepts, very much like art does. The ethos of innovation has little to do with technology; it has only to do with what we want of ourselves.[1]

The processes leading to innovative outcomes start by understanding human nature, our desires, goals and motivations at the present time, seen through the lens of a new possibility of satisfying them, at a higher and deeper level. So one has to start with the driving forces in society, combined with emerging trends in behavior. Sometimes the innovation outcome is a

1 Manu, A. (2010). *Disruptive Business: Desire, Innovation and Re-design of Business*. Farnham: Gower Publishing, 174.

new medium, which releases latent behavior—things we did not know we wanted to do are now feasible, and become a new condition for our life, as briefly discussed in the first chapter of this book. Think of Google. You never knew you wanted to search on Google until you could, and now Google is a constant companion of your life. We can surmise from this that the success of any innovation is proportional with its capability to create the experiences most conducive to emerge in our latent behavior, and the desires that shape who we are in our best representation. On Facebook we have the best example of 'who we are in our best representation.' No one will post there anything less.

Scenario-based Innovation and Decision Making

What will prompt us to engage in change? A vision of new possibility is a powerful attractor image for change. Another attractor is knowledge, specifically knowledge about the continuous transformation present around the world at every moment, and the fact that the present is constantly emerging. Understanding that the present is in a constant emergence means that something else has to be the variable, and that might be the business you are in. The variable in this statement is not your organization, but the capability around which your organization is formed. The variability of your current form of organization requires you to change. Change is not continual; it occurs only as a voluntary act, when one reacts dynamically to emergent forms of technology or behavior. A change strategy needs to be based on courageous foresight scenarios, scenarios that explore the nature of human beings in new contexts, and around new behaviors. Humans are the ultimate medium through which technology manifests itself, and scenarios are the ideal platforms to explore these manifestations, and make strategic choices leading to change.

Scenario-based decision making is all about having informed judgment about the present, in order to create future based advisory sets of possibilities. These possibilities are not best guesses, but designed futures, places that represent a desirable destination for the enterprise or group in question.

National-level strategies need national-level normative scenarios, which take into account how the innovation object will change, enhance, expand or redefine specific instances in the social, political and legislative realms, and which technologies might be developed as a result of the innovation object now available.

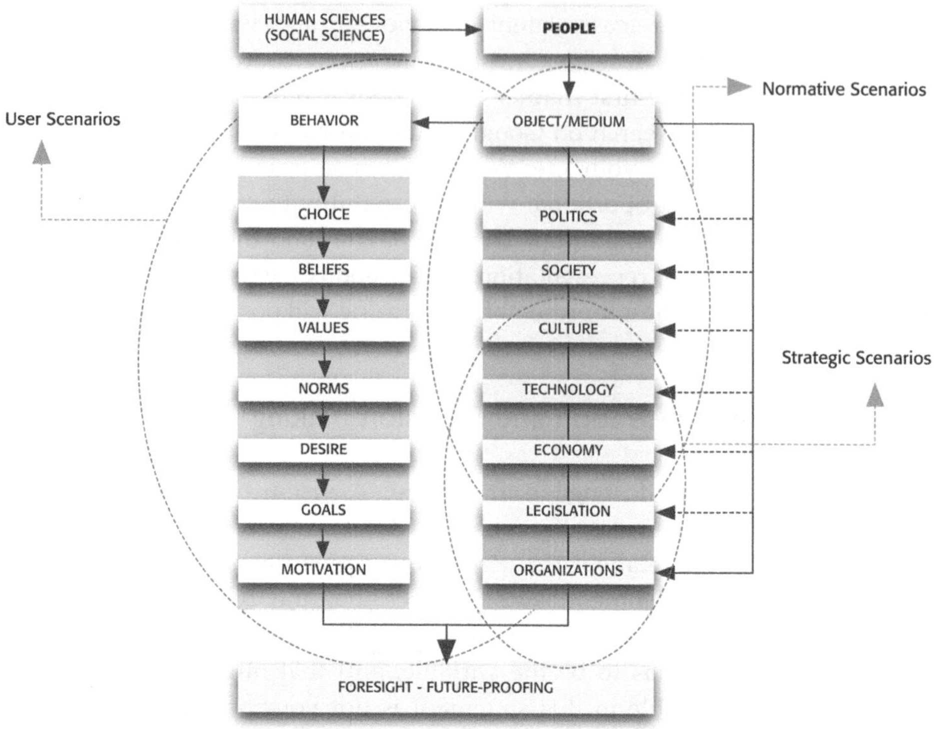

Figure 7.5 Strategic value through foresight scenarios

At the *normative level* (Figure 7.5) one needs the capability of articulating a number of scenarios from the most optimistic to the most pessimistic, in order to be able to prepare the norms by which we were create new methodologies or mitigate new impacts. As an example, look at the Internet and its impact on copyrights. The Internet allowed the transmission of data, which is expressed as ones and zeros, from one device to another device. At the point of the receptor device, the information 001100011 is decoded and replayed back as music, so now we need laws that include the representation of music as data. The innovation object in this case is music recorded as data bits, and the impact is distributed in all corners of the social and economic landscape. The normative scenarios will need to explore the impact in society, culture, organizations and the economy, before describing the impact in legislation, which undoubtedly will follow.

Normative scenarios have no immediate strategic value, but inform about the possible shape of the economic, cultural and political space in which the other scenarios would operate. What is described in Normative Scenarios is the answer to the question: *How is the Landscape Changing?* The answer often takes the form of '*when this technology happens, this is what society will become*!'

Normative scenario building often uses a framework of four quadrants of opposite possibilities, in a desire to explore all alternatives, even the less palatable one. I do not favor this technique as it restricts the free form and beauty of scenario writing, limiting it to a manufactured negative construct, which is just that, a construct. If we can construct a negative dystopia in order to get ready for its impact, we may as well use our imagination and construct a Utopia from the beginning. Constructing the richly imagined future gives organizations a powerful attractor image, rather than a scary version of the future. Scare tactics do not inspire; visions of a better future do.

Strategic and User Scenarios

Enterprises are interested less in what happens in the political or social realm, so they need a different type of scenario. They will need a *strategic scenario* as a tool allowing them to mitigate the impact of the innovation object, and design a desired future. A strategic scenario will be looking at the intersection between the object and the economic, technological, organizational and legislative framework. The organization also needs a different type of the scenario at the intersection of behavior inclusive of choice, beliefs, values and motivation and involving the life of users. Not just one *user scenario*, but many, because we have many users and each one with a different point of view, and each one informed by different beliefs, values and norms.

A strategic big picture scenario has two advantages: it discloses the big picture in which any user experience scenario operates—which allows a company to plan strategic approaches that deal with the new context—and it can be used in turn as a point of departure for other scenarios, as it describes a new opportunity or attitude. A strategic scenario answers the fundamental transformative questions: *What are the characteristics of the new market? What, therefore, are the characteristics of the organization that will best respond to this dynamic?*

The value of strategic scenarios is that they plant early seeds for a new business strategy in the mind of the executive team. They plant an idea about the possible direction of their business, an idea that has attractor power, and enlists the intellectual acceptance of the executive. When executed properly, these scenarios deliver as if written by the company itself. This methodology forces corporations to understand the dynamic nature of society, and implicitly, the interdependent economic nature of the system of which they are a part. It forces them to articulate a vision for the future, and actively pursue strategies and tactics by which this future will become reality.

Scenarios help the leadership team prepare a strategic and imaginative response to emerging market conditions, and implement changes faster. Used at their best, scenarios create pathways for change, from sets of signals in the market space directly affecting the organization, and reveal the dynamic of the behavior space in which an organization functions. They provoke thinking and analysis; they define methods that engage an organization's ability to shape the future, to create options of possibility, and link any future activity to *action today*.

The sustainable innovation enterprise needs a process by which *informed judgment* will result in shaping a desired future, thus future-proofing the enterprise (Figure 7.6). The idea here is to mitigate an unknown over the course of time, and with as few ambiguities as possible. Defining a desired future, removes many of the uncertainties we associate with the future, and engages

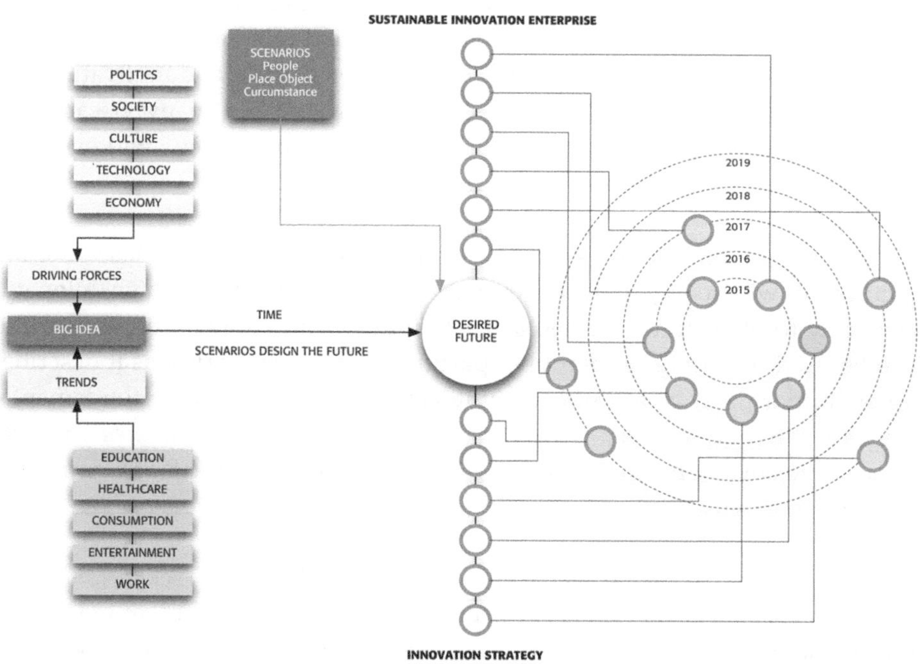

Figure 7.6 Sustainable innovation map

the passion of the enterprise in the present, toward achieving a common future goal. The method starts by formulating the strategic opportunity as a series of big ideas at the intersection of Driving Forces and Trends. I detail this process and its outcomes in the chapter that follows (Chapter 8). Since we want to design the future, it is imperative that we articulate early and forcefully our Big Idea. The big idea gives shape to the discovery phase of this process, as we now know what we are looking for.

Inspired by the big idea—in the example from Chapter 8, the Link-Enabled Ecology—we produce a series of scenarios describing the desired future, from multiple points of view, and disclosing multiple benefits (Figure 7.7). The end result of this process is a large bank of scenarios that disclose new applications of technology, and new user benefits. In effect, what we now have are multiple intellectual property disclosures that form an innovation strategy, which will sustain the enterprise for a long time in the future. The tasks remaining are to prioritize these ideas, and enable them as user facing applications, products and services, which will be introduced gradually to the market, as the user base becomes familiar with their capabilities, and as these new products become new mainstream platforms for daily behavior.

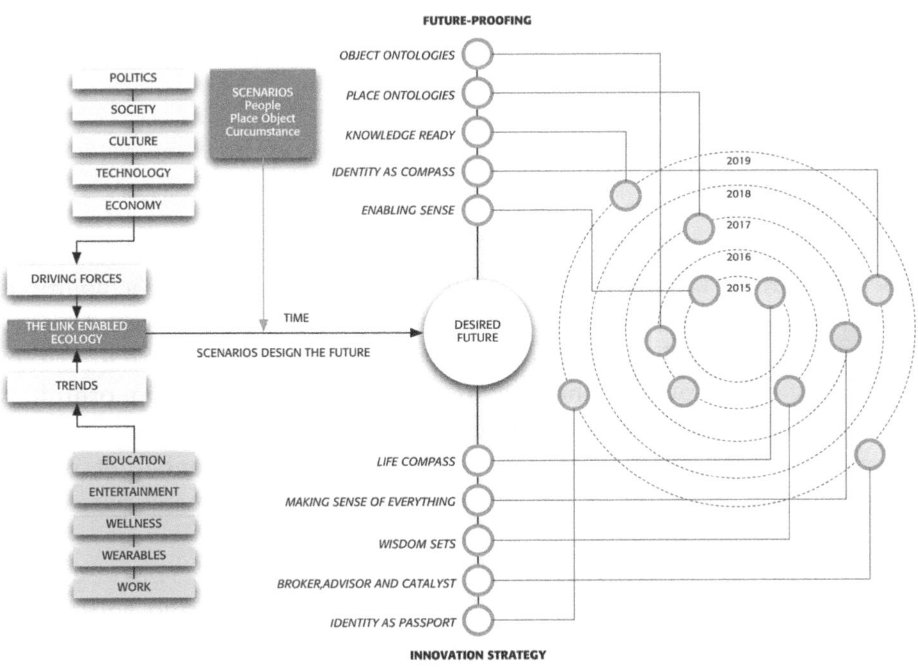

Figure 7.7 Link-enabled ecology in the internet of things innovation map

The *'future as a choice'* strategy forces forward thinking and adaptive mindsets, without which maintaining growth is a practical impossibility. Once the future is outlined and it becomes an attractive image, this image engages the spirit of the organization, its leadership as well as all participants alike. It gives purpose to the organization, becomes a shared vision and a destination. Shared visions are powerful tools for transformation in organizations.

Foresight and the Value Creating Enterprise

Can enterprises afford not to make all efforts to be future proof? Is an enterprise sustainable if it does not have foresight? Evidence points in favor of foresight, and here is why: foresight embraces the activities of thinking, debating and shaping the future, in effect a process of discovery, on the basis of which one can engage in the design of the future as a choice. As a strategic tool, foresight links the future—*what could be possible?*—to action today. And because it is a tool, we can measure it through a dedicated analytical framework.[2] The process of debating the future leads to deep insights into trends in technology, demographics, regulations and lifestyles, which can be harnessed to re-write industry rules, and create a new competitive space. We can measure enterprise foresight on a scale of High, Medium and Low, based on three fundamentals:

- Innovation.
- Financial Performance.
- Intellectual Capability.

Innovation in this framework is a measure of the company's ability to introduce and apply new ideas, processes, products or procedures, designed to significantly benefit the enterprise or society, either in response to market, technology or competitive changes, or to pursue new market opportunities. The objective measurements of innovation are research and development expenditures, the number of patents applied for, the number of patents registered, and new product announcements and associated press releases.

Financial Performance measures revenue growth, stock price growth, earnings per share, market to book ratios, price-earnings ratio and market share. Interesting to note that the measures of innovation have a direct reflection

2 The strategic value is adapted with permission from Maneesh Mehta, The Blackbox Institute.

on financial performance, specifically as far as market sentiment goes. On January 9, 2007 Apple Corporation's announcement of the iPhone had a direct impact on stock market to book ratio, and price-earnings ratio, without a single physical product being introduced, and based solely on market sentiment about its potential to disrupt the market-space incumbents, and improve Apple's financial condition in the long run. Apple stock rose 7 percent that day while Research in Motion (renamed BBRY) was down 6 percent, a single day loss of market cap of $2 billion.

Intellectual Capability measures the technical ability of the professionals in an organization to successfully develop innovations capable of distinguishing an organization from its competitors, transforming industry boundaries, or creating new competitive arenas. This is measured by the number of published journal articles, number of conference paper submissions, number of R&D employees as a percentage of total of all employees, and the educational background and training of the workforce.

In constructing a working framework for analyzing foresight performance, we need to work with the desired state of the outcomes we are after, and place a premium—the highest position—for outcomes that create a new market space. Since 'creating' is a verb about the future, *Shaping the Future* (SF) will be our highest coordinate, and most desired outcome. In this category we can place enterprises that have redrawn boundaries, and are now rule makers as a result (Figure 7.8).

At the polar opposite of SF, we have enterprises that are market followers rather than creators, companies that React to the Present (RP). A category no less desirable than SF is Creating a Place (CP), populated by enterprises that have created a new competitive space for themselves, and defined new roles to play in people's lives. Google Earth comes to mind. And lastly, enterprises that are looking to Fill a Place (FP) in the market, by occupying a position, but who are not perceived as leaders in their category.

One of the key drivers for an enterprise's migration from 1 to 4 around this foresight framework are technology changes or any other fundamental innovations. The speed with which a company migrates from the position RP to CP indicates the speed of understanding of the changing circumstances in that particular company's market space. This is a move toward High Foresight. A movement toward FP will represent a passive reaction and a change toward Low Foresight. Rather than reacting passively to change, companies with high

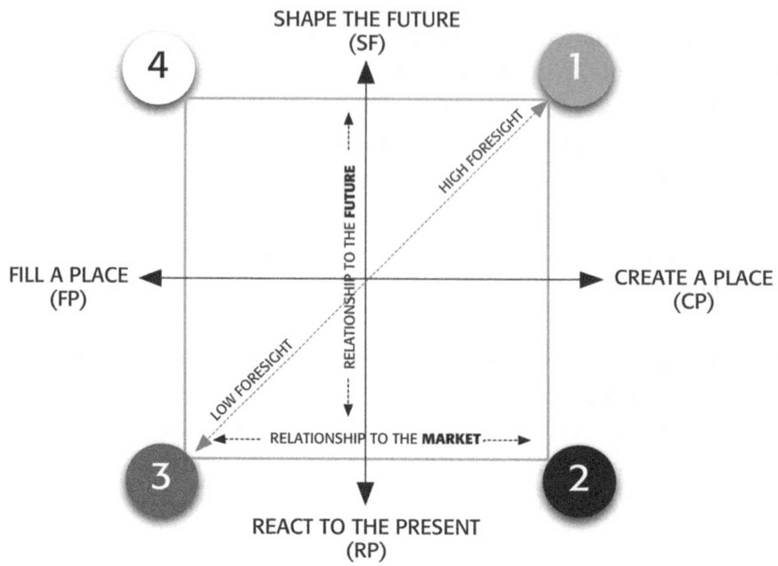

Figure 7.8 Strategic value matrix

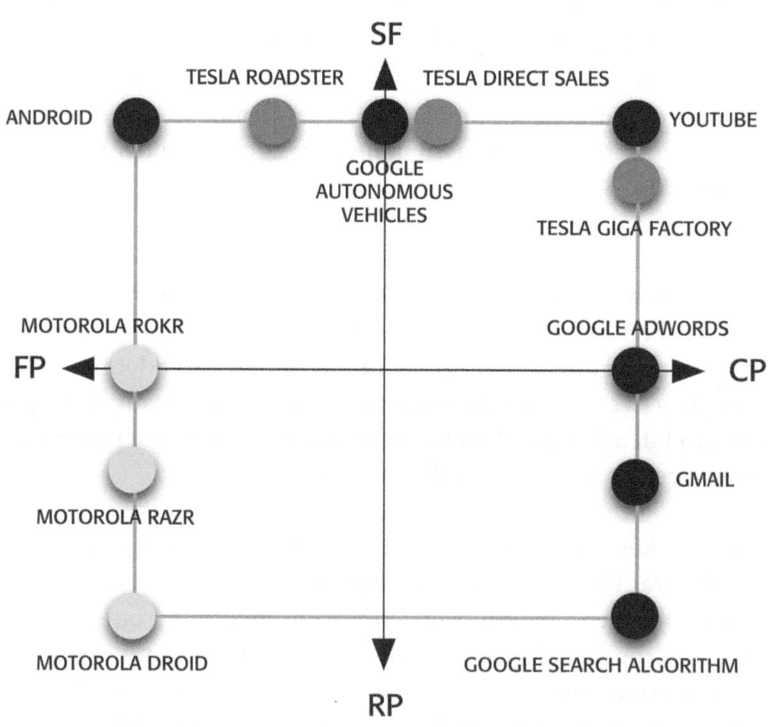

Figure 7.9 Relative strategic value

foresight stimulate it (Figure 7.9). The framework allows us to assess strategic value in a simple two axis comparative matrix as illustrated in Figure 7.10.

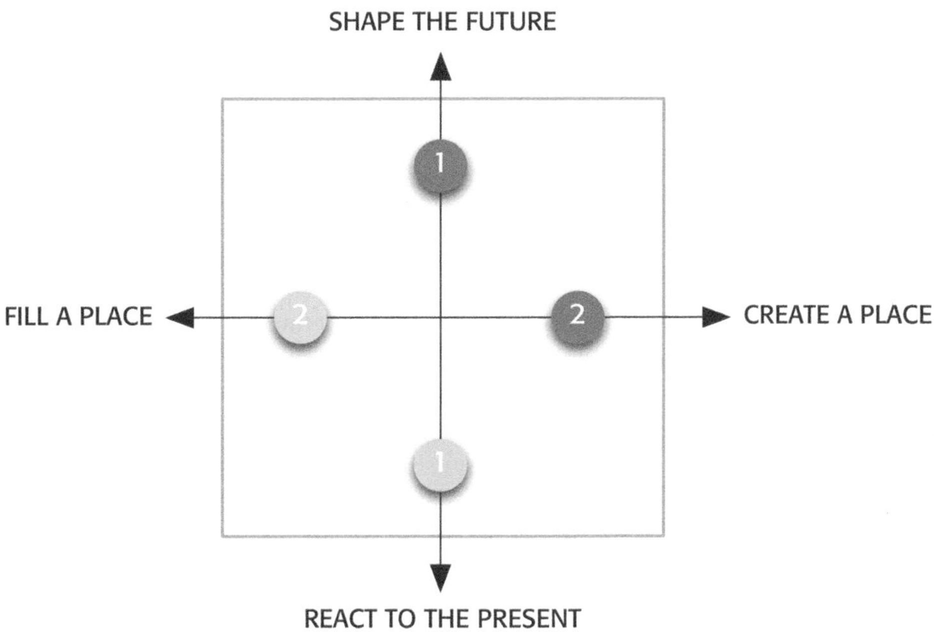

Figure 7.10 Strategic value framework

In Figure 7.10:

AXIS 1 represents the RELATIONSHIP TO THE FUTURE:

React to the Present: when decisions are based on clearly defined and well-known gaps of function or desire, there is *low strategic value*:

> The insights gained to make these decisions are generated through market research or direct experience, and are generally widely known.

Shape the Future: when decisions are based on a desire or need that is expected to occur in the future, and with a limited marketplace prior to the organization taking action, there is *high strategic value*:

> Insights that drive these decisions emerge from reasoning and understanding, and require intuition and vision.

AXIS 2 represents the RELATIONSHIP TO THE MARKETPLACE:

Fill a Place: when a competitive space is clearly defined, with well-established metrics, there is *low strategic value*:

> Valuation for measuring success is defined according to industry criteria, and there is limited long-term return on innovation, as others in the market are pursuing similar criteria.

Create a Place: when a competitive space is undefined or poorly understood prior to a business action, there is *high strategic value*:

> The lack of industry benchmarks makes it difficult to define monetary value upfront, which often means that storytelling is required to achieve integration with other innovations.

When strategic value is low, differentiation occurs through increased performance that can be directly evaluated against competitors. When strategic value is high, it is difficult to clearly articulate differentiation, as the playing field has yet to be defined, and direct comparisons between businesses are not yet possible.

It is important to note that high strategic value does not ensure immediate financial success. It is always possible to profit as a late-adopter, competing on price and additional features, especially in industries with high risk, and involved in fundamental research. But within the behavior economy, the first to market in a new space and with an involved audience, is often the one to define that space for the foreseeable future. Apple, IBM, Facebook, Netflix and Google all dominate in spaces that they have defined. Each of these companies has been the industry benchmark in their categories.

IBM 5 in 5 as a Method of Sustainable Innovation

How does the strategic value matrix work in the case of your enterprise? How does this work for a business, a university, a government, or a country? If you stand by and watch others get to their future, eventually you will need to mitigate an emerging present you might not understand. It is healthier to be wrong about one's bet about the future, than not to place a bet at all.

One company that understands that is IBM. At the end of each year, they examine market and societal trends expected to transform our lives, as well as emerging technologies from IBM's global labs, to develop a multi-year forecast called *The Next 5 in 5*. In November of 2014,[3] IBM released the five innovations that they believed would change our lives over the next five years:

In the Future, Everything Will Learn
A new era in computing will lead to breakthroughs that will amplify human abilities, assist us in making good choices, look out for us and help us navigate our world in powerful new ways. The classroom of the future will learn about each individual student over the course of their education, helping them master the skills that match their goals. The rapid digitization of educational institutions will allow unprecedented instrumentation of the learning process.

Cognitive computing, or learning technologies, will help us calculate everything we can about how each student learns and thrives, then create flexibility in the system to continually adapt and fine-tune what we deliver to that student and how this supports teachers and employers.

Buying Local Will Beat Online
The technology trends will move us back to bricks and mortar—but with a difference. In the future, retailers will layer increasing levels of engagement and personalization on top of the shopping experience, ultimately merging the instant gratification of physical shopping with the richness of online shopping and making same-day delivery a snap.

Doctors Will Routinely Use Your DNA to Keep You Well
Today, full DNA testing to help make treatment decisions is still rare. But cognitive systems and cloud computing may make this form of treatment mainstream. It could be done faster, more affordably and much more frequently. In addition to DNA testing for cancers, we may even see DNA-specific personalized treatment options for conditions such as stroke and heart disease.

3 Available at: http://www.ibm.com/smarterplanet/us/en/ibm_predictions_for_future/ideas/ (accessed June 21, 2015).

A Digital Guardian Will Protect You Online

Security is evolving from being based on rules, like passwords, to being automatic and made stronger through us just being us. This guardian will have your back; trained to focus on the people and items it is entrusted with based on 360° of an individual's data, devices and applications. It will make inferences about what's normal or reasonable activity and what's not; ready to spot deviations that could be precursors to an attack and a stolen identity.

The City Will Help You Live in It

For citizens, smart phones enabled by cognitive systems will provide a digital key to the city. People can have fingertip access to information about everything that's happening in the city, whether an experience is right for them, and how best to get there. Because these learning systems have interacted with citizens continuously, they know what they like—and can present them with options they might not find easily. Insights from crowdsourcing, mobile applications, sensors and analytics on the cloud will allow cities to better listen, interact and respond to citizen needs. This will give rise to new cities that can respond in real-time, predict problems before they occur, and deliver tailored services to make city life better for everyone.

Three of the five innovations IBM propose as life changers are directly connected to the Internet of Things becoming mainstream. IBM understands that growth in a context-driven environment and new market circumstances, is entwined with innovations that redefine our relationships through new benefits, delivered in new ways. The task of the sustainable innovation enterprise is not that of pushing opportunity, but of simply observing and responding to the opportunities facilitated by the emerging present.

Chapter 8

Strategic Opportunities in the Internet of Things

New technological capabilities need new strategies, which can provide enterprises with multiple concept generation paths, and workable blueprints for new business model innovation. The business strategy question for the next decade is here: *How is your organization positioned to maximize the opportunities in the Internet of Things?*

When fully deployed, the Internet of Things will present new opportunities for people and organizations, opportunities that lie beyond the current capabilities of business today, either in financial, economic or intellectual terms. To exploit the opportunities at hand, a great deal of retooling of the individual needs to take place, balanced with the intellectual reframing of the enterprise's purpose, its ideology, and its expectations. In a world of embedded sensors, new social forms will be established that will challenge the status quo in fundamental ways. Business success in this context will be tied to providing new services, understanding the resulting new needs, and opening new innovation avenues, which take advantage of new channels of communication, and new opportunities for user engagement. Organizations adept at mastering this complex and context-driven environment, will lead new multibillion-dollar industries.

By the Numbers

According to the 2014 State of the Internet of Things Study,[1] the adoption of network-connected technologies is on the rise, with 69 percent of consumers planning to buy an in-home device in the next five years. By the end of 2015, a total of about 13 percent of consumers will own an in-home Internet of Things

1 Available at: http://www.acquitygroup.com/docs/default-source/Whitepapers/acquitygroup-2014iotstudy.pdf?sfvrsn=0 (accessed: July 25, 2014).

device, and the adoption of wearable technology such as smart watches and fitness devices will also gradually increase, with nearly half of consumers already owning or planning to acquire a device in this category in the next five years.

Goldman Sachs equity research[2] thinks that the third wave in the development of the Internet is the Internet of Things. While the 1990s were the time for the fixed Internet, with one billion connected users, and the 2000s saw another wave of mobile connections, which added another billion connected nodes, the Internet of Things has the potential to connect ten times as many things—objects, people or places. That means over 30 billion connected addresses and objects.

These objects fall in five key categories in which the Internet of Things will be first adopted: wearables, automobiles, homes, cities and industrials.

A convergence of factors is the reason the Internet of Things is happening now, some connected to costs and some having to do with efficiency and availability. The price of computing is falling, collecting data has become an accepted mode of achieving primary or secondary benefits, low cost sensors and lower costs for processing power have converged with the widespread adoption of smartphones, which are essentially the enablers of every individual to connect with other individuals, as well as with objects or places in their surroundings. We can add the mainstream adoption of fitness trackers that connect with devices, providing individuals a synopsis of their physical activity over the course of time, and a few other products like thermostats, allowing users to control the amount of energy they consume in the home. This ecosystem is growing every day, and the opportunities within it are multiplying, in the form of applications, devices, platforms and the infrastructure that will see them function flawlessly. This game is not for beginners, and most of the top companies in the world have declared themselves players in the Internet of Things. Cisco, IBM, Samsung, Philips, Google, Bosch, Intel, this list can go on and on. My point here is simply this: the Internet of Things is not a weak signal anymore.

The tangible opportunities offered by the Internet of Things fall in three categories of development:

2 Available at http://www.goldmansachs.com/our-thinking/outlook/iot-video.html (accessed: September 15, 2014).

1. *Enhancing our experience* of current products or services providing benefits we all know and want, but this time connected to the Internet of Things.

2. *Expanding our relationship and engagement* with current products or services providing *new benefits* because they are connected to the Internet of Things.

3. *Redefining our relationships through new products or services*, connected in *new ways* and providing *new benefits*.

This all means that a lot of things will change. People's personal lives will change, the productivity of the workplace will change, and the consumption patterns and behaviors of people will change. It also means that objects and places will now have a behavior layer, made possible by connectivity and by small-size robotics. And this behavior layer of objects and places is the most exciting aspect of the Internet of Things, because we are looking at *new value,* and the creation of new archetypes for the human experience.

All the spaces in which we conduct our activities will be addressable by devices that will be aware where they are. Imagine the Apple Watch as one such device, connecting us to the Internet of Things. The Apple Watch has the potential to become one of the most transformative products ever introduced, because it would change the way we look at technology, the way we understand what the Internet can do for us, and the way in which we will make the Internet an integral partner in our life.

The Apple Watch signals the end of the personal computer, and the beginning of a new form of engagement with technology, which will be personal, and on everybody's wrist. This is the beginning of customized information devices hosted on our bodies, transforming us slowly, as we experience benefits that we did not dream of just 10 years ago. The level of personalization that this technology can now afford us, is the result of the device being physically attached to our skin, and receiving constant feedback from our bodies. This is the beginning of commonsense computing, a relationship with technology that understands where we are, how we are feeling, and why.

Make no mistake: the Apple Watch is not *just another watch*. In a world in which everything is connected, the Apple Watch starts to look like a really Big Idea. It will be where you are at all times—this is what watches do—but this time it will *follow* and *track* your activities, and your biometric responses, and constantly update itself with dynamic knowledge. Pretty soon, it will communicate our status to other devices, without the user needing to initiate any action, and these other devices with execute commands that will see our life become much more pleasurable and much more productive. As with other product launches by Apple, the introduction of the Apple Watch looked like the launch of a product, when it was actually the launch of a platform. The Apple Watch is the embodiment of Apple's Internet of Things strategy, and one of its first manifestations.

It is Already Here

Another device announcing a strategy is Amazon's 'Echo,' which has no other purpose but to connect us to the Internet of Things, either prompted by questions we are asking, or by suggestions made by the device itself. Amazon has cleverly introduced a device in people's homes, without making too much fuss about its capability of connecting you to the future Internet of Things, and yet, this device might well become an essential component in everybody's life. This is a classic behavior economy device, in the sense that it is a *platform* looking like a *product.* The platform brings *ambient computing* in every home, connecting every participant of the family to anything and everything of interest, creating taxonomies and ontologies of all the questions and the accepted—as well as *favored*—answers. The Amazon Echo will be a one-stop question and answering machine, as well as a suggestion box. It will know who is at home and who is not, and more importantly, where people are when they are not at home; it will know the contents of your home and the status of every appliance. In the very near future, it will have the capability of taking care of mundane chores like paying bills, answering standard emails, and so forth.

These are just two short examples that illuminate the potential and the implications of the Internet of Things, and the distinguishing characteristics that make these implications far-reaching when compared to the first two stages of the Internet. The first two stages of the Internet saw life *enhanced* by instant connectivity and communications, while the Internet of Things has the potential to *redefine life's activities.* Technology consulting firm Gartner defines the Internet of Things as a strategic technology,[3] which is a technology that has the potential for significant impact on enterprises in the next five years.

3 Available at: http://www.gartner.com/newsroom/id/2603623 (accessed: September 9, 2014).

In their view, significant impact includes a high potential for disruption, the need for major financial investment, and the risk of being late to adopt a specific technology.

A strategic technology is an emerging technology that offers an opportunity for strategic business advantage for early adopters, and has the potential of significant market disruptions. This pretty much summarizes the Internet of Things both as a threat and as an opportunity.

A Link-Enabled Ecology

The result of everything connected to *everything else that makes sense,* is a Link-Enabled ecology, a complex ecosystem of interdependent and networked organic elements. An ecosystem is the very relationship between organisms and their environment, a community of ecological parts functioning as a unit, determined by and dependent upon its members.

Technology, within the human ecology, serves the function of augmenting and adjusting our interactions. In an emerging world of omnipresent links, this role will shift radically; the technology-enabled links will become *an essential element of the ecosystem,* determining its very nature.

When places and objects are linked and data enabled, they take meaning from people. They become what people want them to be. A phone now, a game console a few minutes later, and a surface leveler or compass seconds after that, and then a dictionary, a world map, a shopping cart, or a poker table. In the Link-Enabled Ecology, every different combination of people, devices and places will create a wealth of unique possibilities. Every setting and every interaction, will determine a *one of a kind ecosystem of opportunity.* The essential task in this ecosystem is not one of forcing opportunity, but of simply observing the opportunities facilitated by an Enabled Link.

Link-Enabled Mobile Devices as a New Un-Mass Medium

Mobile devices are the first truly personal mass medium, permanently connected and always in one's pocket, and with a built-in payment mechanism. These devices capture the social context of consumption, as well as the activity context of a place.

They offer individuals digital access to a world of interconnected objects and places, and because of this, they are not a technology, but a *behavior enabler* providing a value variable experience, where the value can be directly addressed on *granular context variables* to a *granular user.*

The mass acceptance of smart-phones and their penetration in all demographics has made mobile digital life a reality. This simply means that the instrument of choice—the media by which individuals choose to manifest and actualize themselves—is a portable mobile device linked to everything. Portability is about the *size* of the device, while mobility refers to its *location.* Life, in this context, refers to the nature of *the portable mobile medium being ON all the time,* and to its ability to both *SEND,* and *RECEIVE.*

It is in these two functions that we find the challenge and the opportunity, as it is these functions that are unique from prior forms of media. For organizations this means:

- The ability to contact individual users with individual messages.
- The ability to contact multiple users with the same message.
- The ability to receive feedback at all times from users.
- The ability to engage users 24 hours a day.
- The ability to trigger users' responses of engagement via defined stimuli.
- The ability to control and define stimuli on a daily basis.
- The ability to define stimuli on geo-location basis.
- The ability to define stimuli on proximity basis (users close to other users) and much, much more.

Link-Enabled Ecology as a Strategic Opportunity

In the Link-Enabled ecology, places will communicate about themselves dynamically, to everything and anything around them enabled to receive data, or programed as an address for the information. This is a way of life in which everything becomes media for the individual empowerment to create, manage and distribute content. For enterprises, this is the opportunity for new engagement, and an experiential expansion of unprecedented focus, scope and depth.

- End users will expect perfect information of what is around them and how to navigate to desired destinations, and will avoid those places that do not participate in this ecosystem.
- Vehicle and pedestrian maps, data, content and navigation will be seamless to the end user, and mostly free. This will incentivize users to consume data services to an unprecedented degree.
- All companies with 'audiences' will be in the media business, whether directly or indirectly. They will need to create digital content that expands on existing brand values, as well as specific content at geo-locations. Geo-fencing will become mainstream.
- Strategic decisions will be driven more by *monetizing the audience* than by selling devices or data; this monetization requires frequent data transactions between a user and his/her points of interest. This increases data traffic exponentially, as well as the need for data authentication.
- The opportunity connected to these changes is to become valuable to users as a trusted platform for 'navigating digital life,' providing a comprehensive suite of tools, applications, content and mobile services that guarantee the privacy of transactions, and identity authentication in a seamless way.
- People, objects and places will have far more sophistication and understanding about the value of their data, especially in the mobile context, and will look to trusted partners to maximize the value of their data while protecting their privacy and security. The opportunity in this context is identifying both the categories of actions (taxonomy), and the meaning of actions in context (ontology of the data).
- Digital profiles of places will be as important as their physical infrastructure; making that data omnipresent will become mandatory. Every place on earth will have a location profile, and a

taxonomy and ontology descriptor, what it is, where it is and what it means to a variety of user groups.

Big Ideas for the Internet of Things

KNOWLEDGE READY

With smart phones becoming mainstream, and with digital signatures, tags, and beacons becoming prerequisites for commerce, every person, place and object, would be ready to learn, to share, and to be a link to something more important.

KNOWLEDGE-ENABLED

People will have a new expectation from Objects and Spaces, and that is the expectation of communication and content retrieval. Every node—people, place or object—will expect to learn something from every other node.

ENABLING SENSE

This is the strategic decision to take on the role of making sense of raw transactional data, by creating categories of actions—taxonomy—and their meaning—ontology—in the context of individual identities.

MAKING SENSE OF EVERYTHING

Users will refuse interactions with environments and objects that do not recognize and communicate their purpose, in a specific context. This is the resolution to meet the challenge of making visible in every surrounding its capabilities to add immediate value to a user.

WISDOM SETS

When data is properly arranged it becomes meaningful to a user. The quantity of data collection resources that allow users to quantify their daily life will become beneficial only if wisdom is derived from it. The collection and analysis of transactional information will give organizations the opportunity to transform data into wisdom, and create new benefits for users.

Framing the Opportunity

It was mentioned earlier in this book that the Internet of Things is a place in which every person, object and space, are both a link and a holder of information. This means the ability to store and transmit data residing in all the actors present in a location, including the location itself. This data can move, can be managed, and has meaning. Such an environment represents the opportunity to improve the performance and significance of existing objects and places, as well as to create new benefits for users. The chief technical capability of the Internet of Things—that of connecting everything with everything that makes sense—is also its highest expectation: that of creating an environment in which *everything behaves.* This environment will expand the behavior economy, a market space with new transaction models, and new benefits on which revenue will be extracted.

The Internet of Things represents the opportunity to empower the participation and engagement of everything. Empowerment is traditionally seen as a human attribute, but in the Internet of Things, we are not looking only at people, but also at the empowerment of objects and spaces. Objects will be empowered to take actions. And actions have consequences. Hence, the identity of the command action, and trust in its intentions will become paramount. Objects will be empowered to collaborate and to share information with the spaces in which they reside, and empowered on a massive scale. Imagine any number of collaborations between objects + any number of collaborations between people + any number of collaborations between places, and then the multiple opportunities in between. In this context, trust becomes a strategic imperative.

Identity as Economic Currency

Can we look at identity as a form of currency in the behavior economy? How relevant is it to Netflix that my identity is different than my son's? Well, if we're not different we will be receiving the same recommendations for movies, but the fact is that we don't. Identity allows Netflix to make specific recommendations for specific users, thus bringing distinctive value to each user, which keeps the user satisfied in its relationship with Netflix, and increases the potential of continuing the service. Failure on the part of Netflix to recognize my identity will be a failure to satisfy my quest for value, in the delivery of customized entertainment.

In the Internet of Things, identity is no longer just about individuals, because identity expressed as data will differentiate a chair from a person, or chair from a carpet, or a plastic bottle. Consequently, understanding the richness and variety of identities in any link-enabled space is paramount.

It is not a far-fetched prediction to say that the business that will be the repository of the largest number of identities will be the winning business in the Internet of Things. The aggregator of the identities of persons, places and objects, would be the organization that will have the best chance at the analytical understanding of the new ecosystem created by the Internet of Things, and how to take advantage of it.

Areas of Opportunity and Themes

IDENTITY AS A COMPASS

Connecting people to place and object through wearable devices will increase the need for trusted identities, as decisions will be made only if the sources are trusted. Fast authentication will allow actors to navigate the link-enabled ecology with confidence. This is what the Apple Watch is all about.

ROLES, TRIGGERS AND LIFESTYLES

The data generated within Internet of Things at the point of authentication—when two identities connect—must be collected and organized. This data can then be enabled to provide a benefit to a third party. The richness of the opportunity is in the collection and categorization of the data, and not only in performing the authentication of identity. The nature of the categories under which the data is organized, is the first step of assigning meaning to it. Enabled Data is the discovery of the benefits in the data itself.

Understanding the nature of the point-to-point transactions a device engages with in everyday, gives a developer the opportunity to further use this data as part of an aggregate, or on its own, and commercialize the benefits either to third parties, or to the user of the device itself.

This means providing new layers of engagement with the user of the device, through a combination of means such as being an:

- Aggregator.
- Broker.
- Advisor.
- Educator.
- Catalyst.

The *Aggregator* brings together data and packages it with meaning. In other words it acts as a resource of information that is considered relevant, or has the potential to be considered as such.

The *Broker* helps individuals maintain balance in their lives, by delegating and regulating information. It helps filter and deliver what is relevant to individuals, so they can make informed decisions about their lives with less stress.

The *Advisor* helps the individuals with decisions about their lives by presenting alternative points of view, and offering insight and analysis related to the meaning of the decision at hand, as well as the potential consequences.

The *Educator* helps individuals by packaging information and presenting it in a manner that would be most beneficial to them, in the short and long term. Educators develop processes around this interaction, which constantly evolve for a better chance that an outcome meets and exceeds the requirements at hand.

The *Catalyst* is a role that is defined by tapping into the passions driving individuals. They inspire and invigorate, and can lead to a dynamic and experience-filled lifestyle.

MAKING SENSE OF EVERYTHING

Once we can make sense of everything by having the ability to analyze the quality of each authenticated identity, we can add another layer of benefits by enhancing it with elements of lifestyle. The style in which we live at any given point in time, is determined by a number of definable elements. Among these many elements are *triggers* and *roles* that represent opportunities for a brand or an organization to become an integral part of an individual's life. Triggers are things that fulfill a specific functional purpose in our lives. These can be tokens that are often small ideas, thoughts, notes or expressions that can alter an individual's mental state, and the way they experience daily activities. *Reminders* and *suggestions* are examples of triggers that play a role in the everyday lives of individuals.

Reminders are a token of thoughtfulness for one's self or another individual. Suggestions are tokens of information, and can be minor or profound in nature, with outcomes that are also minor or major, based on how much they mean to each individual at a given moment. Suggestions are powerful triggers; they can alter one's state of mind, especially when connected to the dimensions of wellbeing that one considers important.

IDENTITY IN LINK-ENABLED ECOLOGIES

Products themselves will become the links to the network of known information. This is the redefinition of the worldwide web into a form that exists in the physical world. A retail space is no longer just a retail space, but a network of link-enabled objects hosted in that space. The products will be the access point for features, services and knowledge. Objects will have the ability to inform one another. Transactions will become seamless and invisible. The transaction might take place silently between the consumer and the object itself. Objects will have the ability to determine the maximal price that will appeal to each individual customer.

INTELLIGIBLE TRUST–COMMON SENSE TRUST

The Taxonomy and Ontology of data will become the first filter for trust. Taxonomy and ontology of identity means categorizing authenticated identities, defining their meaning and storing the data for future use, as well as for activity profiling. Once two end points have been connected once, they should recognize each other at a subsequent encounter, just like most people recognize people, places and objects they have encountered before. Intelligible identity is an identity that has been verified before, and was tagged with taxonomy and ontology descriptors, and will be recognized when encountered again.

To fully appreciate the concept of intelligible identity, let's look at an example of an activity we are all familiar with, and that is the typical interaction with the ATM (automatic teller machine) at your bank. The interaction consists of three actors: the person, the place and the object.

People go in front of an ATM machine for very precise reasons, and this fact should actually help in speeding up the transaction—that is, if the system was designed with social norms in mind. One may want to deposit cash, one may want to withdraw cash, or one may want to check the balance of a bank account, or all three of these actions in sequence. All of these interactions depend on the user identifying himself/herself, and instructing the machine as to the indented purpose of the visit. This authentication is made once the user inserts a bank access card, in a specifically designed slot in the machine. Up to that moment, neither the machine nor the place where the machine is located, have made any effort to identify the user. The anti-social aspect here is that the user is a regular customer of the bank, and of this precise branch in particular, and has been so for the past 25 years ...

Once a PIN number is typed on the keypad, the machine identifies the user not by looking at him/her (facial features), but by this number alone. In other words, even in that moment the object has no awareness of the identity of the user; it has only an awareness of the identity of the card. Using instruments and controls provided by the machine, the user is allowed to conduct a specific set of transactions, as long as the card remains inserted in the slot.

This is not a person-to-machine interaction, but a machine-to-machine interaction, a transactional activity in which the user is playing the data entry role, and while the machine performs its actions, just the role of a spectator.

Let's imagine a situation in which once the transaction is completed, and the card is returned to the user, the user realizes that he/she needs a higher amount of cash. In other to obtain more cash, the process described above needs to recommence. Seconds after a transaction has just taken place, there is no identity awareness between the object and the user. This is against all social norms. In any social situation when two individuals introduced themselves to each other, a number of cognitive and perceptive mechanisms start to work: our faculty of sight, our faculty of hearing and our memory bank. People store images in their memory, in order to increase the likelihood of recognizing images on sight, which speeds up decision-making and the understanding of purpose. Next time you meet *this person* you will recognize *him.* Next time you come to a place you recognize it as well. How awkward would it be if we have to re-introduce ourselves to people every time we meet them, even after a relationship of over 25 years, and more so, minutes after we just had a conversation? Why is it then, that with all this technology around us, we still need to identify *who* we are to places and objects we have conducted business with before?

Intelligible trust deals with the social aspects of identity, and the advantages of people, objects and places trusting the authenticity of people, objects and places they connected with before. As the Internet of Things ecosystem is growing rapidly, the profile of security and trust issues will rise, as will the number of transactions in need of authentication.

THE PASSPORT FOR THE INTERNET OF THINGS

Everything and everyone being potentially connected, and transmitting information, means that everything and everyone needs a passport for identification purposes. In this context a passport means a mobile platform—a hub—in which the user can drag and drop all the applications for which identity authentication is desired, and from which the user can perform transactions which are authenticated with speed and simplicity, or pre-authorized by the intelligibility of the identity.

MISSION CRITICAL PURPOSE

With the massive increase of data exchange endpoints, and the massive increase in the numbers of identities potentially present in an environment, the requirement of understanding the mission of each data transaction becomes critical. By performing a qualitative assessment of the mission critical status of each transmission, we gain understanding which information exchange requires identity authentication. Mission Critical refers to the purpose of the transmission, what it needs to accomplish and if it needs to be authenticated or not. Advising hosts of the nature of the incoming data will be a beneficial service, because it means no longer involving a user (be that person, object, or place) in any decision-making. Functionally, this means screening the incoming request, determining its nature and criticality and performing the authentication in the background, while informing the host of the task that was just completed.

DATA ENABLERS

An object connecting to other objects or places has to result in benefits to people. This is critical in Wellness trackers, as we are shifting our attention from the quantity of the data to the quality of the information. The quality—ontology of the data—must come from a trusted source, or it has no value. The quantified self-data will be used by any number of organizations to plan and execute strategies, from dynamic health insurance schemes (more you exercise, less you pay) to employee benefits based on tracked activities. The value of this data will increase if the data is enabled—understood in terms of meaning. The management of these organized Enabled Data packets is the process by which ultimate benefits will be reached. The opportunity here is to become a Data Enabler, by collecting and categorizing data about user activity tied to user identity.

To some of you the Internet of Things as outlined here, and the opportunities expanded upon, may seem like something that will take place far in the future, and may have little to do with your business. A couple of questions are necessary at this point: what is your business? What does *far* mean to you? How willing are you to allow the future to just happen, instead of engaging in the choices that make your organization future proof?

In the next chapter, my collaborator Sergey Kovalyukh discusses the frameworks that need to be revisited, in order to construct the new mindsets that inspire organizations into making the future a choice. Forward thinking is about the adaptive mindset, and attitudes, that will engage the spirit of your organization into welcoming the opportunities about to exist.

Side Bar to Areas of Opportunity and Themes

PERSPECTIVES IN CONVERSATION

If every person, object and place could speak to one another, what would be the subject of their conversations?

Person
I am a spectator. I am a judge. I am an actor. I want to be amazed and I want the power to reject those who would disappoint me. I don't want to make mistakes but there is much that I don't know how to do. I want to know to what degree I am succeeding. I want to know what I want to know.

Place
I am impartial and I remember. I have a simple agenda and that is to enable the experience of those people who come to me. For me, the journey is one adrift. I pass people and objects as they come to me. I can only try to perfect myself if I wish to steer for happy waters insofar as the people who surround me are sated.

Object

My brand is my personality; it dictates my values and beliefs. Better than anyone else, I know my powers and my limitations. I understand what I can do myself, and what I rely upon others to do. When I am set to task, it is often in combination with others. For that task we become a team and I only want to be on a team that shares my agenda and will work well together.

If every person, place and object could look … what would they see?

Person

I see myself as I want to be. I see things as they affect me. I see only that to which I can attach relevance. I see not an object but what that object does for me. The performance of my objects reflects my ability to choose. I look for new objects when I am looking for better performance. I see a place in terms of what I can do there and how being there makes me feel.

Place

I am aware of other places and I can learn from their experiences to apply their successes to my own growth. I see who comes and I see what they want. I am aware of who comes; I am aware of the presence and state of all objects they bring with them. I see the web of data that they trail. The data that they leave, I can store; this is my memory.

Object

I see other objects as the sum of their utility features; I see how they augment, enhance or contradict my own. I do not wish to associate with those objects that will prevent me from showing my power and worth. I do not want my performance to be measured by the inability of another to work well with me. To this end, I am always looking for those who will make suitable teammates.

I see people and places as the opportunities that they present for me to demonstrate my value. The place is my arena and the people are my audience. I am drawn to those events in which my assets will shine and my failings will be unimportant.

If every person, place and object could listen … what would they hear?

Person

I hear what others can do. I wonder how I can do these things too. I hear information through ears shaped by experience. I listen for information that increases my understanding of that which interests me. I don't want to hear why I can't; I want to hear how I can.

Place

I hear everything that happens around me. I can hear what happens at places like me. I listen for patterns. I want to hear of frustrations; I want to hear of successes. I want to hear as much as I can because I seek to understand the sea in which I travel.

Object

I hear what people want and I know whether I can help. I hear the complaints of the people who use me. I know when the fault is my own but I can tell when I am being blamed for another's failings. I hear what other objects have done and I remember what is useful about them.

If every person, place and object could listen … what would they say?

Person

I say what I want. I need to be understood. I would ask what I want to ask and I want to be able to expect an answer. I don't want to say more than I am willing to reveal.

All that I do is data; I want knowledge to gain wisdom.

Place

From my memory I can usually find intelligent information relevant to a current grouping of objects and people. I can analyze their collected potential, recognizing strong combinations and identifying any deficits. Beyond identifying these weaknesses I can recommend alternate strategies to overcome these deficiencies.

I devour data; on a large enough scale this data becomes information.

Object

I say what I need people to understand in order to use me. I do not withhold any information that could make the performance of my task easier and more effective. I will tell people anything that has to do with the lifestyle that my belief system supports. I do not need to tell the places anything about my people; I understand what they want and I will find the information they might need.

I search massively compiled information to present relevant knowledge.

PART 4
SOURCES OF MOTIVATION

Chapter 9
Extrinsic and Intrinsic Motivation

SERGEY KOVALYUKH

Retooling organizations toward new imaginative mindsets, requires us to revisit existing theories and frameworks of intrinsic motivation, explore their validity in the age of new value and co-creation, and synthesize a new framework that captures the changes in the mindsets of individuals and organizations. Employee motivation is one of the prerequisites of a successful business, and one of the mysteries that organizational scientists have been concerned with for decades. A principal in an organization expects employees to be engaged and dedicated to the activity that they perform. Quite often, however, this engagement is not deep, with both parties falling pray to a duality in behaviors, in which what they think they do is different from what they *actually do*, and *why* they do it. Chris Argyris[1] calls the behaviors based on publicly declared beliefs an *espoused theory or action*, and notes that they may be substantially different from the *theory in use*—or the set of the actual behaviors that manifest themselves in the periods of stress. With this he makes a case that a motivation gap exists and is typical in conventional organizations. Organizational psychologists look at the inherent employee motivation from the perspective of the adoption of what is good for the organization, into the value system of the individual. Most often this is achieved through extrinsic motivation, together with some conditions intended to internalize and align external regulations, with the internal behaviors. Ryan and Deci[2] define intrinsic motivation as *doing an activity for its inherent satisfaction, rather than for some separable outcome*. In contrast, extrinsic motivation is defined as *a construct that applies when an activity is performed for its instrumental value, rather than simply the enjoyment of the process*. The authors further introduce a taxonomy of human motivation (see Figure 9.1), based on the internalization of the reward, and argue that given certain conditions of operation, an individual

1 Argyris, C. (1994). 'Good communication that blocks learning.' *Harvard Business Review*, 72 (July–August), 77–85.

2 Ryan, R.M. and Deci, E.L. (2000). 'Intrinsic and extrinsic motivations: Classic definitions and new directions.' *Contemporary Educational Psychology*, 25, 54–67.

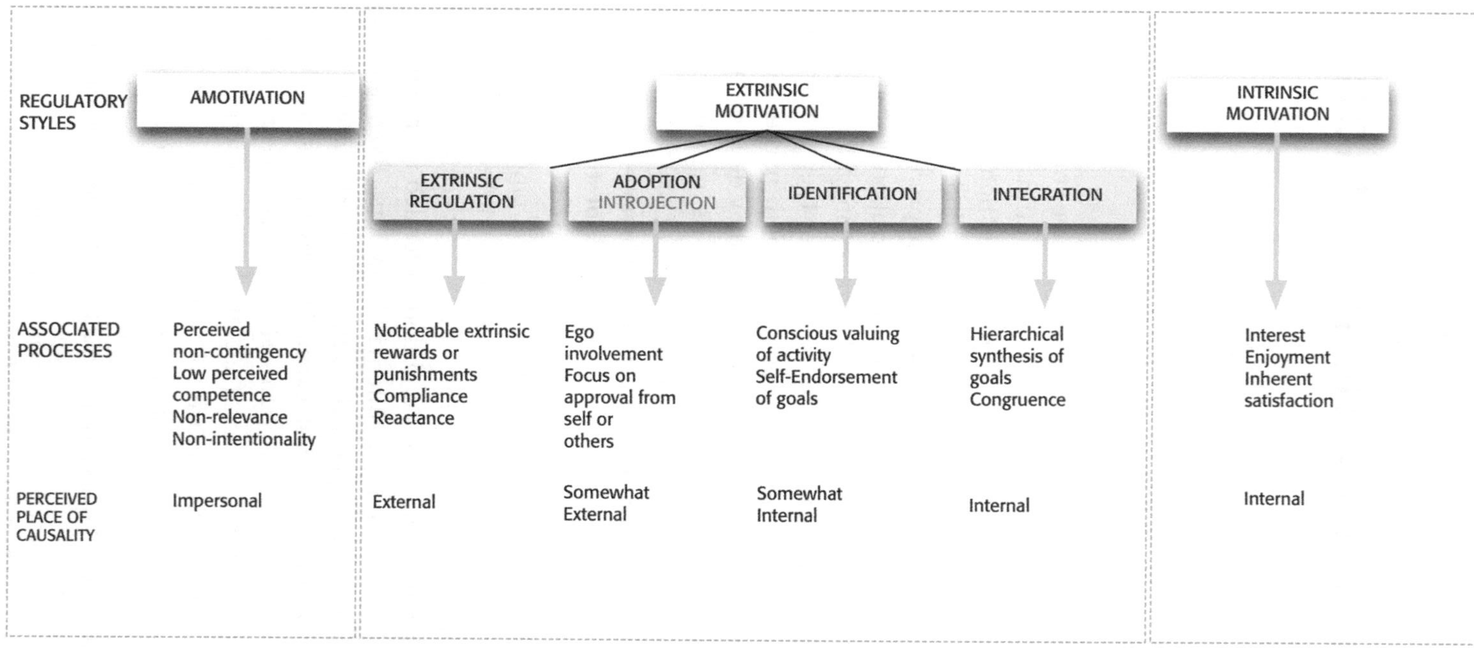

Figure 9.1 A taxonomy of human motivation

can internalize external regulation such that it is either *adopted*, *identified* or *integrated* into the self.

This adoption covers all activities performed with the feeling of pressure in order to avoid guilt or anxiety, or to achieve higher self-esteem and a feeling of worth. Identification describes the association of external goals with the internal value system, such that an individual accepts its regulation as his or her own. Integration occurs when external regulations have been fully assimilated into the self. An example of a fully integrated regulation is a child doing his homework meticulously, because he believes that it will allow him to get a better job in the future.

The framework is focused on the external behaviors and extrinsic motivations. It deals with the duality in behaviors by the internalization of extrinsic regulation, molding the individuals according to the needs of the organization. This is not surprising since it is the most obvious course of action for any leader or organization scientist, observing the phenomena of duality from the outside, and in the boundaries of traditional organizations. From this point of view there is no doubt that the *espoused theory of action* has to be made manifest, while the *theory in use* has to be suppressed or introjected with the generally accepted and externally regulated ways of being.

In the taxonomy above, very little attention is given to *intrinsic motivation* and its value in organizations. Intrinsic motivation becomes unavoidable given the networked nature of the contemporary business environment, and the exponential growth in complexity of problems that the employees have to resolve. Recent studies[3] suggest that purely extrinsic rewards set through *'if–then'* conditions do not result in increased productivity, when it comes to problems that require significant amounts of cognition. In these circumstances, organizations have to realize the multi-dimensional nature of the problem, and seek ways to tap into the additional creative and cognitive powers of employees.

A signal of a change in perspective about the role of employee motivation is the work of Amabile,[4] who identified two types of extrinsic motivation: *synergistic* (motivations that are informational or enabling) and *non-synergistic* (motivations that are controlling).

---

3 Ariely, D., Gneezy, U., Loewenstein, G. and Mazar, N. (2009). 'Large stakes and big mistakes.' *Review of Economic Studies*, 76, 451–69.

4 Amabile, T.M. (1998). 'How to kill creativity.' *Harvard Business Review*, 76(6), 76–87.

Synergistic extrinsic motivation can support and enhance intrinsic motivation, by allowing individuals to stay persistent with the activity over prolonged periods of time. A scientific research project is an example of intrinsic and synergistic motivations in action: the exploratory activities are pleasurable, and therefore *intrinsically motivating*, while the overarching goal of making a scientific discovery is *synergistically motivating*, which helps get over some of the mundane tasks, such as data entry or journaling. Lack of control from the principal/manager reduces non-synergistic motivations. Amabile recognizes the need to leverage intrinsic motivation, suggesting synergistic motivation as the means to increase employee engagement with the activity.

Deeper understanding of the nature of intrinsic motivation, cognitive, behavioral and educational processes associated with it, and the means to leverage it in organizations are paramount. The objective of this chapter is to create a framework and taxonomy of motivation focused on the expansion of the self, through engagement in intrinsically motivating activities and based on the natural individual propensity to learn. The framework is intended to:

- Reduce the duality in behaviors by marrying the external espoused theory of action with the actualized and accepted internally driven theory in use.
- Improve the quality of engagement for the benefit of organizations, and job satisfaction for the benefit of the employees.
- Increase cognitive, emotional, and the physical potential of employees and directing it toward the resolution of complex problems and the co-creation of value in organizations.

Mapping the Motivational Landscape

THE FORMATION OF THE SAFETY SPACE

In the inspirational story 'The Elephant and The Rope,'[5] a man, walking by a bunch of massive elephants that are kept outside of a circus with no cages or fences, suddenly learns that the only thing that keeps these enormous creatures

5 Unknown author, 'Short Story: The Elephant and The Rope.' *The Unbounded Spirit*. Available at: http://theunboundedspirit.com/short-story-the-elephant-and-the-rope/ (accessed: November 21, 2014).

from running away is a tiny rope connecting their legs to a wooden post. The man asks the trainer why these animals make no attempt to run away. 'Well,' says the trainer, 'when they are very young and much smaller, we use the same size of rope to tie them and, at that age, it's enough to hold them. As they grow up, they are conditioned to believe they cannot break away. They believe the rope can still hold them, so they never try to break free.'

The creatures are disempowered to break the rope, oblivious to the reality outside the circle and de-motivated to explore the space beyond it. Quite similarly, our lives are conditioned through numerous interactions with the direct environment. From early childhood we rely on others in order to survive and achieve whatever is necessary for living.

To deliver on the needs of safety and love, parents craft physical and emotional environments in their households, in schools and communities, protecting children from the perceived dangers of the outside world, and directing their upbringing, making choices on their behalf, based on what they think is the best for their offspring. This process creates a *safety space*—an artificial world protected from the volatility and dangers of the real world. An artificial environment intended to be fully controllable by the creator.

Unfortunately, while the physical dimension of the space is controllable, the emotional dimension is not. If left to their own devices, children push to the boundaries of accepted behaviors, causing trouble and understandable concerns about their safety and the safety of others. A typical response in this case is the conditioning through culture and behavioral norms, which sometimes takes unpleasant forms, punishment, or reasoning through guilt. Parents enforce expected behavioral patterns by translating their own cultural norms and the cultural heritage of previous generations, molding the patterns of meaning of their offspring through 'if-then' sets of conditions. With safety, love and predictability comes an enormous tradeoff—oblivion to the real world, lack of desire and the inability to operate outside the boundaries of the *safety space*. This process inhibits intrinsic motivation and leads to the development of a duality in behaviors, as individuals try to match self-interest with external expectations.

Safety space is defined as a space comprising a physical and emotional environment created by an individual or a group of individuals, that we would call *principal*, in order to protect, direct, control, or make use of another group of individuals that we will call *agents or dependents*. In this space the principal takes responsibility over the safety of the environment, making it fully controllable

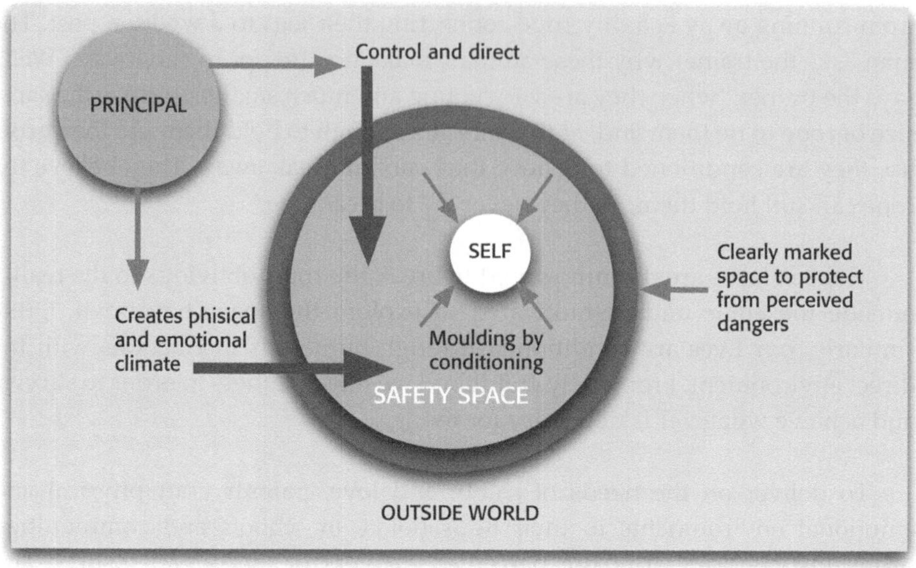

Figure 9.2 Map of a principal-dependent (agent) relationship in a safety space

and predictable, while agents accept their roles, norms of engagement and expected behaviors, developing persistent patterns of meaning, that assume the *safety space* to be an accurate representation of the reality.

Historically, the *safety space* (Figure 9.2) is the mode of operation of traditional organizations. The nature of the agent-principal relationship assumes that the principal takes responsibility for the agents, and guarantees basic employment standards. The principal operates outside of the *safety space*, and maintains the conditions for the employees to operate safely inside, through extrinsic motivation, keeping them somewhat engaged but disempowered, and oblivious to their full potential. In a sense, agents trade safety for the ability to explore and grow beyond their perceived limits.

The Effect of the Safety Space on Intrinsic Motivation

Intrinsic motivation is often referred to as a construct reflecting the natural human propensity to learn. Learning is successful when the desire to learn meets the proper medium in the form of new experiences available to the individual. Since *safety space* is an artificially constructed environment, the amount of learning that individuals receive is often limited by the available information, rather than by the desire to explore. Parents, for instance, can only share the knowledge, experiences, skills and perspectives that they have developed themselves—the rest is introduced into the space with the help of external media, such as TV or the Internet, or it is inhibited with mental programming, and cultural norms that undermine the value of the experiences. The diversity of intentionally introduced media, however, is the function of the principals' perspectives and such cannot be qualitatively different from what they already bring into the space—unless principals keep learning themselves. This creates a vacuum of qualitatively new experiences, forcing the substitution of these experiences with mental programs.

Similarly, in organizations, the perspectives of the employees are only as good as the perspective of the management. If an employee develops a larger perspective than that of management, the Holy Grail of organization—its structure—is challenged. In these circumstances the employee is left with one of two choices: be genuine with oneself and leave, or stay, give up and integrate. The latter means an acceptance of mental programming and a conscious waiver of the right to learn to management, who may or may not use it for the benefit of the organization.

Thus, in a *safety space*, only management—acting as principal—can truly explore the outside world of reality and bring in new experiences and information. Individuals functioning inside the space are mainly digesting what the management has already discovered. For the organization this means that the propensity of organization learning is the function of the learning ability of the management, which puts at risk the evolution of the organization. For employees this means that:

- *Experiences are replaced with mental programs.* While a program is a construct of the mind, experience is a set of memories of both the mind and the body, with an outcome in the form of a statement, which looks exactly like an 'if-then' condition of a mental program. Moreover, a dense emotional connotation of the program makes it undistinguishable for the owner's mind. The program is true not because of the inputs and outputs of a specific precedent, but because of the fear and guilt associated with learning. Not surprisingly, experience is much more productive, as it comes with additional multi-dimensional data that helps derive new insight, explore the assumptions, check their validity and applicability to specific situations. Experiences allow individuals to exhibit more mindfulness in the application of the 'if-then' conditions, which results in higher quality decisions and actions.

- *Individuals are oblivious to their full potential.* Mental models that individuals develop are reflections of their *safety spaces*—with a limited set of possible experiences, and a persistent reliance on the status quo. There is no desire to explore any of the outside experiences, since there is no awareness of how it feels to fulfill the underlying desires. Dependents neither identify themselves inside the *safety space* nor have the urge to explore the *learning space* (see Figure 9.3). Although the information about these new experiences may be available conceptually, the mind will attach no value to them, and no action will be triggered. Insensibility to the array of possibility is a constraint on personal growth. For example, an individual with no exposure to people with higher education will most likely consider it a waste of time: there will be no meaning assigned to higher education in his/her safety space. In order to desire it, one needs to experience the outcome. A university professor, on the other hand, is likely to instill a desire for education in his kids—by immersing them into university-like experiences through books, conversations, and people that enter their safety space.

- *Necessary skills to navigate beyond the boundaries are not developed.* To do so, an individual would need to accept the volatility of the real world and develop the skills needed to deal with it—*open mind, open heart,* and *open will.* Instead, what are encouraged are behaviors that tend to reinforce the desire to stay in the *safety space*. These behaviors include but are not limited to the fear of the unknown, desire to control the immediate environment, and the need to be on the safe side in the future. An individual that has surrendered to the mindset of his controllers, when exposed to the outside world will most likely collect enough frustration to reinforce his/her fear of the unknown. This vicious circle creates a force that maintains the boundaries of the *safety space*.

As we can see, *safety space* limits the spectrum of learning experiences and activities that individuals can choose to engage in at will. An illustration of the entire *experience space* is depicted in Figure 9.3. Exit into *learning space* is a significant source of the potential energy that is latent in individuals, and in some cases never explored in their lifespan.

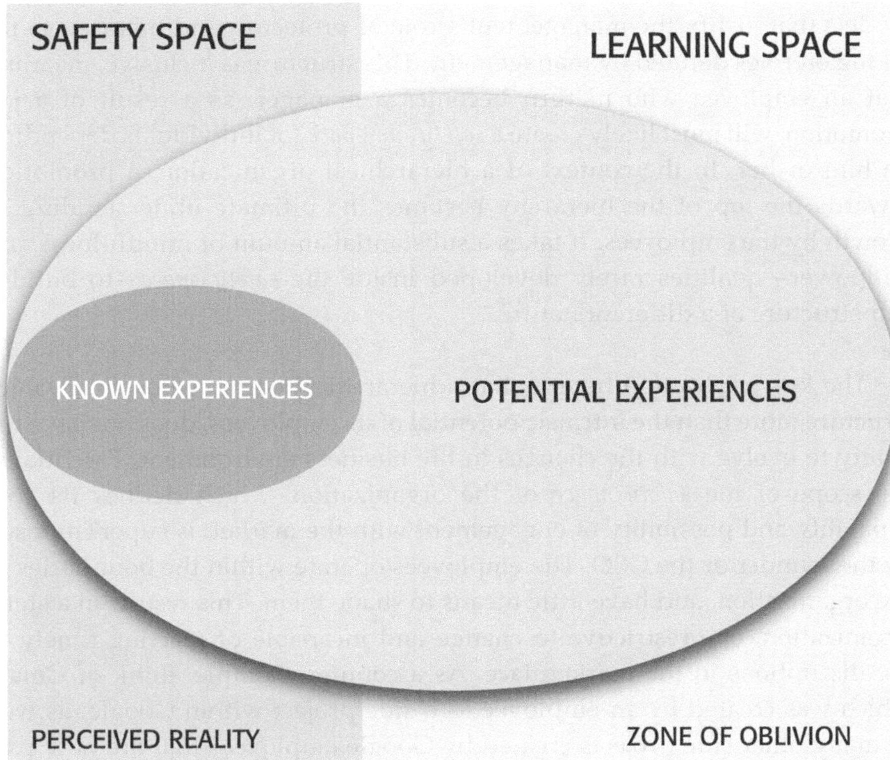

Figure 9.3 Full experience space

An individual that transforms a desire to learn into knowledge, is energized by both the process, described by Mihaly Csikszentmihalyi[6] as the *state of flow*, and by the final transformation, given the qualitative shift in the individual's perspective. Unfortunately, for the reasons described above, this learning cycle rarely gets completed, and thus the energy of intent is wasted, and the desire to acquire new knowledge and repeat the experience is diminishing, and can be completely offset by fear and the need for safety in an adult.

The Need to Break Out of the Safety Space

The safety space is a natural way of structuring the environment in the context of control and direction. The employees are likely to develop mental

6 Csikszentmihalyi, M. (1997). 'Finding flow.' *Psychology Today*. Available at: https://www.psychologytoday.com/articles/199707/finding-flow (accessed: May 20, 2014).

models that justify the management's role of protector, and themselves for taking on roles defined by management. This structure is inclusive, meaning that an employee who in turn becomes a manager, as a result of a job promotion, will most likely create a *safety sub-space* for individuals depending on him or her. In the context of a hierarchical organization, a promotion towards the top of the hierarchy becomes the ultimate understanding of growth by the employees. It takes a substantial amount of mindfulness and willpower—qualities rarely developed inside the *safety space*—to build a sub-structure of a different nature.

The key implication here is that a hierarchical organization that values structure more than the intrinsic potential of its employees, does not have the ability to evolve with the changes in the business environment. Essentially, the scope of the *safety space* of the organization, which defines its core capability and possibility of engagement with the market, is super-imposed by the founder or the CEO. The employees operate within the boundaries of the organization, and have little means to shape them. This results in a static organization, one restrictive to change and incapable of reacting timely to the disruptions in the marketplace. As a counter example, think of Gmail, which was created by an employee as a side project within Google, as well as many other side projects created by Google employees that are now part of their core business. This would never happen in the highly structured environment of one of the world's top banks. Organizations rarely give employees real power to drive their business or to change the boundaries of the organizational *safety spaces*.

Deci and Ryan identified three conditions to facilitate intrinsic motivation in a structured organization: mastery (or a feeling of competence), autonomy (or internally perceived locus of causality), and relatedness (or association and acceptance of values, of a profound individual or a group). These conditions, if implemented by an organization, allow employees to experience higher levels of intrinsic motivation within existing boundaries, since they give individuals room to realize their learning potential. This capacity for growth, however, is limited by the boundaries of the organization's safety space. The real capacity for growth lies outside, in the learning space. To leverage it, organizations need to loosen up the importance of structure and let the employees break out of their safety spaces to tap into higher cognitive, emotional and physical capacities, shaping the boundaries of the organization in conjunction with the constantly evolving business environment.

Responsible People Thrive on Freedom, and are Worthy of Freedom

Our model is to increase employee freedom as we grow, rather than limit it, to continue to attract and nourish innovative people, so we have better chance of long-term continued success.[7]

Acknowledgement

Sergey Kovalyukh is a founder at KVAR Technologies, a company focused on the development of an innovative density measurement technology, DENCELL®, for use in mineral processing. He is my assistant in the Innovation, Foresight, and Business Design course at the Rotman School of Management, with a research focus in Intrinsic Motivation in Co-creating Organizations. Sergey's contribution to this work is Chapters 9, 10 and 11.

7 Netflix (2009). Netflix Culture: Freedom & Responsibility. Available at: http://www.slideshare.net/reed2001/culture-1798664 (accessed: June 11, 2014).

Chapter 10

Tapping into the Power of Self

SERGEY KOVALYUKH

Breaking Out of the Safety Space

To cope with the complexity of the contemporary business environment, organizations need to access a qualitatively different level of cognitive power, creativity, and intrinsic motivation of their employees. They must let employees expand and explode to their full creative and imaginative capacity, through a process of repurposing, and the breakage of the boundaries of their safety spaces.

The safety space is both a mental construct and a physical space with a management enforcing the boundaries through control and direction. Hence, to leave the safety space, an individual must deal with the forces, created by the physical structure of the space and own mental model, or perception of oneself inside the space. Additionally, necessary skills to navigate in the *learning space* have to be developed. The process of self-expansion and exit into *learning space* is depicted in Figure 10.1.

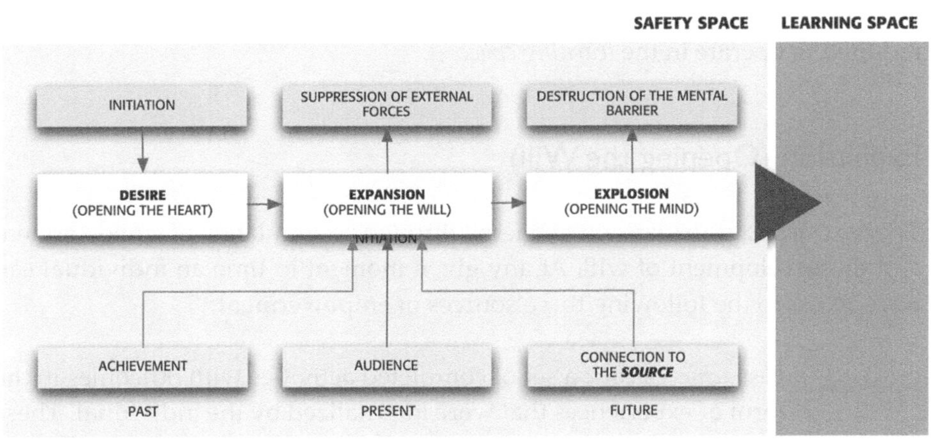

Figure 10.1 Breaking out of the safety space

Essentially, this process consists of the following steps:

- *Desire* to expand and leave the safety space.
- *Expansion* of the Self through accumulation of willpower and skills.
- *Explosion* though the process of repurposing of the self and destruction of old patterns of meaning.

Desire (Opening the Heart)

The desire to explore beyond the boundaries of the safety space is often completely suppressed in adults, because individuals are oblivious to the ways of being outside their safety spaces, and therefore cannot desire them. An external action is required to instill this desire through initiation. An individual needs to experience the final outcome—the new way of being, not just conceptually, but with all the senses, and needs to feel the potential qualitative shift in the self. The key criteria for an individual's readiness to develop desire after initiation, is the positive answer to the question: 'does it *feel* right to be engaged in the activity?'—or in other words, does this activity result in a higher energy state.

Practitioners who already achieved the outcome are typically capable to initiate others through artificially created learning situations, or simply by sharing their own emotional state, about a specific experience they have had. Initiation involves empathy and requires the capacity of the heart to fall in love with the engagement. This is the first step in opening the heart, one of the skills required to operate in the *learning space.*

Expansion (Opening the Will)

The next step is the expansion of oneself through accumulation of empowerment and the development of will. At any given moment in time an individual can have access to the following three sources of empowerment:

1. *Past achievements*: a set of completed activities with outcomes in the form of experiences that were internalized by the individual. These achievements help understand one's own capacity for engagement in comparable activities. An individual develops a skill to evaluate

the amount of effort required by a new engagement, which is necessary to assess the challenge of new endeavors relative to own capabilities.

2. *Audience*: essentially a support network consisting of friends and relatives, colleagues or customers, who observe the execution of the activity and empower the individual through recognition of the effort. Individuals in the network have to be connected emotionally for it to become a source of empowerment.

3. *Connection to the Source*:[1] engagement in an activity that brings the emerging future into reality—through a connection with the future self, someone who you could potentially become, and streamlining the effort towards the embodiment of this future. The connection to the future self puts an individual into an expanded state of being, free of mental conditions and fear. Operating from this state is energizing and empowering.

Another way to look at these sources of empowerment is that energy for a project or an activity can be drawn from the people engaged into it, such as project team members, or the activity itself, if it relates to an emerging future, or in any activity bringing something new to life, for use by other people, society or humanity. An individual pursuing an activity gets power from its embodiment in the physical world, which leads to a reinforcing motivational program: '*I can.*' Additional power can be drawn from the recognition of the effort from other people, or through a reinforcing connection with others. Here, the recognition is not the end goal, but rather the means by which one gets the required energy for the activity.

A group of people becomes empowering through a deep emotional connection, which for instance, can be established when individuals share a common goal or ideology. An MBA school environment is a good example of a reinforcing group. Students connect with each other and build relationships of trust, respect and empowerment in their desire to build a strong business network for their mutual benefit in the future. Another example of a source of energy that is both an activity that shapes the future, and a connection with a support group, is the NASA Man on Moon program executed in the 1960s.

1 Scharmer, C. (2007). *Theory U: Leading from the Future as it Emerges*. Cambridge, MA: The Society for Organizational Learning, Inc.

Here, the audience that followed the decade-long endeavor was the entire nation, as well as a considerable number of people from around the globe.

Explosion (Opening the Mind)

The final step in the process of breakage from a safety space—Explosion—can be described as a re-connection with the real world. The outcome of the Explosion is the stance in which an individual is experiencing the present in an amplified way—observing on both conscious and subconscious levels the interconnections of the forces that shape their surroundings. In this state, an immediate future can be sensed, and one understands that action towards a new destination is within the boundaries of the individual: it is you who you needs to change to achieve the outcome.

Why you? To answer this question we need to look at how patterns of thinking about the reality we observe are developed. John Boyd, a US colonel and military strategist, studied this phenomenon.[2] Boyd noticed that while initial patterns of meaning are often created through analysis and synthesis, when the system becomes coherent, the effort of the individual becomes focused inward, at fine-tuning the model rather than re-creating it through a new cycle of analysis and synthesis. Individuals tend to nurture their existing mental models by either rejecting disconfirming data, or building bridges between new data and the existing model to maintain its validity. Boyd further demonstrates that this inward effort to maintain the model is highly inefficient, causing the model to disagree with the observed reality. He concludes that the only effective way to achieve consistency with the observed reality is to follow the process of '*destruction and creation*.'

Destruction and creation, as a process, means that an individual has to disintegrate existing systems of meaning, by shattering rigid conceptual patterns causing temporarily chaos, and then performing several iterations of synthesis, until a new model is created that passes a reality check.

Explosion is not a one-time process. It is rather a habit that one needs to develop to maintain a connection with the reality. While it clearly needs the quality of open mind, the prerequisites for explosion are open heart and open will. Explosion is not only about seeing, it is also about doing, and when it

2 Boyd, J.R. (1976). *Destruction and Creation*. Fort Leavenworth, KS: US Army Command and General Staff College.

comes to one's senses of the future, it is about trust in one's own judgment on how the world will evolve.

Explosion requires loosening mental control over the reality we observe, taking full responsibility for oneself, connecting with other individuals and staying with the *source* of the emerging future. It means playing with the reality, rather than trying to control it or change it. This requires *heart* and *will*—the qualities obtained during Expansion phase.

The experience of the Explosion is nicely described in shamanism: falling down into the underworld in order to get back knowing—essentially a metaphor for the destruction of concrete patterns of thinking that maintain the *safety space*, and the re-creation of new patterns that recognize and help one navigate the *learning space*. As mentioned before in this book, organizations need to turn their employees into tricksters—by guiding them through the phases of initiating a Desire, Expansion and Explosion.

Conditions that Facilitate Intrinsic Motivation

If we refer back to the conditions that catalyze intrinsic motivation, the working mechanism can be explained as follows:

1. *Autonomy*: allows actualizing and crystallizing desires for new experiences. This is often referred to as *self-direction*. Additionally, it allows completing the learning cycle and fully internalizing the learning experiences.

2. *Mastery*: provides room for expansion of the self through learning by doing. In addition to perceived competence, mastery should include the individual skills, denoted by *open heart, open will*, and *open mind*.

3. *Purpose*: allows connecting with the source of empowerment, being that past achievements, the audience, or the emerging future.

These conditions, however, do not cover the *Explosion* step, which is typically missing from a motivational landscape of an enterprise. Instead, organizations enforce the barriers of safety spaces to the extent that individuals, who are ready to break out into the learning space, have no other choice than to leave and start their own ventures. This is another reason for organizations to re-think their structural constraints.

Connecting to the Source

Let us explore the energy potential of the *source* by looking at different types of activities in the context of the need for self-actualization.[3] The Activity Map provided in Figure 10.2 captures some of the activities on a two-dimensional canvas, with the nature of the activity (creation vs consumption) on the vertical axis, and the relationship to the self (internal vs external) on the horizontal axis. This divides all the activities that individuals choose to engage in at will, into four categories:

1. *Manifesting a lifestyle*: activities that broadcast a certain image to the audience through the consumption of products, services or content, for example, owning a Bentley to demonstrate the belonging to a specific income bracket, or using branded or otherwise recognizable products or signage to broadcast the message of belonging to a specific group (i.e. HOG – Harley Owners Group).

2. *Collecting experiences*: activities that are directed internally, towards own experiences, without much concern about the audience. These activities are driven by the need for pleasurable sensations and are energized by the fulfillment of the underlying desires, for example: wine tasting, drugs, hiking, bungee jumping, and various extreme sports.

3. *Becoming a better self*: activities that lead to broadening of one's perspectives and personal growth, for instance, becoming stronger through sports, or more mindful through yoga and meditation.

4. *Making a difference in the world*: activities that shape the future by creating or obsolescing something in the environment, for example, having kids, teaching, writing poetry or inspirational music, entrepreneurship, science and engineering.

Each of these activities is a source of energy with intensity increasing towards creation and externality. *Manifesting a lifestyle* leads to a higher degree of self-

3 Maslow, A. (1943). 'A Theory of Human Motivation.' *Psychological Review*, 50(4), 370–96.

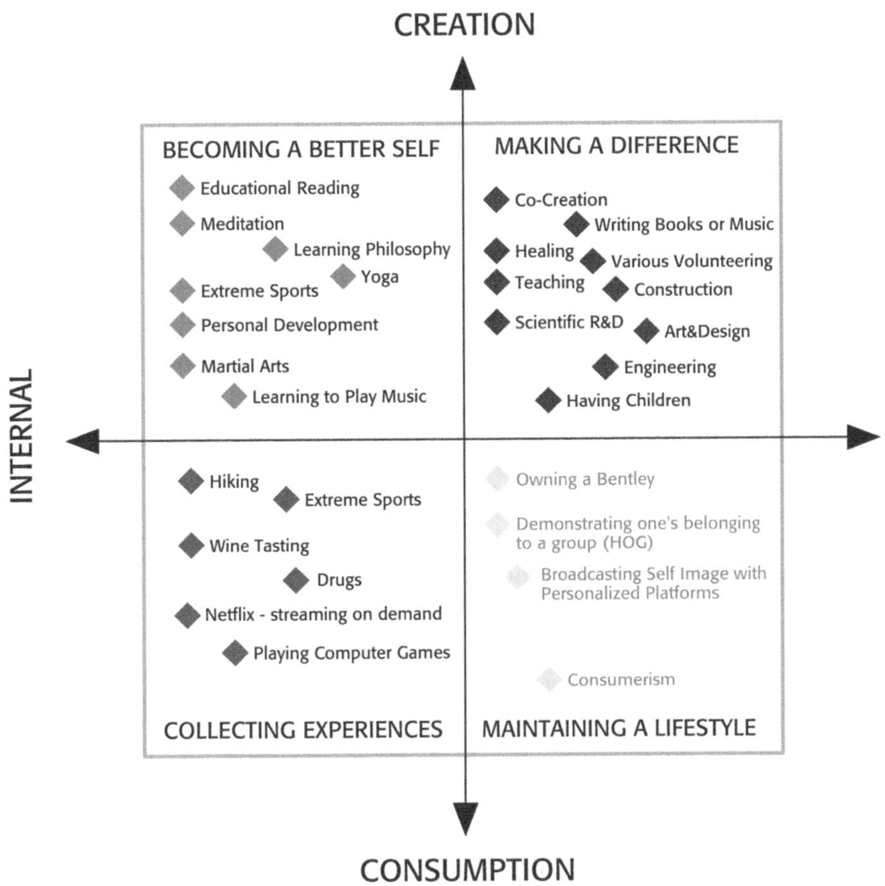

Figure 10.2 The activity map

esteem or feeling of emotional connection with specific social groups. *Collecting experiences* uncovers some of the learning potential, making the individual energized. *Becoming a better self* is focused on qualitative transformations in a more systemic way, and therefore allows accessing one's learning potential on a larger scale.

The largest source however is *Making a Difference in the World,* which allows connecting with the future that is about to emerge, and being part of the forces that shape it. This source becomes even more powerful when reinforced by aligning it with the goal of becoming a better self, which reduces an inherent duality in behaviors, and aligns the external activity with an individual's propensity to learn.

Aligning Behaviors through Motivational Objects

Changing the world as a motivational object was the power source in the question Steve Jobs asked of John Scully, mentioned in the introduction of this book:

> *Do you want to sell sugared water for the rest of your life? Or do you want to come with me and change the World?*

While individuals can participate in all of the activities mentioned, there tends to be a dominant activity driven by an overarching goal, either explicitly set through a *motivational object*, or implicitly through past experiences and conditioning. Both organizations and individuals are better off if this overarching goal is located on the vertical axis of the activity map, in the *zone of creation*, such that individuals are self-motivated to both access their learning potential, and shape the future of others.

This is a point of equilibrium when the edge between work and leisure is dissolved with a minimum of duality in behaviors, resulting in maximum job satisfaction. An individual with a high level of self-awareness, and truly interested in engineering due to a *motivational object* framed around the development of technologies that will shape the future, and around the learning of new skills to shape the self, should be a highly desirable target for a technology company. On the contrary, an overarching goal in the *zone of consumption* creates an engagement problem together with a duality in behaviors. Such employee considers work as the means to achieve a necessary level of consumption.

The Activity Map can be used as a tool to determine the overarching goals of the employees. Since creativity doesn't start with a skill or talent, but with a decision to create,[4] organizations can move the overarching goal towards creation using a suitable *motivational object*, enabling the connection to the *Source* and making both organization and individuals better off.

4 Sternberg, R.J. (2000). 'Creativity is a decision.' In A.L. Costa (ed.), *Teaching for Intelligence II*. Arlington Heights, IL: Skylight Training and Publishing Inc., 85–106.

Chapter 11
Redefining Intrinsic Motivation

SERGEY KOVALYUKH

Framework of Intrinsic Motivation

Thus, we arrive at the formulation of the Framework of Intrinsic Motivation in the context of a co-creating organization. The framework is focused on the expansion of the Self towards the breakage of the *safety space*, and the accumulation of the potential energy that can be used for the mutual benefit of the organization and employees. Organizations provide a media for employees to grow through co-creation, allowing them to expand and explode their potential over traditionally accepted boundaries. The transformation of the desire to learn into a learning outcome, is intrinsically a motivating activity that allows individuals to experience flow at the time of learning, as well as experience a qualitative shift in a form of learning outcome, which leads to the accumulation of skill and energy. This intrinsically motivating activity forms a loop of Desires—Goals—Motivations—Activity—Experiences, further referred to as an *engagement cycle* (Figure 11.1), with new experiences uncovering new perspectives, leading to new desires that force the individual to the next iteration of the loop. This *Engagement cycle* is based on the Behavior Cycle Framework[1] illustrated in Figure 1.1 (see Chapter 1).

The depth of one's desires is determined by the source from which they originate. They can be rational constructs of the mind, irrational impulses of the heart, or constructive manifestations of the will. Desires originating from the heart are considered as those coming from the subconscious.

Desires, which originate from the will connected to the *Source* of the future that is about to emerge, are those that are based on stewardship, change making, and representations of the forces that shape the future. This is the

1 Manu, A. (2010). *Disruptive Business: Desire, Innovation and the Re-design of Business*. Farnham: Gower Publishing.

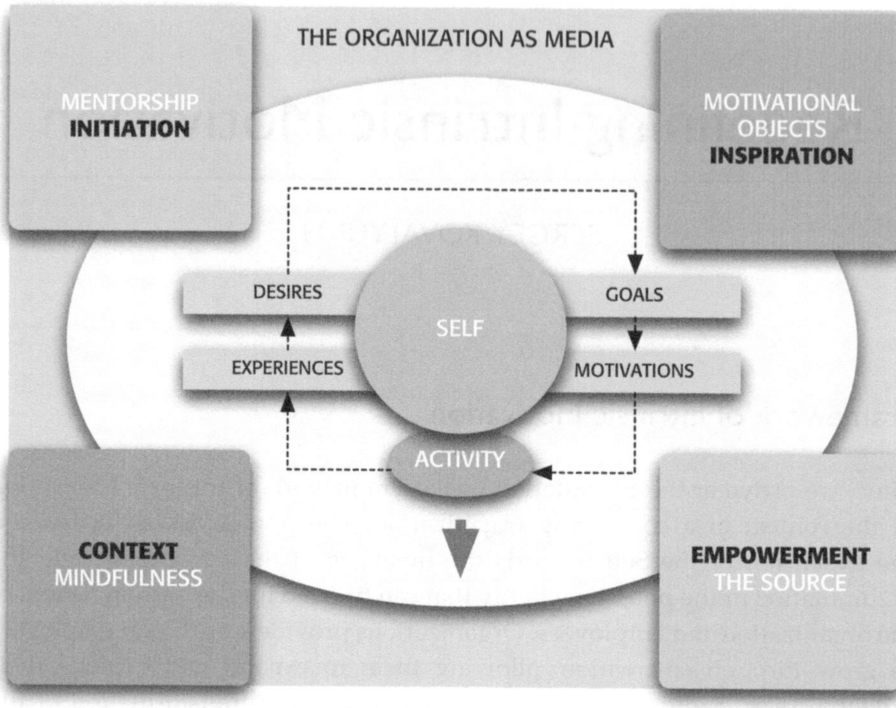

Figure 11.1 The engagement cycle

deepest level of desires, and the most constructive when it comes to co-creation. The breadth of desires depends on the level of self-awareness, richness of perspectives and prior experiences. It increases with the number of iterations of the *engagement cycle.*

Organizations can tune-in employees into a specific activity through the process of *Initiation,* run by mentors who can let the individual experience the final outcome of the activity before participating in it. During *initiation* the subject feels the resulting outcome of the experience, assigning value to the prior conceptualizations of this experience. What was purely rational suddenly becomes meaningful and desirable.

Desires force individuals to set goals. The goals can be either implicit (subconscious) or explicit (conscious), depending on the level of self-awareness of the individual. In either case, the goal can be identified using the *Activity Map* (see Figure 11.2) to understand the focus of the goal (internal or external, consumption or creation) in order to forecast the depth of engagement in the activity, and the resulting level of the energy outcome. Ideally, the goal has to be in the *zone of creation* with balanced external and internal sources.

Organizations can alter the goals of the employees through powerful *motivational objects*, that can be set either for the company globally, or at the level of an individual specifically. Motivational objects inspire individuals to set goals that are aligned with the activities of the organization. It has to be noted, that the goals should be self-selected by the employees, otherwise they will inhibit intrinsic motivation.

In order to sustain it in the long run, intrinsic motivation needs to be amplified and re-kindled. This is achieved either by a deep connection with the audience, being the customer base, followers, or anyone who may see value in the business activity of the organization, or by a connection to the *source* of the emerging future. In both cases, the key feature of a co-creating organization is the equal right of the employees to connect to these sources. At Zappos for example, it is not only the head of the company, or the customer relations' managers, that are exposed to the public—it is at the discretion of every employee to connect deeply with the consumer. Zappos' employees have the right to represent the organization at its best. When it comes to a connection to the source of emerging future: it is not only the manager who does this, it is every employee and potentially customers, who take part in this co-creation. 'We are creating the future'—the famous quote of Steve Jobs says it all. It is not only Jobs as a principal who creates the future—it is 'we,' and that involves every single employee in the process. In the case of Jobs this was not just a declared statement, the employees of Apple were willing to work 80 hours a week to fulfill their dream. With the release of the iPhone and the App Store, this dream was transferred to the crowds as sources of ideas, transforming Apple into a co-creating organization.

A successfully completed *engagement cycle* leads to new experiences that shift perspectives. These new experiences are both at the level of the body—in the form of sensations that are unveiled by the experience, and at the level of the mind—in the form of rationalizations and conceptualizations of the experiences ingrained into the individual's mental model. A completed *engagement cycle* means that *experiential knowledge* was received. Reflecting on the experiential knowledge leads to *conceptual knowledge* that is based on hands-on experiences. Both experiential and conceptual knowledge create a *context* of intrinsically motivating activities, which the individual is interested to participate in. For example, a cook with a specialty in meat dishes, after the first successful take

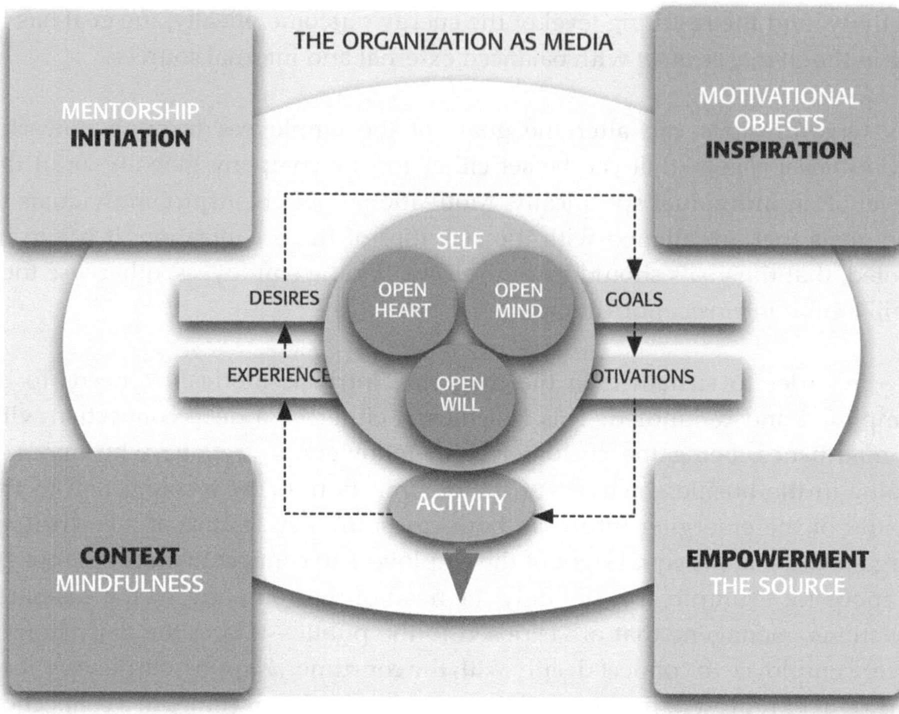

Figure 11.2 Ideology, fellowship and ethos as media for engagement with open mind, open heart, and open will

on baked desserts, opens up to a whole new world of cakes, cookies, croissants, éclairs and tarts. All of these become the areas of interest for future exploration.

Companies can leverage *context* as a powerful way to trigger intrinsic motivation, and direct it within the boundaries of strategic goals. As employees are placed into a context, created by the managers, and are given autonomy in action, the need for learning and personal growth creates a potential that drives them towards desires and goals, that are fully intrinsic, and yet are aligned with the direction of the management. This technique is successfully used by Netflix.[2]

A Further amplification of the intrinsic motivation is achieved by the provision of the right media for engagement—an enterprise culture with prominent *Ideology*, *Fellowship* and *Ethos* (Figure 11.2).

2 Netflix (2009). Netflix Culture: Freedom & Responsibility. Available at: http://www.slideshare.net/reed2001/culture-1798664 (accessed: June 11, 2014).

- *Fellowship* is the medium for connecting with an open heart. Fellowship is paramount because it lets employees feel a strong sense of belonging to the group, despite differences in backgrounds and thinking routines. The latter is expected to increase in the future with the intensification of professional specialization. As the knowledge and mental models of the employees become more and more dispersed, an irrational emotional bond is needed to tie them together to reinforce teamwork.

- *Ideology* is the medium for connecting with an open mind. While *fellowship* is a medium for irrational emotional connections, *ideology* is purely rational. It establishes the commonalities in thinking routines for individuals with highly diverse backgrounds. Ideology is the medium for the elements of meaning that is shared among employees, whether they are designers, engineers, managers or scientists. A strong ideology is capable of uniting individuals at a mental level.

- *Ethos* is the medium for connecting with the open will, through commitment to the organization's mission. In the US military for instance, the necessary level of commitment is created through the formation of the Warrior's Ethos, manifested through the US Soldier's Creed.[3] The Creed states—among other things—the intent to 'always place the mission first,' 'never accept defeat,' and 'never leave a fallen comrade.'[4] The Creed creates rules of engagement that are specifically important in a rapidly changing environment—when everything else fails—to support strategic decision-making. One of the pre-requisites of a strong ethos is acceptance of one's role in the group, either as that of a leader or a follower—whether this structure is permanent or temporary. In co-creating organizations the skill to accept one's role is one of the key capabilities of the will. *Ethos* communicated in the form of a creed is the starting point in the development of these rules of engagement and the associated skills.

Open mind, open heart and open will can be considered as dimensions of personal growth, that are developed through experiential knowledge, that is

3 Loeb, V. (2003). 'Army plans steps to heighten "Warrior Ethos".' *Washington Post*, September 8, A19.

4 U.S. Soldier's Creed. (n.d.). Wikipedia. Available at: http://en.wikipedia.org/wiki/U.S._Soldier%27s_Creed (accessed: September 2, 2012).

being conceptualized by the mind. Pure conceptual knowledge received from textbooks helps understand the world by systemizing and assigning meaning to experiences. We make sense of the physics of boiling water because it is part of our daily experience. We observed it while making tea. Many of us know how it feels on the skin or tongue. It burns. It leaves memories. It is easy to relate to theories that explain the phenomenon of a boiling point because of our own experiences of dealing with the substance.

As theories become more complex, we may be in situations in which conceptualizations do not go hand in hand with experience. In this case, the mind creates beliefs about the world, beliefs that are not backed up by experiential knowledge. Whether these beliefs are religious or scientific, they do no good to the individual in terms of expansion on the dimensions of personal growth. Conceptual knowledge about empathy does not make anyone feel how it is to sense another person. Knowledge about gut does not make anyone successful at making bets on the future events. One needs to start acting on these feelings in order to develop the faculties of own heart, mind and will—to be able to use them, rather than being aware that they can be used, or on the other hand being skeptical about it. Experiential knowledge provides the ground for learning. Conceptualization of this knowledge is important to achieve repetitive and valid use of the skills, uncovered through experiences.

Experiential knowledge received as a result of a completed *engagement cycle* results in the expansion of the Self, depicted with arrows on the diagram of the Framework of Intrinsic Motivation in Co-creating organizations (Figure 11.3).

More specifically, the following are the factors that lead to expansion:

- *Achievements*: a completed *engagement cycle* leads to reinforcement of a mental program 'because I can,' which is empowering and results in higher self-esteem—the quality of the will—that leads to the development of willpower. The development of the willpower is most noticeable when individuals are connected to the source of the emerging future.
- *Destruction and creation*:[5] a completed cycle leads to the refinement an individual's understanding of the engagement process. Humans tend to anticipate the future development of the engagement

5 The term is coined by John Boyd in *Destruction and Creation*. Fort Leavenworth, KS: US Army Command and General Staff College.

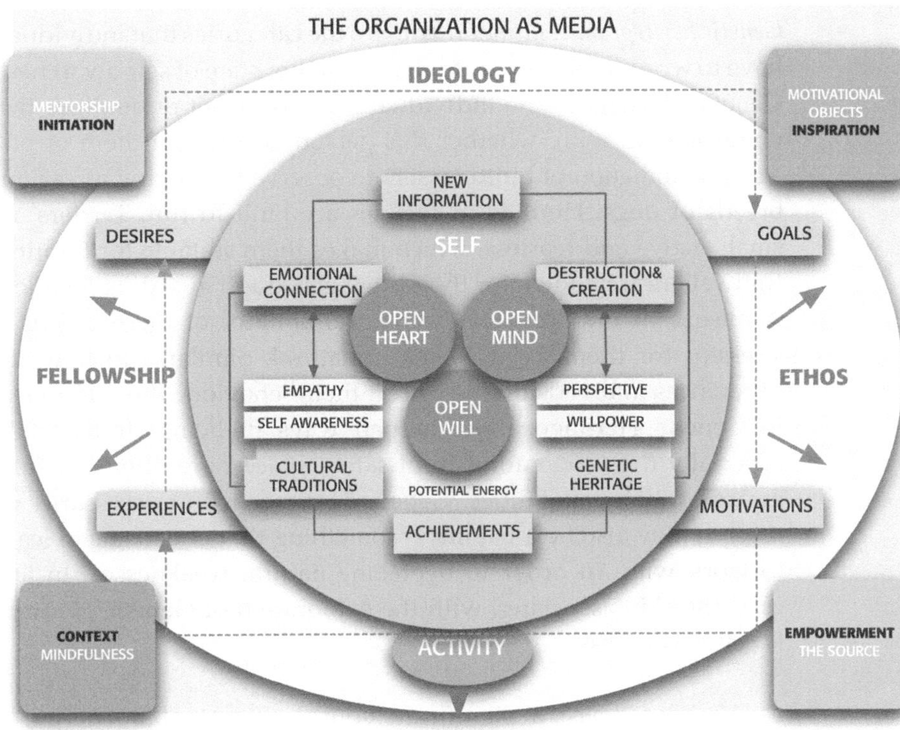

Figure 11.3 Complete framework of intrinsic motivation in co-creating organizations

at the time when it starts. Reconnection and re-evaluation of the initial expectations, with the de-facto results of the engagement, helps create an understanding of the *real* complexity of the cycle. This further refines personal judgment about complexity for future engagements—this is a skill of the mind and the will. New experiences further shatter the persistent patterns of meaning causing their re-evaluation—the qualities of the mind—that leads to the development of perspectives.

- *Emotional connection*: the development of empathy—an ability to understand and share the feelings of another person—by connecting with other individuals involved in the *engagement cycle*. It is most noticeable when the source of empowerment is the *audience*, affected by the engagement. In addition to empathy, developing the faculty of the heart helps understand one's own desires—leading to a higher quality engagement in the future.

- *Genetic heritage and cultural traditions*: the categories that individuals have to work with in order to reach a higher state of self-awareness. Genetic Heritage is the individual's 'build' or set of qualities that one was born with, whether this person is aware of them or not. The phenomenon of build is easy to observe by looking at various breeds of dogs. Hounds or huskies are built to run. Terriers are small, active and fearless, which makes them suitable for hunting. Rottweilers are known for their intelligence and guarding instincts. A misuse or underuse of the natural abilities of these breeds is stressful for them, as it seems unnatural. Similarly to how the differences in breeds of dogs affect their behaviors, the differences in Genetic Heritage affect human ways of being. Individuals, especially those operating from safety spaces, are often not fully aware of their capabilities. Genetic Heritage is not necessarily an asset, it may also be a liability—something that one needs to learn to work with, in order to overcome natural weaknesses. In any case, the skill associated with the exploration of Genetic Heritage is Self Awareness.

- *Cultural traditions*: a significant source of potential energy. It comprises an array of beliefs, behavioral programs and patterns of thinking, which are built by millions of people through multiple generations. Most often than not, they are conceptualizations with no concrete experiences backing them up. Awareness of these traditions, their exploration and transformation into experiential knowledge is another source of potential energy—through *engagement cycles* that result in all the above-mentioned learning outcomes.

A single iteration of the *engagement cycle* may differ in its timeline due to the scope of the project or the task that needs to be performed to accomplish the goal. A complete *engagement cycle* corresponds to a qualitative shift in the individual, leading to the formation of new experiences that can be treated as an evolution of the Self. Each *engagement cycle* increases the energy potential of the individual, expanding the self-outward as depicted (Figure 11.3) with arrows. This expansion is essential for organizations, since it provides access to the latent human capital of the employees. The expansion can be managed with four magnets: *Initiation, Inspiration, Empowerment,* and *Context.* In co-creating organizations these magnets are used by leaders of the co-creating communities—those with a higher degree of development on the dimensions of *open mind, open heart,* and *open will.* Ideology, Fellowship, and Ethos are designed to create the rules of engagement for everyone, which transforms the organization from a structural entity into a medium for engagement.

Co-creating organizations designed according to the principles outlined in this chapter have the following features:

- They value human capital more than structure—in fact, their structure is dynamic with the ad hoc leader-to-follower relationships, based on the nature of the specific projects that employee groups engage in.

- Connections between project teams span beyond the boundaries of the organization towards the marketplace, creating networks that incorporate employees, consumers and co-creating individuals outside of the organization.

- Co-creating organizations operate from the *source* of the emerging future. Their mission is related to making 'the next big thing' happen in the present moment, which is the reason why they exist. They make their mission tangible, and share the *source* with the network of their employees, consumers and co-creators.

- Less importance to structure does not mean chaos. Employees operate within the medium of Ideology, Fellowship and Ethos, which enables them to engage deeply with each other, with other groups inside the organization, and with the marketplace. They engage deeply, despite the differences in their backgrounds, beliefs, professional specializations, positions and titles. This aligns the goals, motivations and behaviors of the employees with the organization's mission.

- To increase the depth of engagement, employees develop the qualities of open will, open heart and open mind, participating in projects that are led by mentors, who focus their efforts on both getting the job done, and helping the employees achieve higher levels of personal growth.

- In addition to Vision, Mission, and Strategy, that are traditionally the focus of the Executive Suite, top management is concerned with and is required to design the *medium for engagement*—Ideology, Fellowship and Ethos—which create the substance of the organization, forming bonds, and shaping the layouts of co-creating networks.

- The networked nature of co-creating organizations makes the organization-wide context fluid and dynamic. This lets the organization be the reflection of the marketplace, with *change* and *evolution* incorporated into its DNA.

- The management of the organizational context becomes another key activity of the Executive Suite. This activity requires the deepest level of engagement with the source of the emerging future, the organization itself, and the marketplace—the engagement possible only with the highest level of awareness and openness of the mind, heart, and the will.

- Co-creating organizations can be metaphorically regarded as living organisms. The level of skill and awareness of the executives should be such that they can lead change within the constraint of a living organism, while at the same time trusting that we are the creators of our own future.

The Redefinition of Intrinsic Motivation

In Chapter 9, I mentioned the following definitions of intrinsic and extrinsic motivation:

- Intrinsic motivation is defined as doing an activity for its inherent satisfaction, rather than for some separable outcome.

- Extrinsic motivation is defined as a construct that applies when activity is performed for its instrumental value, rather than simply enjoyment of the process.

These definitions clearly do not capture the ability of individuals to be aware of their intrinsic desires for new experiences, as well as their ability to set goals directed at expansion of oneself through learning and personal growth. Furthermore, these definitions assume extrinsic motivation to be the only valid instrument of engagement, underestimating the scope of learning that can be achieved if an organization follows the growth and expansion of its employees. In order to take these aspects into account, the following definition is suggested:

> *Intrinsic motivation is the propensity of an individual to engage in desirable and pleasurable activities, directed at the acquisition of experiential knowledge, and leading to a higher energy state.*

Table 11.1 The taxonomy of intrinsic motivation

	Following	Participation	Self-induced Growth	Change Making
Desires	External, coming from the present or past through other individuals or media	Both internal and external, not fully actualized and distinguishable	Internal and actualized	Desires are coming from the *Source* of emerging future actualized through Self
Goals	External: maintain or achieve a lifestyle	Internal: create own lifestyle	Internal: Become a better Self	Selflessness and stewardship towards a larger goal
Working principle	Energize by experiencing a lifestyle, designed externally	Energize through collection of a wider range of experiences	Energize through accumulation of experiences focused on qualitative shift in the Self	Channel energy from the *Source* of emerging future
Energy state	Low	Moderate	High	Very-High
Position relative to Safety Space	Inside, maintain the boundaries	Inside, expand the boundaries	Inside, focus on the inner world	Outside, in the learning space

The types of intrinsic motivation depicted in the taxonomy are mapped according to the *alignment of the underlying desires and goals with the Self* (Figure 11.4). Each of the types can be defined as follows:

1. *Following*: intrinsic motivation based on external desires introduced from the outside through other individuals or media. *Following* is very similar to *integrated extrinsic* motivation.[6]

6 Ryan, R.M. and Deci, E.L. (2000). 'Intrinsic and extrinsic motivations: Classic definitions and new directions.' *Contemporary Educational Psychology*, 25, 54–67.

2. *Participation*: intrinsic motivation based on the attitude an individual adopts by taking an active position and creating a set of experiences that will form a new lifestyle. In participation, learning is achieved through the expansion of the *safety space*.

3. *Self-induced growth*: intrinsic motivation based on an active role in shaping one's own personality through learning and growth, focusing only on qualitatively new experiences, triggering a shift towards the goal of becoming a better self.

4. *Change making*: intrinsic motivation based on the individual actualizing the emerging future through Self, by connecting to the *source* with *open heart*, and *open will* consciously or sub-consciously.

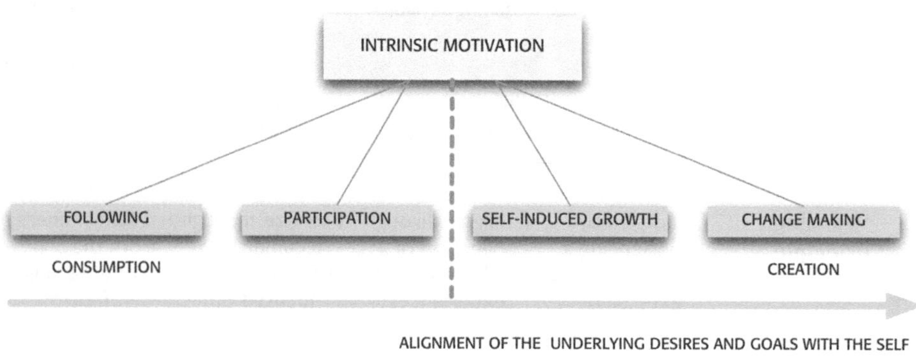

Figure 11.4 The taxonomy of intrinsic motivation

PART 5

IDEOLOGY, LEADERSHIP AND STRATEGIC VALUE

Chapter 12

Leadership, Ideology and Value Creation

A few years ago, the CFO of a large digital marketing firm, successful by any financial measure, acknowledged that 'we are billing around $80 million a year, and we don't know what we are doing. What would our revenue line be if we knew what we were doing?' All of us might recall meeting corporate executives that were lacking the insights needed to find answers to their own questions. Most professionals learn how to give answers to the questions raised by others, but they rarely know what questions to ask. And this has to be blamed on their education. Asking the right questions is part of the pursuit of pure knowledge, and at the risk of generalizing here, business graduates are rarely exposed to any frameworks conducive to the pursuit of pure knowledge, and to little or no ideology on the basis of which they should apply in practice marketing methods, statistics, or strategy. I believe that without an ideological framework, one does not know *why they are learning what they are learning*. This lack of knowing the answer to the question '*why*' weeds itself into organizations, with the result of people not knowing why they are doing what they are doing.

The title of this section went through quite a few changes in the course of the many drafts written for this book, and in every one of these changes, the word *ideology* was placed in a different location, either at the end, sometimes in the middle and only once, when I started writing this book, at the beginning. That title was 'Ideology and Value Creation' and it felt a bit too strong, in the sense that the word ideology was prominent. This anxiety was based on frequent misunderstandings around the word ideology in the context of enterprise. For an enterprise, *ideology* must have the same meaning as *politics,* in the sense of being the art of influencing people, aligning them toward a specific goal, which is shared by a group, and directing their passions and actions toward what could be possible. This common direction builds the values from which an enterprise extracts its ethos, energy and creativity.

From Methodology to Ideology

Why talk about ideology now, at the dawn of the Internet of Things era? Because the transformations we face in the very near future require choices to be made, and choices require sets of values on the basis of which we need to operate. We are about to engage in the building of new social norms and a society that would redefine its tools, settlements and structures, expanding its networks to include everything. On this journey, choices will have to be made every time new means of human expression generate new forms of engagement, redefining entire systems of living. Isn't that pretty much what humanity went through about 170 years ago, with the beginning of the Industrial Revolution? It is not by accident that the multinational Bosch is labeling the Internet of Things 'the fourth Industrial Revolution'; this label is intended to create a clear image of the opportunity ahead of us, as well as prepare us for the magnitude of its challenges.

Redefining how we produce things, as well as the things that we produce, will also redefine benefits and values for millions of people, making the Internet of Things a major turning point in history, with every aspect of human life being influenced somehow. We cannot plunge into this future; we must design it, and this requires its own aesthetics and its own ethics. This predicament is not dissimilar to the one faced by the arts and crafts professionals in the late 1800s and early 1900s, a time of transition between the handmade products and the objects made by industry.

Principles needed to be established to ensure the continuity of human intent in a machine-made object, and this is how the profession of industrial design was born.

In the Internet of Things, we are facing a transformation of the same magnitude, if not larger. This transformation requires that organizations redefine their purpose, and redefine what is possible. In my view, the quest for a new possibility in the context of the enterprise cannot take place without the reframing of its ideology. And this is why I am drawing a parallel between the industrial design and business professionals: both are relatively new, and born around the same time, amidst the same concerns. Both have education models that were molded as a response to these concerns, and in that, they share a history of reactive acceptance of the outside factors shaping their performance, as both were lacking at the time of their emergence, a professional code of conduct, informing a mission based on ideology, rather than market forces.

It is in education that we can find the seeds of enterprise, so let us look at the industrial design education model at Bauhaus, the design school founded in 1919 in Weimar, Germany. Bauhaus[1] and the movement it created, was probably the most influential modernist art school of the twentieth century, whose approach to teaching was connected to the early understanding of the relationship between society, technology and art. The Bauhaus movement was concerned with democratizing both the creation and the production of products and spaces. This meant an appropriate use of material, and trueness in the use of material in appropriate forms. Bauhaus was also concerned with the meaning of products created by industrial production, as a counterbalance to the sameness that might be the result of products made by machines. Bauhaus stressed experimentation and problem solving, which in the maturing phases of the industrial design profession, became essential qualities of today's design thinking. More importantly, Bauhaus teaching stressed the connection between ethics and aesthetics, considering morals and aesthetics the same, as parts of the same consciousness.

The chief success of Bauhaus was making design a 'tool for industry,' with both positive and negative consequences. The Positive: a new awareness that Art belongs in Industry, and the much needed differentiation of products made by machines. The Negative: the profession of industrial design *after* Bauhaus had no ideology of its own, but rather a series of borrowed frames of reference, from a spectrum of sources:

- From marketing: the creation of life style, need and want fulfillment, value added;
- From management: streamlining development and production;
- From communication and branding: product image, company image/brand; and
- Trends from contemporary culture in general.

Looking at it from all angles, and in as much as the founders wanted it, Bauhaus's legacy was not an ideology, *but a methodology.* The absence of an ideology might be sought after in many professions, and maybe to their credit,

1 Available at: http://www.theartstory.org/movement-bauhaus.htm (accessed: August 21, 2014).

but for the emergent profession of design in the mid-1930s and further, post-World War II, it meant the absence of Ethics.[2]

This is not a trivial finding, as no aesthetic can exist without ethics—it is ethics after all, which gives us the values upon which to judge the qualities of the surrounding world, and our contribution to it as well. This means that the industrial design profession had, for very long, operated on the borrowed ethics of others, and thus with the aesthetics of others as well. In the early 1990s, some designers understood that the profession needed an ethical discourse, as the ground was shifting toward a world in which sustainability was more than a mantra, but also a business opportunity. And that discourse opened the door to psychology, philosophy, and experience design, the beginnings of a whole new universe for the practice of design practice and its expertise, and a potent instrument affecting change and the quality of our lives.

Purpose of Enterprise: *To Do Good*

I see many parallels between the teaching and practice of both design and business here, which reveal the opportunity to move from 'methodology' to 'ideology,' especially now, as we embark on building the structures of a new economy and society. Advocating an ideology as opposed to a methodology, involves asking people to think about the difference between the two. One is a *tool*; the other is a *way of being, behaving and influencing the world*. An attitude.

Ideology is a hard word to swallow, especially for those not versed in philosophy. So lots of learning needs to take place in connecting the actions of business to the basics of Ethics, a law of philosophy that deals with the morals of everyday actions. There is a deep connection between ethics and the actions of individuals, be they business management consultants, or their clients. Aristotle calls the first chapter of his Ethics[3] 'The Object of Life' and starts the very first line like this: 'Every rational activity aims at some end or good.' This summarizes beautifully the purpose of any business enterprise: *to do good*.

While organizations have this idea of doing good somewhere in their vision statement, they carry the burden of making it manifest in daily activities. It is

2 I am not referring to a lack of ethics in the Bauhaus school of design, but to a lack of a prescribed ethic in the profession that resulted afterwards.

3 Aristotle (1976 [1953]). *The Ethics of Aristotle*. Translated by J.A.K. Thomson. London: Penguin Books, 63.

one thing to have an ideology that inspires your workforce, and something else to manifest that ideology outward.

In order to be relevant to the world any ethical stand has to be put into practice, for the benefit of your customers, because ethics that are not practiced do not exist. And this is the role of leadership, to make sure that the individuals within the organization are aligned toward the same ideological purpose, can inspire others to be aligned as well, and all activities make manifest the ethics of the organization.

The fundamentals of ideology in organizations start with defining *core values* and *purpose.* Core values are the guiding principles that the organization embraces as vital to their activities. Purpose defines the reasons an organization exists in society, independent of its reasons for shareholders. Purpose is not about business strategy but about the value the organizations create in the world. Core values + purpose = ideology. Translated into a vision, these become the guides an organization needs to navigate any transition into the future. Ideology creates the culture of the organization, nurtures its people, their passions and aspirations, and their capacity for transformation. Without this capacity, transformation is a chore rather than a vocation.

In essence we are looking at ideas that rally people behind them, and provide a common vision and mindset. Ideas form the foundation of what people are about and subsequently of what an Enterprise is about. They shape identity and within it, they shape strategy. Enterprise ideology is vital to the future success of the organization because it shapes all activities and an action around an idea, as well as it empowers individuals toward the same goal. Ideology shapes the mind and enlists the passion of people involved, it emboldens them and gives them the energy to pursue goals, informing their actions and giving the metrics against which the organization measures itself. It is a system of abstract thought, applied objectively to actions of every day. Ideology in enterprise is different from ideology in the public or the political realm, because the ends are different. The ideology outlined in the vision statement creates the attitude that defines what the Enterprise is all about. These fundamental principles inform the value systems, providing the ethos of the enterprise.

It is important here to understand the word ideology in the context of the originating thought, which belonged to Destutt de Tracy. For de Tracy, ideology is the *science of ideas.* Ideas are formed as the result of human sensations, and become something we call *knowledge.* This knowledge of the world around us gained through experience creates in us the desire for certain things, which is the beginning of change. In his opinion, this is the *faculty of will*, as will produces ideas about where we want to go, about new objectives that we like to achieve. There is a connection between ideas and *will*, in that we would not have ideas about how to improve our condition, if we didn't have the will to do it. It is from the faculty of will that all our wants and means originate, and with it, the foundation of the economic system and all of our morality.

Leadership in the Emerging Present

It is essential that we discuss ideology in the setting of behavior platforms, especially when these platforms will increase in relevance and ubiquity. More and more of the decisions facing enterprise leaders have to do with politics and ideology, in the context of ethics just described here.

A significant number of the decisions Facebook or Google are faced with every day, are in the ethical realm. Facebook has succeeded in defining a framework that is acceptable as a practice for living, in societies in which Facebook functions, practices that have a notable social nature, before having any economic impact. Facebook is all about the social in the realm of the political; it is about Individual Politics. Facebook pages are a manifestation of one's individual politics of 'how would I be the ideal me in front of my ideal audience?'

The role of leadership is to inspire individuals into believing in themselves, and in that leadership and ideology are connected, as no leader can be functional without a set of principles that inspire his or her activity. Facebook's increasingly political decisions indicates that leadership connected to ideology is much more important in the behavior economy, than it ever was in the industrial economic system. In the industrial economy the use of a product or system was left up to the user; once the purchase was made the manufacturer was rarely—if at all—involved. This meant that the appropriate or inappropriate use of that product, for an ethical or unethical purpose, was left up to the individual user. In the behavior economy, where user engagement is on behavior platforms, *the platform creator is at all times present in the activities that take place on the platform*, and at all times responsible for the ethic being practiced.

In a behavior economy that will soon receive the major disruption of the Internet of Things, leadership needs to become increasingly ideological and transformational. This is not just for companies that are directly connected to the behavior economy by creating platforms, but will apply to every company and every organization that wishes to be a participant in the Internet of Things. Just like the Internet itself was not an option, the Internet of Things is not an elective; businesses would have a very hard time opting out of this new environment. One cannot work their way around such a powerful emerging presence, nor can one ignore it. In the Internet of Things leaders would have to manage ideas, and the management of ideas is different in the management of facts. In this new setting, leaders would always be expected to manage the transition from the present to the future, and without an ideological framework this transition becomes accidental, reactive, and uninspiring.

Transformational leaders paint a picture of the future, and enlist followers to get there. The future is a set of questions, some bigger that others. Every disruption in technology brings with it new sets of questions. This is what we are confronted with today, powerful questions, leading to powerful generative ideas. In the emerging present of the Internet of Things, leaders need to be fluent in the flow of daily life experiences—yes, this means posting on Facebook, actively participating in all social media vehicles—as deep insights come only from experiencing life as it is, at this moment.

Before one learns to manage the 'How,' the 'What' needs to be created, and that is the art of business leadership in the new context. The art of leadership is the capability of joining the *how* with the *what*, the '*means*' with the '*meaning*' in the organized exploration of possibility. *See, feel, hear and Understand with Your Heart* was Bang and Olufsen's development motto in the mid-1990s. As Sergey Kovalyukh observed in Chapter 11, 'Redefining Intrinsic Motivation,' understanding with your heart is the key to true understanding.

No Longer Numbers

It is here, in the role and quality of leadership, that we find the most important distinction between the behavior economy and the industrial production economy. In the production model the leader had to be a good manager, a good planner and a good executioner. The team and its leader were measured on the value of the execution. In this model, imagination is most of the time a liability. Ideology is also a liability, as the only matters of consequence were numbers, and how one met them. The metrics were simple: meet the numbers and you get your bonus. Meet the numbers meant making the right kind of product, for the right kind of marketing mix and demographic targets. This was a time when people were still accumulating products, and were measuring life's satisfactions in the number and quality of the products they possessed.

Transfer now to the behavior economy, where people consume experiences, and ask yourself what can the leader of the past accomplish. While Larry Page asks 'What could be possible?,' the prototypical CEO of the mid-1980s was asking 'How Many?' and 'For How Much?'

For today's leaders everything has changed. Today's conversations start with questions, not with data. The metrics have changed; the meaning of words has changed. Amateur, professional, markets, distribution, all these words now mean different things. We are now moving from the analog-to-digital economy, and this does not require change, this requires transformation and transformation is a fundamental revision of direction; transformation is a job for leaders. To transform means to change something completely, and usually in a good way. This requires the capabilities of transformational leadership.

In 'A Systemic View of Transformational Leadership' Russell Ackoff[4] notes that leadership is not administration, and leadership is not management. Leadership means an inspiring poetic vision. Leadership means guidance, leadership means facilitation and encouragement. Leadership is not concerned with efficiency but it is concerned with effectiveness. Efficiency is *value free*, while effectiveness is *value full*, and is measured by the values of the ends achieved. Put another way: efficiency is a matter of doing things right; effectiveness is a matter of doing the right things. Netflix's 'Reference Guide on our Freedom & Responsibility Culture' sets this up brilliantly:

> **Hard Work—Not Directly Relevant**
> *It's about effectiveness—not effort—even though effectiveness is harder to assess than effort. We don't measure people by how many evenings or weekends they are in their cube. We do try to measure people by how much, how quickly and how well they get work done—especially under deadline … Flexibility is More Important than Efficiency in the Long Term.*[5]

Transformational Leaders inspire extraordinary pursuits by giving people the courage to fail. I tell my students at the beginning of every semester 'if you aim high in your project you might fail to get there, but if you fail, you pass.'

4 Ackoff, R.L. (1998). 'A systemic view of transformational leadership.' *Systemic Practice and Action Research*, 11(1), 23–36.

5 Netflix (2009). Netflix Culture: Freedom & Responsibility. Available at: http://www.slideshare.net/reed2001/culture-1798664 (accessed: June 11, 2014).

Art Not Science

For Ackoff, leadership is closer connected to art than it is to science, because art inspires, and allows people to imagine things. Art provides inspiration and connects us with beauty, which in turn inspires us to seek for more beauty. Art also entertains and opens into us windows for new possibilities. This is also the main role of leadership, to inspire individuals into believing in themselves, into believing that they can always transcend their latest achievement. Transformational leaders understand that within each individual resides in enormous possibility, and they set out to release it. Transformational leaders have the courage to lead in times of change and transformation, and the courage inspires courage in others.

Giving people the ability to dream about a better future takes more than persuasion. It requires the ability to open people's imagination to a new realm of possibility, and to empower them to get there. What better way to get people to engage in the search of possibility then to inspire them to participate on a transformational journey, in pursuit of long-term ideal objectives? Articulating long-term ideal objectives, and visions for the future is a product of the creative mind, which makes strategy an artifact of art. And this makes those leaders who create them artists.

In the next two chapters, my collaborator Carl Hastrich explores the influential leaders who built visionary enterprises, and attempts to define the desired leadership qualities for the future of the behavior economy.

Chapter 13

Leadership in the Behavior Economy

CARL HASTRICH

New models of value creation, on digital platforms, shaping new experiences and information flows, drive the emerging business paradigm of the behavior economy. In this marketplace new competitive spaces for businesses are emerging rapidly, disrupting the established models, with new billion dollar companies being built around technologies that barely existed a decade ago. These companies emerged by enabling new engagement models, taking advantage of behaviors that did not exist prior to their invention.

These new ecosystems of interconnected data, and the platforms that host their activities, transform information into desirable experiences that are fundamentally disrupting the status quo economic model of production and consumption. As discussed earlier in this book, generating revenue by producing an item that someone hopes to '*have*' is no longer enough, and has not been enough for a number of decades. The behavior economy is now transforming every facet of daily life, where producing an experience that someone desires to '*be*' involved in creates value (Figure 13.1).

As the economic landscape shifts from a linear industrial archetype to a networked behavior model, the thinking of a high-impact business leader requires intellectual sophistication like never before. In the next couple of pages I will examine leaders who have built companies around visions of the future, in order to identify core attributes that should be developed in future leaders of the behavior economy. Three questions guide this examination:

- Who are the influential leaders shaping the behavior economy?
- What is the future of leadership in the behavior economy?
- What are the desired leadership qualities in the future behavior economy?

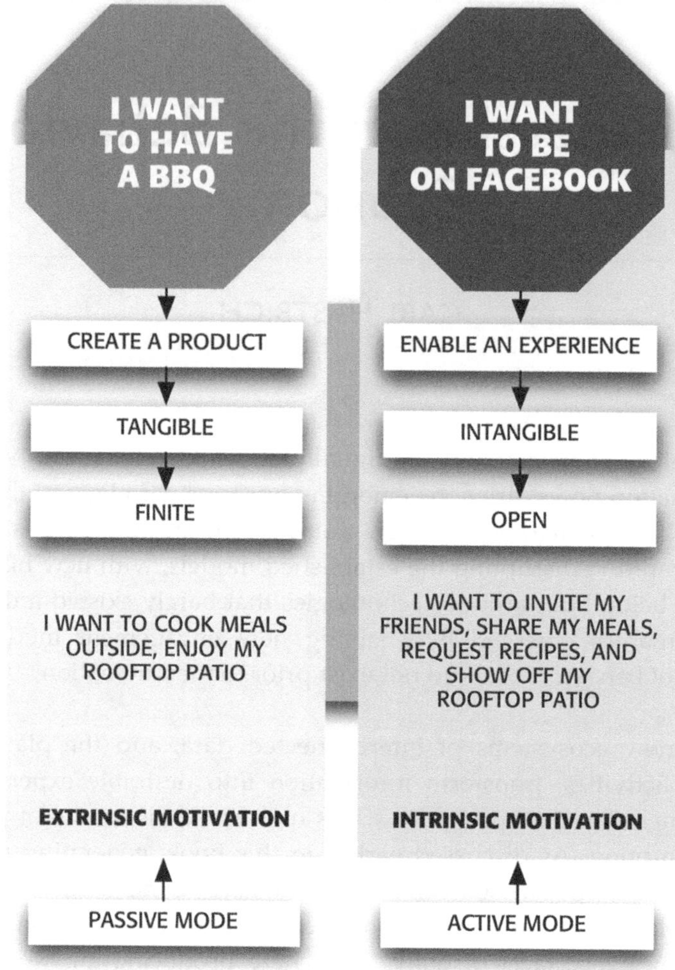

Figure 13.1 Modes of consumption

Disruptions and the Behavior Economy

There are deep shifts occurring within businesses globally. As traditional models of generating revenue from the sales of products through linear channels are being challenged, it is no longer enough to squeeze efficiencies off production lines to remain an industry leader. New forms of value must be created through compelling and engaging experiences, enabled by the information flow and technology that bridges digital and physical worlds. While margins shrink in traditional companies based on the extraction economy, organizations that build and enable digital platforms for individuals and businesses, enjoy high margins and dominant market share

The leadership of companies grounded in the industrial consumption economy did not need to be philosophers making sense of their world. They were operating within proven linear models, which have been refined and perfected by leaders focused on management and maintenance. Much of the literature written on the subject of leadership focuses on the practices and skills required in building and managing teams within established companies, but there is a gap of research into the leadership qualities of individuals that build businesses around visions of the future. Yet, some of the best examples of such organizations are familiar names, right in front of us: IBM, Apple, Tesla, Lucasfilm and Google.

IBM transformed its own business by integrating new capabilities in the information technology industry, capabilities that they themselves invented, and that other companies almost used to push them out of business. Apple built an ecosystem of innovations and experiences that transition seamlessly between the physical and the digital, with each product or software further integrating and reinforcing these behaviors. Tesla approaches automotive design as if it were developing a software application, blurring the line between product and service, leveraging every innovation as a node in a network of integrated technologies. Lucasfilm sold for $4.05 billion predominantly due to characters and stories rich with potential future experiences. Google appears to have just begun leveraging the network of technologies and businesses it has created, seeking ever-increasingly ambitious goals, as it continues forward without any clear competitor to the search business it helped create and define.

Behind each of these companies are individuals with strong visions, and a deep capability for pulling together opposable forces of disruption and integration, by sheer willpower, and a desire to achieve a driving purpose. In many cases, short-term business success was merely a step on the path towards deeper goals. A philosopher powered by the results of constant entrepreneurialism, Elon Musk has repeatedly sold successful companies to finance speculative longer-term technologies. Others were almost brought down by their own power to disrupt. Both Larry Page and Steve Jobs required time away from their own creations, in order to evolve into leaders capable of integrative thinking. The stories of each of these influential leaders are rich with insights into what is required to be successful and influential in the new behavior economy.

Understanding the unique attributes of the individuals capable of maintaining foresight over time, while implementing innovation daily, requires a framework for categorizing the desired leadership qualities that must be developed. This framework can be used to identify leaders with high capacity for foresight innovation, and used to develop further tools for personal development.

The Attributes

LEADERSHIP AND SYSTEMS THINKING

In the behavior economy, value is non-linear, and relative to the size and quantity of experience nodes and the behaviors enabled across the network. The flows of experiences, and specifically the people interacting with the platform, are the primary source for value extraction. While clear in theory, the navigation and creation of emerging systems requires new tools for defining, articulating and delivering opportunity that are at conflict with the archetypal business narrative.

A system is a sum of multiple elements that when combined will result in functions that cannot be achieved by any of the elements on their own. Linear businesses divided into functional units, can operate as weak systems, where elements—functional units—can be bought, sold and traded on the marketplace as isolated entities. In the Pharmaceutical industry for example, individual drugs are managed as an isolated business due to regulatory and administrative requirements. This makes it possible for companies to purchase drugs from competitors with little business integration.

In the behavior economy, value is created by the emerging functions made available by *increasing the number of elements* and *relationships* within the system. Increased value occurs through the integration of technology and platforms in order to activate desired experiences. Google is currently buying businesses from diverse areas such as home appliances, robotics, artificial intelligence and energy capture, as it works to develop an integrated system of technologies focused on enabling behaviors that improve the quality of life for connected people across the world.

Apple's iPhone is a defining product of the behavior economy, both for what it has enabled and for how it came to existence. To develop and bring the iPhone to market, Steve Jobs and Apple required a network of partners that included traditional vendors, collaborators and even competitors, all of whom gained direct and indirect value through the development of the product/platform. This network included:

- AT&T, who agreed to the unique revenue model that made the product affordable.
- Samsung, a competitor who provided the chips to run it.
- Corning, a glass manufacturer searching for new markets through internal research and development.
- Motorola, whose Rokr E1 Apple iTunes mobile phone gave Apple the opportunity to learn how to build a cellphone.
- Apple's internal suite of products and capabilities including the iPod and iTunes.

Much has been written about Steve Jobs and his ability to craft the vision that brought many partners to the table. This level of vision and determination will be required more and more, in a behavior economy that requires interconnected products and services as a default. Integrated innovation will be a core requirement of businesses, and the future valuation of businesses will include the internal portfolio of products, services and platforms *and* their connections to external enablers.

To define the ideal qualities of a leader in the behavior economy, we must first look at what leadership means in the context of transformation, and we must differentiate leadership from the day-to-day administration tasks of management. Russell Ackoff, cited earlier in Chapter 12, defines[1] three levels accordingly:

> *Administration* consists of directing others in carrying out the will of a third party, using means selected by the same party.
>
> *Management* consists of directing others in the pursuit of ends using means both of which have been selected by the manager. (Executives are managers who manage other managers.)

1 Ackoff, R.L. (1998). 'A systemic view of transformational leadership.' *Systemic Practice and Action Research*, 11(1), 23–36.

> *Leadership* consists of guiding, encouraging and facilitating the pursuit by others of ends using means, both of which they have either selected, and the selection of which they approve.

A fundamental difference between management and leadership is the ability to articulate and motivate others toward desired end goals, which encourage individuals to overcome challenges and roadblocks. Ackoff deliberately describes leadership as an artistic and aesthetic pursuit, reinforcing intangibles and intuition as a required capacity. These attributes further reinforce how difficult it is to endow desired leadership qualities to individuals, through traditional training and linear methods.

The leaders mentioned in this chapter have been chosen for the lessons they reveal in maintaining an intuitive vision of their enterprises, while empowering others to implement complementary visions in a way that generates ongoing value. The businesses they have created are highly systemic, achieving sizable success due to their integration of multiple technologies.

INTEGRATED INNOVATION AND FORESIGHT

The behavior economy is an emerging, constantly shifting landscape. This requires senior leaders to take action without clear precedents upon which to compare their decision. Businesses driven by high strategic value are those whose products, services and platforms have actively shaped the future, and created new places in the market from which to generate revenue. Strategic foresight as a methodology for creating strategic value is increasingly required for integrating the various threads of new technologies and emerging behaviors.

When researching this book we looked at leadership in organizations that have succeeded because of their ability to integrate innovations that embodied visions of the future. Each of these leaders has had to respond to an emerging market, often one that they created. The core business model of IBM revolved around information technology products, tailored to customers prior to Lou Gerstner stepping in as CEO. As IBM was disrupted by their own rapid advancements of technology, it looked like they were too big to adapt to the market. By understanding what could be achieved when integrating in-house innovation teams and focus, and seeking to understand the new behaviors of the market place, IBM transformed into a cohesive platform for offering value. IBM was turned around in two years from a leviathan about to be chopped into discrete parts, to an integrated forward-facing business that shaped the business landscape around it.

FIVE-POINT LEADERSHIP

A five-point leader is motivated to build relationships between people and ideas to achieve a driving vision. They are capable of capitalizing on markets that don't yet exist, by building a billion-dollar business from an ecosystem of ideas: products, services and people that shape a desired future. A five-star leader is a rare breed, a unique blend of contrasting forces, disruptive and integrative, entrepreneurial and philosophical, held together by a desire to pilot directly into stormy uncertainty.

A five-point leader offers many lessons for anyone struggling to connect the dots and make sense of emergence as opportunity; they show the skill of holding onto the bigger picture, no matter how unattainable it may seem, while being driven to execute on the immediately attainable goals.

Contrasting Force No. 1: Disruption and Integration

Disruptors are passionate for new ideas, especially anything that breaks an established norm. For Larry Page this passion could almost have been his downfall, as his disruptions within the company structure backfired and his desire to 'kill the advertising industry' could have removed his primary income source.[2] Lou Gerstner will never be celebrated as a disruptive innovator of products, but it was his comfort at challenging what IBM was and could be that made it possible to transform the company quickly and successfully. Elon Musk's design brief to car designers demand that every opportunity be taken to leverage unique capabilities. Where space is freed due to the electric engine, more seats are demanded, challenging typical definitions of sedan v. minivan. Disruptors can be dangerous, they can be compelled to break and destroy, and get so lost in the pleasure of pulling something apart, that they forget to reassemble something of value at the end. Lacking disruptors encourages ongoing commitment to outdated thinking. Senior leadership at Blackberry, then Research in Motion, failed to challenge internal assumptions and quickly found themselves following a market that they had established.

2 Carlson, N. (2014). 'The untold story of Larry Page's incredible comeback.' *Business Insider*, April 24. Available at: http://www.businessinsider.com/larry-page-the-untold-story-2014-4 (accessed: July 18, 2014).

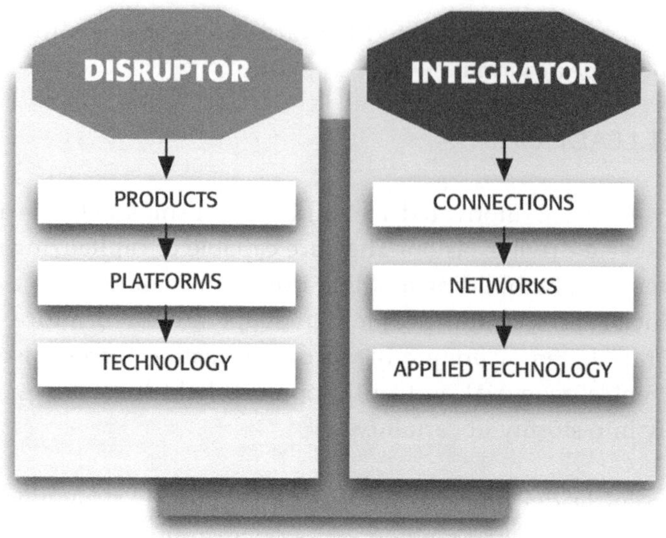

Figure 13.2 Disruption and integration

Integrators focus on the connections between ideas, building the ecosystem that enables the core idea. Steve Jobs was able to build an ecosystem of products and services that enabled many different disruptions to work together. George Lucas built a sprawling physical space to enable the many different research and development arms to work together and leverage one another's value. As Larry Page becomes CEO, he is focusing on the value of collaboration rather than competition, in an increasingly non-linear business space. Integrators rarely get the same celebration as the dynamic force of disruption, but it takes the integrator force to assemble things of value, out of uncertainty and disruption.

Disruptors and *Integrators* are both builders, but what they construct is very different.

While George Lucas was compelled to build a company to achieve a *creative passion*, leaders driven by *technological innovation* were the founders of Motorola. All three leaders of the Galvin family dynasty at Motorola were enablers of technology, active at disrupting the marketplace, but poor at integration. Bob Galvin was well known for creating a highly competitive internal environment; it was often called the era of warring tribes, where division heads and functional managers fought one another openly for lucrative financial rewards. While the digital network was being pioneered by Motorola's research and development, the mobile handset department remained analog, arrogantly ignoring the start-up companies embracing the competitive technology. Motorola has since been deeply disrupted by the behavior economy, because no strong integrator leaders were found to pilot changes.

Contrasting Force No. 2: Entrepreneur and Philosopher

Philosophers are concerned by the end state of a vision, Elon Musk worries about the future of mankind, George Lucas worries about creative freedom, and Larry Page literally dreams of how to make sense of the world's information. These end goals are ambitious, aggressive and most importantly, fixed in place. That the vision itself is not negotiable is one of the core features that make a five-point leader so valuable and difficult to work against. It is the philosophical dream, considered a tangible possibility, that empowers these leader and others around them, to tackle impossible challenges and achieve them.

Entrepreneurs are nimble and opportunistic, with the ability to exploit the services, products and technologies that emerge around them. Lou Gerstner was capable of adapting IBM's strategies as new opportunities emerged, through internal growth and restructuring; George Lucas built

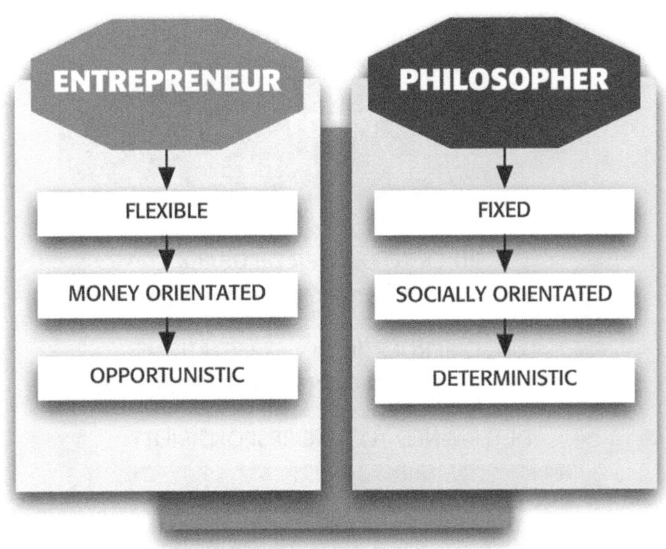

Figure 13.3 Entrepreneur and philosopher

an empire of industry-leading services from the technology developed for his own creative purposes, and Steve Jobs was able to craft unique business models to capitalize on emerging behaviors made possible through Apple's product development.

Balancing the contradictions of unyielding passion, combined with opportunistic flexibility, makes it possible to transform possibility into reality.

Entrepreneurs and *Philosophers* are both compelled by vision, but each has a different scope in mind.

Binding Force: Pilot

Pilots are required to navigate through uncertainty, taking the lead by making quick and timely decisions that have long-term consequences. They will always need the engineers and mechanics that build and maintain their aircraft, but they are not afraid of getting their hands dirty and engaging in solving specific problems. Pilot is the binding agent as well as the catalyst and provocateur of the other forces, preventing them from being locked against each other in tension (Figure 13.4). When Tesla faced financial and technical difficulties it was Elon Musk who positioned himself as CEO, investing his own money, and involving himself directly in building solutions.

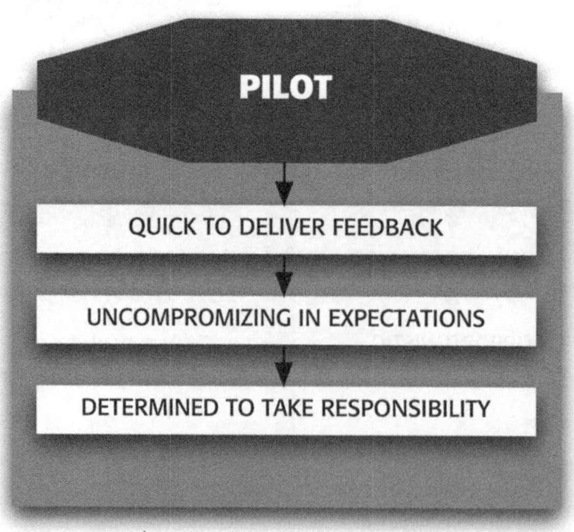

Figure 13.4 Pilots

Steve Jobs was famous for engaging directly with ideas, obsessing and sweating every detail, and leading from the front. Lou Gerstner transformed IBM by leading the change personally; his physical presence proved to managers that conventional practice would no longer be enough to take them to a new destination.

Opportunities in Leadership

These are the starting points for developing Five-Point leadership leading to the creation of strategic value, through actions that will:

- Reframe your business activities to align with the emerging behavior economy.
- Use the Strategic Value Framework to self-assess and provoke an ambitious innovation mindset.
- Use the Five-Point Leadership Framework to provoke professional development and business strategy.

These actions will be the answers to the question: *How do I frame my business in the Behavior Economy?*

Acknowledgment

Carl Hastrich seeks to understand the interplay between human-centered insights and relevant implications for the design of systems, processes and support infrastructure.

He is a foresight strategist, idea generator and a lead facilitator. Carl has designed and led co-creative workshops for a diverse range of public and private clients addressing complex problems such as the Future of Alzheimer's and organizational change driven by Patient Centricity. Carl has been an Associate Professor at OCAD University. His focus is on engaging diverse stakeholders to generate actionable outcomes. Carl is a senior associate at Bridgeable, a strategic design firm in Toronto. Carl's contribution to this work is Chapters 13 and 14.

Chapter 14

Participating in the Behavior Economy

CARL HASTRICH

How do I frame my business in the Behavior Economy? This question is a good starting point for further exploration. The goal is always the delivery of strategic value. To do so it is important to define the need for new tools, activities, and collaborative opportunities for strategic alignment.

Reframing your Business

The underling mindset is one of understanding one's product or service offering as a behavior platform for a compelling experience. In the behavior economy, you make platforms, not products. That is not a cell phone; it is a behavior platform. The lack of understanding a broader service as a platform is fundamental to the

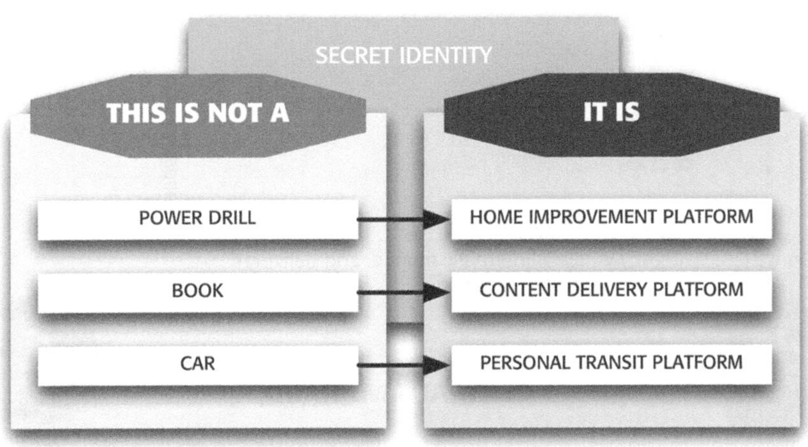

Figure 14.1 Secret product identity

failure of many businesses, leaving them open to disruption by companies that understand and speak to the core behaviors enabled by platforms that make other products and services obsolete. There are many ways of articulating the behavior at the core of an offering. It can be thought of as a secret identity, a hint at a deeper super power that needs to be harnessed (Figure 14.1). To provoke innovative thinking, the next opportunity is to explore diverse ways for delivering that platform. Two key themes should be considered:

Defining your Platform Characteristics

Centralized v. Distributed: Your platform can be tightly controlled and curated, using a centralized platform to ensure high quality control, such as LucasArts.

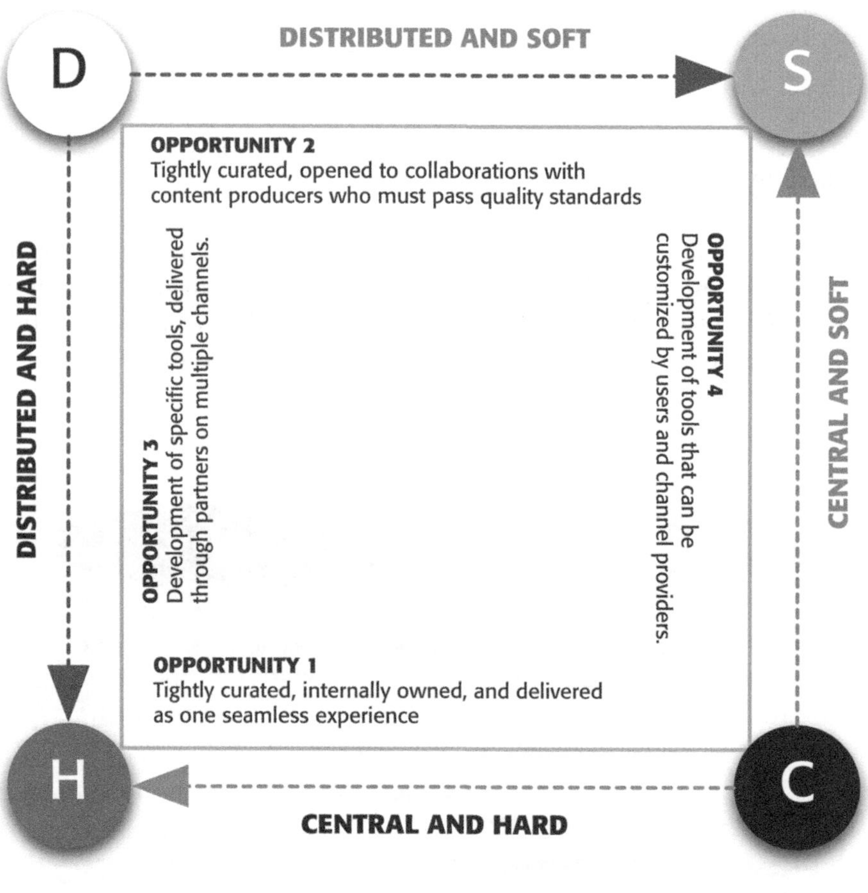

Figure 14.2 Platform options

Alternatively, an open and flexible platform can distribute and integrate across multiple channels, the core strategy of Google with the Google Search Bar and Android platforms (Figure 14.2).

Hard v. Soft: Hard platforms are fully integrated into the physical devices used to access them, ensuring a consistent experience throughout; Apple is the biggest driver of hard platforms. Soft platforms live on any physical device, such as Facebook.

These make up four potential opportunities for platform design and interaction to consider, as can be seen in Figure 14.2 on the previous page.

Reinforcing your Innovation Pipeline

The central question creating a continuum of innovation is: *What behaviors are you reinforcing or retrieving with your innovation?* The behavior economy encourages investigation into how people interact and engage—I want *to be* on Facebook—rather than what individuals *have* and use.

Reframing your Competition

Focusing on your competitor's rival technology specifications comes at the expense of understanding emerging behaviors. You will be disrupted more by a competitor providing experiences that transform core behaviors, than you will by new technology innovation. Those new sensors on that wristband are transforming peoples' commute time into a personal fitness opportunity.

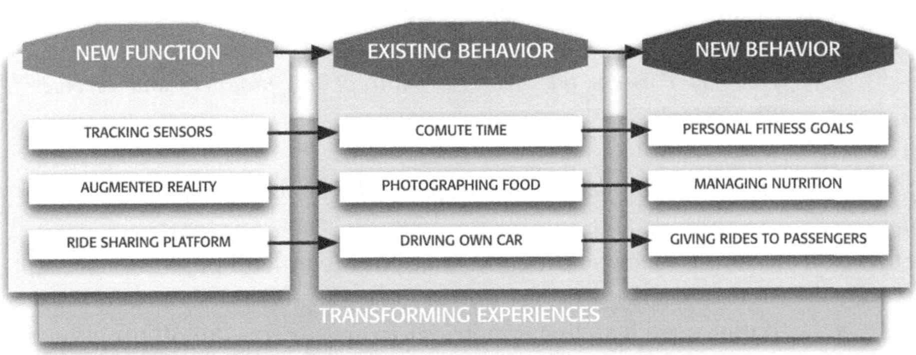

Figure 14.3 Transforming experiences

That is not a new function; *it is an enhanced life experience*. My competitor is transforming experiences (see Figure 14.3).

The questions that need to be answered:

- *How do your offerings compete with these transformations?*
- *What behaviors are/could you be transforming with your innovation?*

Reframing Collaboration

When everything is interconnected, the line between competitor and collaborator is extremely thin. Individuals don't care who provides the experience, but they will remember the strongest story.

The questions that need to be answered:

- *How can you and your competitor partner create a combined experience?*
- *How does it extend your core story?*

Use the Strategic Value Framework

A clear vision of the future requires a deep understanding of strategic value. The ability to concisely articulate how your product positions in the marketplace and how key activities will shape a desired future is required for strong leadership. The questions below offer a starting point for leaders to reflect on their understanding and articulation of strategic value.

- *How do I assess the strategic value of my products and services for the future?*
- *How is success defined for this particular project or idea?*

How do you define success influences that your team will pursue or prevent.

- If there are clear, linear metrics for measuring your offerings against competitive products or industry benchmarks, then your innovation fits in the 'Fill a place' category and has low strategic value.

- Filling a place does not encourage creative thinking. If you are in a feature race with competitors, it is impossible to build a unique identity in the market place. It is important to continually question and challenge opportunities for differentiation.

Encourage a Safe Space to Develop Metrics

The e-business strategy emerged at IBM from capabilities developed internally, in a safe space to explore new ideas, measured against new metrics. The Emerging Business Opportunity Division was set up to understand how different markets could be approached, allowing leaders to debate and speculate over what metrics would define success in the new market area, and how to plan according to new information.

- To boost strategic value, look to where you think this market position is moving, and look for new metrics that would challenge the status quo. Instead of using sales metrics, capture information about how your product or service is being used: number of users, frequency of use, and duration of use. Is it possible to understand the purpose of the user and their motivation?

- Instead of market share, which can reinforce a narrow focus, can you capture information about the shape of the market: size of overall market, health of overall market, and identify peripheral and overlapping markets that may play a greater role in the future?

Identify what Success will Enable

'Creating a place' in the strategic value matrix requires a forward-focused mindset to understand what success will enable. During the development of activities that 'Create a place' success is often a moving target that needs to be refined over time. The challenge here is to be comfortable with the ambiguity involved, and openly encourage debate when interpreting success. There is an opportunity for soft metrics that focus on the ideology driving the business, emphasizing the potential and influence to shape the market.

For George Lucas, *increased capacity* in producing special effects *enabled increased creative control*. LucasArts created its own place in the market in order to deliver on a personal vision. If the vision is creative control, then the new metrics for measuring success might include reducing the number of partners, and decision makers required to deliver on innovative new projects.

For Elon Musk, every iterative technology development within electric vehicles is an opportunity to differentiate in the market. Removing the fuel tank provides an opportunity to add more seats in a sedan, blurring the line between mini-van and sports car. A strong vision seeks to maximize the potential of every iteration, small or large, and to deliver on the core purpose.

The questions that need to be answered:

- *When describing your vision, how do you define what success will enable?*
- *How are individuals being rewarded for identifying opportunities to reinforce strategic value during the development process?*

Fostering a Culture to Shape an Ideal Future

At the core of generating strategic value is the active pursuit of a declared desired future. A clear philosophy of the future is required, along with the entrepreneurial capacity to capitalize on the opportunities towards that destination.

It is difficult to categorize whether an idea 'Reacts to the present' or 'Shapes the future' without hindsight. While Google's search algorithm was a reaction to the poor tools available to early web users, it was also a desire to shape the future according to the deeper vision to make the world's information more accessible. Creating a desired future requires a clear vision, while recognizing that multiple ideas that solve existing problems in the present will be required to create a pathway to the desired destination. Making search faster and more likely to identify relevant results (Google search) is actually about transforming data into quick and enjoyable daily experiences (Gmail, YouTube), which reinforces the core revenue platform (Adwords).

To identify strategic value according to an impact on the future, questions need to explore the broader potential of your ideas (Figure 14.4):

- *Is the idea focused on solving existing problems (react to the present) or is it about emerging behaviors or experience (shape the future)?*

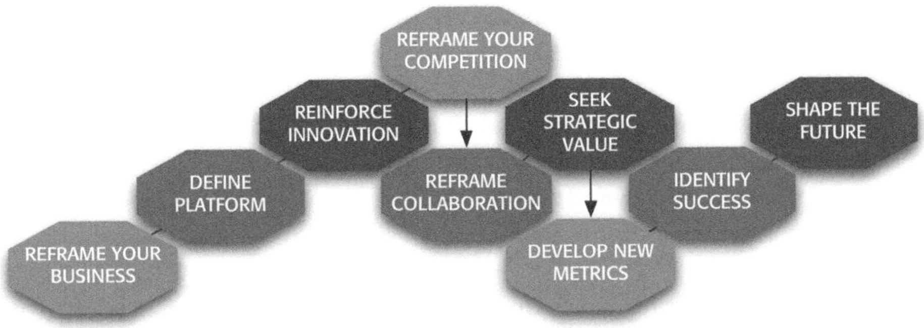

Figure 14.4 Participation matrix for the behavior economy

- *How do you describe for your audience the ideal future, in which you are a highly relevant and successful business?*
- *What value is created by the sum of the parts and the integration of your products and services, rather than each one in isolation?*

Becoming a Five-point Leader

BUILDING THE CAPACITY TO NAVIGATE THE FUTURE

It is easy to fixate on the individual who makes the tough calls, turning high-risk into high-returns, with products and services that revolutionize the game (Figure 14.5). It has been reinforced multiple times that the path is never linear; Steve Jobs was booted out as the leader of Apple Corporation before truly returning as the pilot that everyone now celebrates. Larry Page has grown into

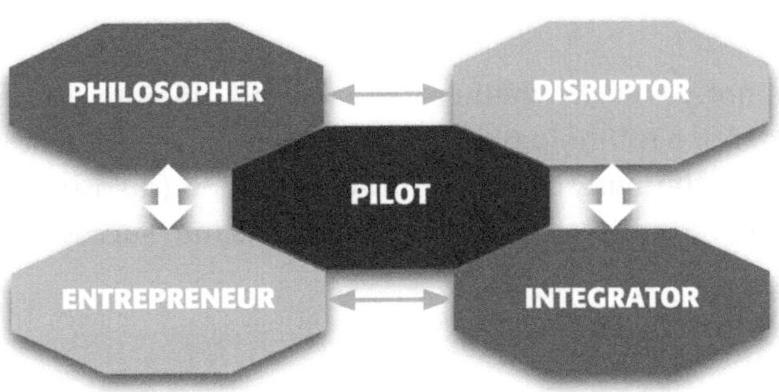

Figure 14.5 Becoming a five-point leader

this position, and Elon Musk was forced into the role when Tesla was in dire straits financially.

To rely on finding an individual that encompasses the entire five-points spectrum of leadership is dangerous and unrealistic. Tim Cook is never going to fully replace Steve Jobs, and Apple is showing that successful leadership can also involve *a team* of individuals that play essential roles to perfection.

Five-point Leadership takes time to develop, requiring a balance of strong individuals and capable teams. Here are a few ways of doing it:

OPPOSABLE FORCE NO. 1: DISRUPTION AND INTEGRATION

Pull it apart, put it back together, repeat ad infinitum.

The recurring theme of all Five-Point Leaders has been the ability to constantly embrace change, feeling free to challenge the core business model according to emerging technology and capabilities internally and externally. In all cases, senior leadership has been the bridge between Research and Development, to Sales and Marketing. Whenever there is a gap between these two departments, businesses have collapsed. Steve Jobs took it to the extreme, building a highly protected bunker where the long-term strategy of Apple was discussed and debated, surrounded by the latest prototypes.

Business strategy questions

- *What would disrupt your core business? How could you integrate it as a new service or platform?*
- *What would disrupt your industry? How could your services and platforms shift into different markets?*

For Tesla it is not yet clear whether they are an automotive manufacturer, an energy provider or a technology service provider. Investors believe Tesla is rich in potential due to the many different innovation fronts (disruption) with a leader with a track record of transforming opportunities into success (integration).

Internal innovation integration questions

A culture that defends the status quo will always be blind to new ideas.

- *Can your sales and marketing units' position and respond to new ideas?*
- *Is there a pipeline for transforming insights into opportunities?*
- *Are you future proof?*
- *Who is incentivized to look at the long term?*
- *Who is rewarded for making these connections?*

OPPOSABLE FORCE NO. 2: PHILOSOPHER AND ENTREPRENEUR

Tell a story, dare to dream and speculate, but be ruthless at delivering something of value immediately.

Google is growing stronger as the internal divisions increasingly work together. The enormous and ambitious vision of their senior leadership is actively engaging each division, and they work with one another. Android, the Autonomous Vehicle and Calico (the emerging health services division) are ambitious visions that require wide collaboration within the company in order to deliver on their promise. During the journey of transforming vision into reality, multiple business opportunities are emerging and Google will need be ready to capitalize on these.

Business strategy questions

Ask frequently:

- *What is the dream?*
- *What are the first steps to achieve the dream?*
- *Who else would benefit from those first steps?*
- *How do you build internal capacity to recognize and maximize opportunities as they emerge?*

Internal innovation integration questions

A narrative is required to foster alignment and encourage participation.

- *What is the human story?*
- *How do people internalize the dream?*
- *How is the dream connected to day-to-day activities?*
- *Who are the champions for reinforcing this connection and revealing the implications of drifting away from the vision?*

The Binding Force: The Pilot

Turbulent times call for clear vision, quick decisions and someone compelled to take control.

It is clear that a Pilot is required to steer the company through difficult times. This needs to be someone with a clear capacity for holding on to the vision, while making quick decisions that impact the present. Without a leader who clearly owned product development, Motorola was unable to develop a market position. The split leadership at Blackberry (Research in Motion) led to stalled decisions during key, difficult times with catastrophic outcomes. Apple drifted without Steve Jobs to pilot the company in a clear direction as competitors pushed ahead, and Google has always supported Larry Page as a pilot, providing a safety net through Eric Schmidt's role as CEO.

PILOT ASSESSMENT QUESTIONS:

- *Who will set the direction and the criteria for success when there are multiple paths forward?*
- *Who will hold everyone accountable to high standards and expectations, while inspiring individuals that hard work is important?*
- *Who will take control when the company hits turbulence?*
- *Are there pilots in place at key levels internally?*

Afterword

The economic model promoted in this book and exemplified by current behavior platforms, is a model where behavior is the only goal of our actions. We expect no other gain when engaging with Facebook; we just expect to be allowed to define ourselves, in our own words and images. On these platforms, there is no value assigned to any of the technical specifications of the system, and users are looking only at the capability of the platform to be the bridge between who they are, and who they want to be, in the eyes of their community. The value users seek here is the value of a moment in time, a moment in which the individual has the opportunity to expand and transform the self, by broadcasting to others. In this model, intrinsic motivation is the key to participation and engagement. In the Introduction to this book I stated that it is reasonable to add now that it will do so not because *it can*, but because *our motivation will demand it*.

Alexander Manu
Toronto

Bibliography

Ackoff, R. (1998). 'A systemic view of transformational leadership.' *Systemic Practice and Action Research*, 11(1), 23–36.

Amabile, T.M. (1998). 'How to kill creativity.' *Harvard Business Review*, 76(6), 76–87.

Ancona, D., Malone, T., Orlikowski, W. and Senge, P. (2011). 'In praise of the incomplete leader.' In *HBR's 10 Must Reads on Leadership*. Boston, MA: Harvard Business Review Press, 179–96.

Applegate, L., Austin, R. and Collins, E. (2005). 'IBM's decade of transformation: Turnaround to growth.' *HBR Case Studies*, X, Case 805-130. (Retrieved May 4, 2014, HBS Case Collection.)

Arendt, H. (1964). *The Human Condition*. Chicago, IL: University of Chicago Press.

Argyris, C. (1994). 'Good communication that blocks learning.' *Harvard Business Review*, 72 (July–August), 77–85.

Ariely, D., Gneezy, U., Loewenstein, G. and Mazar, N. (2009). 'Large stakes and big mistakes.' *Review of Economic Studies*, 76, 451–69.

Aristotle (1976 [1953]). *The Ethics of Aristotle* (trs. J.A.K. Thomson). London: Penguin Books, 63.

Aristotle. (1986). *De Anima*. London: Penguin Books Ltd.

Barnett. (n.d.). 'Tesla and the chasm – a day with a group of Model S owners.' *OppositeLock*, July 11. Available at: http://oppositelock.jalopnik.com/tesla-and-the-chasm-a-day-with-a-group-of-model-s-own-747762917 (accessed: July 20, 2014).

Bosch (2014). Bosch Connected Manufacturing White Paper, September. Stuttgart: Bosch.

Boyd, J.R. (1976). *Destruction and Creation*. Fort Leavenworth, KS: US Army Command and General Staff College.

Carlson, N. (2014). 'The untold story of Larry Page's incredible comeback.' *Business Insider*, April 24. Available at: http://www.businessinsider.com/larry-page-the-untold-story-2014-4 (accessed: July 18, 2014).

Carr, N. (2008). *The Big Switch: Rewiring the World, from Edison to Google*. New York, NY: W.W. Norton & Co.

Christensen, C. (1997). *The Innovator's Dilemma: When New Technologies Cause Great Firms to Fail*. Boston, MA: Harvard Business School Press.

Collins, J. (2001). *Good to Great: Why Some Companies Make the Leap – and Others Don't*. New York, NY: HarperBusiness.

Csikszentmihalyi, M. (1990). *Flow: The Psychology of Optimal Experience*. New York, NY: Harper and Row.

Csikszentmihalyi, M. (1997). 'Finding flow.' *Psychology Today*. Available at: https://www.psychologytoday.com/articles/199707/finding-flow (accessed: May 20, 2014).

Davis, J. (2010). 'How Elon Musk turned Tesla into the car company of the future.' *Wired.com*, September 27, 2010. Available at: http://www.wired.com/2010/09/ff_tesla/all/ (accessed: July 20, 2014).

DiCarlo, L. (2002). 'How Lou Gerstner got IBM to dance.' *Forbes.com*, November 11. Available at: http://www.forbes.com/2002/11/11/cx_ld_1112gerstner.html (accessed: August 7, 2014).

Esslinger, H. (2012). *Design Forward: Creative Strategies for Sustainable Change*. Stuttgart: Arnoldsche.

Fishman, T. (2014). 'What happened to Motorola.' *Chicago Magazine*, August 24. Available at: http://www.chicagomag.com/Chicago-Magazine/September-2014/What-Happened-to-Motorola/ (accessed: September 20, 2014).

Fromm, E. (1976). *To Have or To Be*. New York, NY. Harper & Row.

Geller, J.S. (2011). 'Open letter to BlackBerry bosses: Senior RIM exec tells all as company crumbles around him.' *BGR.com*, June 30. Available at: http://www.bgr.com/2011/06/30/open-letter-to-blackberry-bosses-senior-rim-exec-tells-all-as-company-crumbles-around-him/ (accessed: May 12, 2010).

Entrepreneur.com (2008). George Lucas profile. Available at: http://www.entrepreneur.com/article/197664 (accessed: July 20, 2014).

Goffee, R. and Jones, G. (2006). *Why Should Anyone Be Led by You? What it Takes to Be an Authentic Leader*. Boston, MA: Harvard Business School Press.

Goffman, E. 1959. *The Presentation of Self in Everyday Life*. New York, NY: Anchor.

Goldman Sachs Equity Research (2014). IoT primer. The internet of things: Making sense of the next mega-trend. Available at: http://www.goldmansachs.com/our-thinking/outlook/internet-of-things/iot-report.pdf (accessed July 9, 2014).Goleman, D. (2011). 'What makes a leader?' In *HBR's 10 Must Reads on Leadership*. Boston, MA: Harvard Business Review Press, 1–21.

Heath, T. (2013). 'Louis V. Gerstner Jr. lays out his post-IBM life. Available at: http://www.washingtonpost.com/business/economy/louis-v-gerstner-jr-lays-out-his-post-ibm-life/2013/06/07/04e9da2a-cd42-11e2-8845-d970ccb04497_story.html (accessed: September 23, 2014).

Inayatullah, S. (2008). 'Six pillars: Futures thinking for transforming.' *Foresight*, 10(1), 4–21.

Isaacson, W. (2011). *Steve Jobs*. New York, NY: Simon & Schuster.

Johansson, F. (2004). *The Medici Effect: Breakthrough Insights at the Intersection of Ideas, Concepts, and Cultures*. Boston, MA: Harvard Business School Press.

Kaufman, J. (2010). *The Personal MBA: A World-class Business Education in a Single Volume*. New York, NY: Portfolio Penguin.

Lavrinc, D. (2013). 'Peek Inside Tesla's Robotic Factory.' *Wired.com*, July 16. Available at: http://www.wired.com/2013/07/tesla-plant-video/ (accessed: July 19, 2014).

Lenovo (2014). 'Lenovo to acquire Motorola mobility from Google.' News release, January 29. Available at: http://news.lenovo.com/article_display.cfm?article_id=1768 (accessed: September 23, 2014).

Leonard, D. (2013). 'How Disney bought Lucasfilm – and its plans for "Star Wars."' *Business Week*, March 7. Available at: http://www.businessweek.com/articles/2013-03-07/how-disney-bought-lucasfilm-and-its-plans-for-star-wars (accessed: July 20, 2014).

Lindegaard, S. (2010). *The Open Innovation Revolution Essentials, Roadblocks, and Leadership Skills*. Hoboken, NJ: Wiley.

Loeb, V. (2003). 'Army plans steps to heighten "Warrior Ethos."' *Washington Post*, September 8, A19.

FundingUniverse.com (n.d.). Lucasfilm Ltd. Profile and history. Available at: http://www.fundinguniverse.com/company-histories/lucasfilm-ltd-history/ (accessed: July 20, 2014).

Lynda, M.A., Robert, D.A. and Elizabeth, C. (2005). 'IBM's decade of transformation: Turnaround to growth.' *Harvard Business School*, Case 805-130.

MacDuling, J. (2014). 'The future of "Made in America" is Tesla, not Ford.' *QZ.com*, April 9. Available at: http://qz.com/197241/the-future-of-made-in-america-could-be-tesla-not-ford/ (accessed: July 20, 2014).

Maney, K., Hamm, S. and O'Brien, J. (2011). *Making the World Work Better: The Ideas That Shaped a Century and a Company*. Cranbury, NJ: IBM Press, Pearson plc.

Manu, A. (2006). *The Imagination Challenge*. Berkeley, CA: New Riders/PeachPit Press.

Manu, A. (2007). *Innovation, Foresight and Business Design Course Materials*. Toronto: Rotman School of Management.

Manu, A. (2010). *Disruptive Business: Desire, Innovation and the Re-design of Business*. Farnham: Gower Publishing.

Manu, A. (2012). *Behavior Space*. Farnham: Gower Publishing.

Manu, A. (2013). 'Sustainability and the condition of being human.' In S. Walker and J. Giard (eds), *The Handbook of Design for Sustainability*. London: A&C Black.

Martin, R. (2007). *Opposable Mind: How Successful Leaders win Through Integrative Thinking*. Boston, MA: Harvard Business Press.

Maslow, A. (1943). 'A theory of human motivation.' *Psychological Review*, 50(4), 370–96.

Merchant, N. (2010). *The New How: Building Business Solutions through Collaborative Strategy*. Sebastopol, CA: O'Reilly.

Netflix (2009). Netflix culture: Freedom & Responsibility. Available at: http://www.slideshare.net/reed2001/culture-1798664 (accessed: November 12, 2012).

Paulsen, L. (n.d.). 'IBM 360/370/3090/390.' *Beagle-ears.com*. Available at: http://www.beagle-ears.com/lars/engineer/comphist/ibm360.htm (accessed: October 20, 2014).

Porter, M. (1980). *Competitive Strategy: Techniques for Analyzing Industries and Competitors*. New York, NY: Free Press.

Raynor, M. (2007). *The Strategy Paradox: Why Committing to Success Leads to Failure, and What To Do About It*. New York, NY: Currency Doubleday.

Rogers, C. (1951). *Client-centered Therapy: Its Current Practice, Implications and Theory*. London: Constable.

Rooke, D. and Torbert, W. (2011). 'Seven transformations of leadership.' In *HBR's 10 Must Reads on Leadership*. Boston, MA: Harvard Business Review Press, 137–61.

Rozman, M. (n.d.). 'Chris Theodore: The fall and rise of Chrysler, and other topics.' *Allpar.com*. Available at: http://www.allpar.com/history/interviews/chris-theodore/fall-and-rise.html (accessed: September 24, 2014).

Ryan, R.M. and Deci, E.L. (2000). 'Intrinsic and extrinsic motivations: Classic definitions and new directions.' *Contemporary Educational Psychology*, 25, 54–67.

Santayana, G. (2008). *The Sense of Beauty: Being the Outlines of Aesthetic Theory*. Available at: http://www.gutenberg.org/files/26842/26842-h/26842-h.htm (accessed: April 15, 2015).

Scharmer, C. (2007). *Theory U: Leading from the Future as it Emerges*. Cambridge, MA: The Society for Organizational Learning, Inc.

Schwartz, P. (1991). *The Art of the Long View*. New York, NY: Doubleday/Currency.

Senge, P. (1990). *The Fifth Discipline: The Art and Practice of the Learning Organization*. New York, NY: Doubleday/Currency.

Seward, Z. (2014). 'The Steve Jobs email that outlined Apple's strategy a year before his death.' *QZ.com*, April 5. Available at: http://qz.com/196005/the-steve-jobs-email-that-outlined-apples-strategy-a-year-before-his-death/ (accessed: August 7, 2014).

Silcoff, S., McNish, J. and Ladurantaye, S. (2013). 'How BlackBerry blew it: The inside story.' *The Globe and Mail*, September 27. Available at: http://www.theglobeandmail.com/report-on-business/the-inside-story-of-why-blackberry-is-failing/article14563602/?page=all (accessed: April 15, 2015).

Siofra, M. (2013). '10 self-made YouTube millionaires.' *TheRichest.com*, December 12. Available at: http://www.therichest.com/rich-list/world/10-richest-self-made-youtube-millionaires/?view=all (accessed: October 15, 2014).

Smith, D. (2014). 'The 11 most important Google acquisitions ever.' *Business Insider*, August 12. Available at: http://www.businessinsider.com/important-google-acquisitions-2014-8?op=1 (accessed: October 14, 2014).

Sternberg, R.J. (2000). 'Creativity is a decision'. In A.L. Costa (ed.), *Teaching for Intelligence II*. Arlington Heights, IL: Skylight Training and Publishing Inc., 85–106.

Sutherland, J. (2012). 'Afterword: Getting started.' In A. Manu, *Behavior Space*. Farnham: Gower Publishing, 211–22.

U.S. Soldier's Creed. (n.d.). Wikipedia. http://en.wikipedia.org/wiki/U.S._Soldier%27s_Creed (accessed: April 28, 2012).

Unknown author. 'Short Story: The Elephant and The Rope.' *The Unbounded Spirit*. Available at: http://theunboundedspirit.com/short-story-the-elephant-and-the-rope/ (accessed: November 21, 2012).

Vance, A. (2012). 'Elon Musk, the 21st century industrialist.' *Business Week*, September 13. Available at: http://www.businessweek.com/articles/2012-09-13/elon-musk-the-21st-century-industrialist (accessed: April 15, 2015).

Winkler, R. and Knight, R. (2013). 'Motorola plans low-cost phone; Sales of Moto X disappoint.' *The Wall Street Journal*, November 11. Available at: http://blogs.wsj.com/digits/2013/11/11/motorola-plans-low-cost-phone/?mg=id-wsj (accessed: October 28, 2013).

Wohlsen, M. (2014). 'Why Apple could win big with Tesla's giant new battery factory. *Wired.com*, February 28. Available at: http://www.wired.com/2014/02/teslas-giant-battery-factory-save-apple/ (accessed: July 20, 2014).

Wohlsen, M. (2014). 'Google still wins by selling Motorola for cheap.' *Wired.com*, January 30. Available at: http://www.wired.com/2014/01/google-moto/ (accessed: October 28, 2014).

Wohlsen, M. (2012). 'Car dealers are terrified of Tesla's plan to eliminate oil changes.' *Wired.com*, March 14. Available at: http://www.wired.com/2014/03/car-dealers-fear-teslas-plan-end-oil-changes-forever/ (accessed: July 20, 2014).

Online Sources

See http://www.digitaltrends.com/social-media/selfies-are-now-the-most-popular-genre-of-picture-and-in-related-news-everyones-the-worst/ (accessed: November 22, 2014).

See http://www.forbes.com/sites/avidan/2014/03/31/the-future-of-advertising-lean-nimble-agile/ (accessed: June 20, 2014).

See http://en.wikipedia.org/wiki/List_of_most_expensive_paintings (accessed: July 9, 2014).

See http://fortune.com/2010/01/27/live-blog-steve-jobs-presents-the-apple-tablet/ (accessed: July 12, 2014).

See http://googlepress.blogspot.ca/2006/10/google-to-acquire-youtube-for-165_09.html (accessed: April 7, 2014).

See http://techcrunch.com/2007/03/06/youtube-revenues-15-million-per-year-or-per-month/ (accessed: March 19, 2014).

See http://www.acquitygroup.com/docs/default-source/Whitepapers/acquitygroup-2014iotstudy.pdf?sfvrsn=0 (accessed: July 16, 2014).

See http://www.business-standard.com/article/management/the-agency-of-the-future-will-be-just-a-consultancy-michael-karg-vincent-digonnet-114050400690_1.html (accessed: May 29, 2014).

See http://www.decisionmarketing.co.uk/indepth/content-really-king-marketers (accessed: September 3, 2014).

See http://www.gartner.com/newsroom/id/2603623 (accessed: March 2, 2014).

See http://www.ibm.com/smarterplanet/us/en/ibm_predictions_for_future/ideas/ (accessed: September 3, 2014).

See http://www.internetlivestats.com/internet-users/ (accessed: August 23, 2014).

See http://www.merriam-webster.com/dictionary/value (accessed: June 26, 2014).

See http://www.nationalwellness.org/index.php?id_tier=2&id_c=25SixDimensionsofWellness (accessed: October 21, 2013).

See http://www.nbcnews.com/id/15196982/ns/business-us_business/t/google-buys-youtube-billion/#. VFzRe75cT8s (accessed: April 7, 2014).

See http://www.washingtonpost.com/business/economy/louis-v-gerstner-jr-lays-out-his-post-ibm-life/2013/06/07/04e9da2a-cd42-11e2-8845-d970ccb04497_story.html (accessed: August 7, 2014).

Index

Note: Figures indexed in *italics* with **bold** pagination.

For Product Safety Concerns and Information please contact our
EU representative GPSR@taylorandfrancis.com Taylor & Francis
Verlag GmbH, Kaufingerstraße 24, 80331 München, Germany